The Complete Art & Science of

Sausage Making

Healthy Homemade Recipes from Chorizo to Hot Dogs

Tonia Reinhard
MS, RD, FAND
with
Brendan Reinhard & Brent Mitchell

Robert
ROSE

For complete cataloguing information, see page 262.

Disclaimer
The recipes in this book have been carefully tested by our kitchen and our tasters. To the
best of our knowledge, they are safe and nutritious for ordinary use and users. For those
people with food or other allergies, or who have special food requirements or health issues,
please read the suggested contents of each recipe carefully and determine whether or not
they may create a problem for you. All recipes are used at the risk of the consumer.

We cannot be responsible for any hazards, loss or damage that may occur as a result
of any recipe use.

For those with special needs, allergies, requirements or health problems, in the event
of any doubt, please contact your medical adviser prior to the use of any recipe.

Design and production: Kevin Cockburn/PageWave Graphics Inc.
Editor: Sue Sumeraj
Recipe editor: Jennifer MacKenzie
Proofreader: Sheila Wawanash
Indexer: Gillian Watts
Step-by-step photographer: Tango Photographie
Food stylist: Gabrielle Bélanger
Prop stylist: Jacques Faucher

Additional photographs: Bangers © istockphoto.com/LauriPatterson; Sweet Italian Sausages
© istockphoto.com/4kodiak; Cajun Boudin Blanc © istockphoto.com/Juanmonino;
Boudin Noir Sausage © istockphoto.com/Shaiith; American Hot Dogs © istockphoto.
com/LauriPatterson; Pepperoni © istockphoto.com/LauriPatterson; Spicy Fresh Kielbasa
© istockphoto.com/ffolas; Cup o' Joe Morning Sausages © istockphoto.com/kirin_photo;
Weisswurst © istockphoto.com/DoraZett; Cabanossi © istockphoto.com/Dar1930;
Athenian Chicken Sausages © istockphoto.com/jerrydeutsch; Spicy Sicilian Sausages
© istockphoto.com/Silberkorn

Cover image: © istockphoto.com/sangfoto

The publisher gratefully acknowledges the financial support of our publishing program
by the Government of Canada through the Canada Book Fund.

Published by Robert Rose Inc.
120 Eglinton Avenue East, Suite 800, Toronto, Ontario, Canada M4P 1E2
Tel: (416) 322-6552 Fax: (416) 322-6936
www.robertrose.ca

Printed and bound in Canada

1 2 3 4 5 6 7 8 9 MI 24 23 22 21 20 19 18 17 16

Contents

Acknowledgments

Many thanks to John Reinhard for help with research and recalling the memories of sausage making with that original son of Barisciano, Italy, Guido Pacifico, who also served on our taste panel as the toughest critic. And many thanks to Faye Woodside, JD, a consummate wordsmith, for her assistance with editing and to Zoe Woodside and Claire and Gea Reinhard for serving as junior members on the taste panel.

We also owe a debt of gratitude to Steve and Sue Francis, owners of the Country Smoke House in Almont, Michigan, for the use of their state-of-the-art test kitchen and sharing their knowledge and love of sausage making (http://www.countrysmokehouseinc.com).

Introduction

"Spaga! Spaga!" I can still hear that word reverberating from more years ago than I care to remember. Even though I never learned Italian, I knew that *spaga* was the word for "string" in the Italian dialect of my parents' small hometown near the foothills of Gran Sasso Mountain in the Abruzzo region of central Italy. The kitchen table set up in the basement was covered in pink bits of meat, and coils of sausage were piled high awaiting my part of the operation: dozens of tiny pinpricks with a long sewing needle. I watched expectantly while my mother fumbled for the string to tie the end of the sausage that my father pushed through the grinder.

Before all the fuss about string would come the endless arguments about how much fat to remove from the meat. My mother was a traditionalist, preferring the time-honored methods of her ancestors, while my father was more forward-thinking. She argued that it tasted better with more fat; he argued that the sausage would dry better with less fat. He also believed that fat was unhealthy.

And then there was the drying chamber debate. The conditions had to be optimal: proper air circulation, cold but not close to freezing. I can still see the coils of pink sausage dangling from long wooden poles hung in the attic rafters. The curing period was relatively short — up to 3 weeks at some point during our Michigan winter.

At the time, I had no idea that this family tradition was an example of one of the oldest sausage preservation methods, relying on the combined effects of bacteria present in the meat, salt, time and proper temperature and humidity conditions to create dried fermented sausages.

More recently, I have found myself buying some of the great new sausages that have hit the market. These products boast interesting ingredients and flavors, contain lower fat and saturated fat, and make very convenient meal centerpieces. But when my husband was diagnosed with several food sensitivities, I had to scramble to replace his favorite foods with foods on the "approved list." I soon found that almost all commercial sausage products contained a long list of ingredients that were incompatible with his very short list of approved foods. And it occurred to me: if only I could control the ingredients that went into the sausages, I could put them back on the menu.

At that point, I didn't imagine I could make my own sausages — my previous sausage-making experience consisted of enthusiastically, if somewhat unartfully, stabbing holes in sausage casings with a sewing needle. Instead, I turned to the professionals at a local custom meat store renowned for producing its own fresh sausages and numerous other specialty meat and cheese products. (I confess that I had an "in," as I knew the sausage production manager and the chef.) I was able to purchase gourmet sausages that were easy on my husband's stomach and my sewing equipment.

Not long after, I read two articles that reinforced my belief that sausages could be a healthy addition to anyone's diet. The first was a peer-reviewed journal article discussing what is perhaps the most typically cited slam against processed meats: the addition of nitrites. The second was a how-to article on making sausage at home, written by a registered dietitian in the dietetics professional magazine *Food & Nutrition*. While there is plenty of controversy about typical sausage ingredients, such as saturated fat and salt, being able to make sausage at home means total control over all ingredients.

For example, people who need to avoid gluten or lactose can easily do so. Indeed, even those who completely eschew meats can make tasty vegetarian or vegan sausages!

Since the specialty sausages had been such a success, I suggested to Brendan, the production manager, and Brent, the chef, that we should come up with more recipes and put together a book. They were both excited about flexing their creative culinary muscles, and I enjoy spreading the word about health and nutrition, and particularly dispelling myths.

The first chapters of this book provide background on the traditions, food science and nutrition of sausages. Next, in Part 2, we cover the equipment needed to make sausages and provide details on the ingredients — some common and some more unusual — you'll need to purchase. We then explain the process of preparing, cranking out and storing sausages using safe practices. Part 3 is the heart of this book: 150 delicious and easy-to-prepare sausage recipes from around the world. You'll find all of the classic, traditional sausages here, as well as some innovative recipes inspired by regional cuisines. In Part 4, we've provided some tips on meal planning and suggestions on perfect side dishes to accompany your sausages. Helpful glossaries and resources round out the book.

If you are not too concerned about the history or science of sausage making, or about the nutrition and health controversies surrounding sausages, and you want to get right to making your own sausages, the best place to start is Part 2, with the how-to chapters on making sausage and food safety. These chapters will give you the detailed information you need to prepare the recipes in Part 3 with complete confidence.

I hope you enjoy making and eating these sausages as much as the three of us enjoyed creating them!

— Tonia Reinhard, MS, RD, FAND

PART 1

THE ART & SCIENCE OF SAUSAGES

CHAPTER 1
A Worldwide Tradition

Although historians do not have a precise date for when humans first made sausages, Homer described the fundamentals of this ancient food around 830 BCE in *The Odyssey*: salting and smoking meats in order to preserve them. The word "sausage" comes from the Latin word *salsus*, which means "salted meat." The early Greeks and Romans stuffed a variety of meats and spices into animal intestines, later more palatably called casings.

Since meat is a nutrient-dense food and is highly susceptible to microbial contamination, it makes sense that our ancestors, by necessity, developed creative meat preservation techniques. We take modern refrigeration for granted, but early humans' need to preserve food was crucial to survival, and many unique food products that we still enjoy today are the result of early human ingenuity in food preservation.

Types of Sausages

So what exactly *is* a sausage? At its most basic, a sausage is a highly seasoned minced meat, usually stuffed into casings of prepared animal intestine. However, the modern permutations on that definition are practically infinite and can even include vegetarian sausages stuffed into a vegetable-based or synthetic casing.

There are several different general types of sausages, which the Food and Agriculture Organization of the United Nations breaks down into the following classifications:

1. **Fresh sausages** are made from fresh meats and are usually not fermented, cured, smoked or cooked. They must be either refrigerated or frozen and cooked prior to eating. Examples include Italian sausages and breakfast sausages. (The majority of the sausages in this book are fresh sausages.)
2. **Fermented (or dried) sausages** are made from cured or uncured, fermented and sometimes smoked meats and are not cooked or heat-processed. Fermented sausages are further classified as either dried or semi-dried sausages. Examples include Genoa and German salamis and pepperoni.
3. **Smoked sausages** are typically cured but not fermented sausages that have been partially heat-processed to reduce their moisture content. Smoked sausages include cotto salami and kielbasa.
4. **Emulsified sausages** are made from comminuted (finely ground) and well-homogenized cured meats, fat, water and seasonings. They are usually smoked and precooked to varying degrees. Some familiar examples include hot dogs, bologna, mortadella and liverwurst.
5. **Cooked sausages** are considered ready-to-serve because they are made from fresh meats that have been cooked or cured and are cooked again after stuffing. They may also be smoked after these steps. Another group within this category (but which can also be considered a specialty category on its own) includes cooked or baked products that are molded into loaves or other shapes instead of being stuffed

into casings. Examples of this type include olive loaf, scrapple and head cheese.

One excellent website, developed by two avid sausage makers, divides the types of sausages into two very clear categories: ready to eat and not ready to eat.

Please note that commercial products in the "ready to eat" category, such as smoked sausages, all state emphatically to "cook before eating" — most likely due to liability concerns, as the manufacturer has no control over what happens to the product once it leaves the facility. However, in the recipes in this book, the smoked, poached and dried sausages have been cooked, brought to the appropriate safe internal temperature or preserved in some other way, and can be safely consumed.

SAUSAGE TYPES

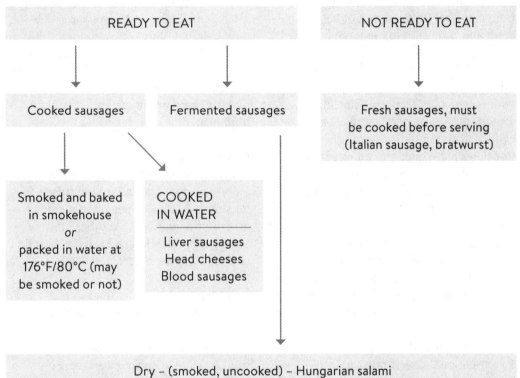

READY TO EAT

NOT READY TO EAT

Cooked sausages

Fermented sausages

Fresh sausages, must be cooked before serving (Italian sausage, bratwurst)

Smoked and baked in smokehouse
or
packed in water at 176°F/80°C (may be smoked or not)

COOKED IN WATER

Liver sausages
Head cheeses
Blood sausages

Dry – (smoked, uncooked) – Hungarian salami
Dry – (not smoked, uncooked) – Italian salami, Spanish chorizo
Semi-dry – (smoked, cooked) – Summer sausage
Spreadable – (cold smoked, uncooked) – Mettwurst

Source: Stanley Marianski, meatsandsausages.com. Used with permission.

The World of Sausages

Many cultures around the world have their own sausage traditions, influenced by distinctive regional culinary touches. The list that follows is by no means comprehensive — and apologies to countries not on the list! — but will give you an idea of the vast array of possibilities when it comes to sausages.

You'll find classic recipes for many of these sausages in Part 3, along with modern renditions of others.

Africa

North Africa's traditional sausage, merguez, is made with lamb or beef, and sometimes a combination of both meats. Merguez is a very spicy sausage that gets its heat from harissa, a hot sauce made with chile peppers, paprika and olive oil. This fresh sausage is grilled and eaten as an entrée or in a sandwich.

In South Africa, the boerewors is made from a coarsely ground mix of beef, game, lamb and/or pork. This sausage is grilled on an open flame.

China

Pork is the main meat used in Chinese sausages. Chinese pork sausages are called lap chong (or lap cheong), which translates to "winter stuffed intestine." Both fresh and dried sausages are popular. Most often, they are enjoyed in combination with rice or noodles. Typical ingredients include monosodium glutamate, soy sauce, cinnamon and sugar. Liver sausage (goin chong) is made with pork liver. The Chinese also make a specialty sausage using chicken liver, sometimes in combination with pork liver.

Czech Republic

Two traditional Czech sausages are jitrnice, a pork liver sausage, and yirtrnicky, which contains various organs along with lemon, cloves, allspice, marjoram and other herbs and spices.

England

Invasions of the ancient Romans and medieval French armies both brought culinary influences that included traditional sausage making. Today, sausage consumption throughout the United Kingdom is over 5,000 tons every year. Perhaps the most famous dish featuring sausages is bangers and mash, which is also enjoyed in Canada, Australia and New Zealand. Mash is simply mashed buttered potatoes. Bangers may be any variety of sausages, although Lincolnshire and Cumberland sausages are favorites. Lincolnshire sausage, named for the county from which it hails, is a coarsely ground pork sausage with a strong sage flavor. In Cumberland sausage, the flavors of white and black pepper predominate, and it has a characteristic chunky texture because it uses chopped meat instead of ground. The colorful term "banger" appears to have originated in 1919, although it has been linked to the years of the Second World War, when rationing forced the use of larger amounts of water in sausage, making them prone to exploding at high heat.

Finland

Many countries make a traditional blood sausage, and in Finland this is the mustamakkara. Recipes often include a mix of pork and beef. Another Finnish sausage, kestomakkara, includes brandy or beer, allspice, cloves and sugar.

France

France has a long history of sausage making. *Saucisse* refers to fresh sausage, *saucisson sec* to dried sausage and *saucisse cuite* to cooked sausage. Some

Haggis

Scotland is famous for haggis, a food almost everyone has heard of but few have tasted. Although not a sausage by the most common definition, it contains sheep organs combined with onion, oatmeal, beef fat and spices, encased in the sheep's stomach.

French specialty products include andouille, boudin blanc, boudin noir, saucisse de Morteau (a smoked sausage) and Toulouse. Andouille is made with tripe and only differs from its smaller cousin, andouillette, in diameter. Boudin noir is the French version of blood sausage, containing pig's blood and bread crumbs, while boudin blanc contains milk and rice. Toulouse is made of pork, red wine, garlic and spices that vary by region.

Germany

The names of many sausages enjoyed worldwide contain the German word *wurst*, a fact that illustrates this country's impact on sausage making. *Wurst* is the German word for "sausage," and the first part of a German sausage name denotes the type of sausage — either preparation style or origin. The "brat" part of bratwurst, for example, indicates that the sausage will be fried. Brühwurst describes a sausage that will be boiled. German sausages can contain any type of meat, although pork is the most common. Other familiar sausages include knockwurst, a smoked beef sausage, and landjäger, a dried smoked beef sausage.

Italy

Italy boasts one of the more extensive sausage repertoires. The Italian word for "sausage," *salsiccia*, is often combined with the name of a region in Italy to refer to specialty sausages from that region. However, many sausages have one-word names such as salami, cotechino, soppressata, luganiga, zampone and mortadella. Pork is the meat of choice, although other meats are also used. In certain regions of Italy, the climate is ideal for making dried sausage, and that tradition has continued to the present day among immigrants to North America, where the addition of cure is highly recommended because of the less hospitable climate.

Korea

Korea's blood sausage, called sundae (pronounced "soon-day"), contains various ingredients stuffed into cow or pig intestines and then boiled or steamed. The most common ingredients for sundae are cellophane noodles, barley and pork blood. Other variations include dried squid and kimchi. Snack sausages are also popular in South Korea — and apparently not just for eating. Some South Koreans, rather than remove their gloves in cold weather, have been known to use snack sausages as iPhone styluses!

Malta

Zalzett tal-Malti is a pork sausage with just a few simple ingredients: salt, black pepper, parsley and coriander. It's prepared in a variety of ways, from grilling to boiling.

Mexico

Mexican chorizo has some important differences from Spanish chorizo, on which it is based. Although it is usually made of pork, it can also be made with beef. Mexican chorizo is sold both loose and in casings; with the latter, the casings are removed before the sausage is added to tacos and other Mexican dishes. Green chorizo gets its name from the striking green color achieved by the inclusion of spinach, chile peppers and cilantro.

Poland

The word "kielbasa" describes any of numerous Polish specialty sausages. Poland has a long history of artisan sausage making dating back to the ancient Roman military incursions in 500 BCE. It didn't take long, though, for Polish sausage makers to add their unique spin, creating world-renowned products. One such product is kabanosy, a dried smoked pork sausage touted as the "finest meat stick in the world."

Long-Lasting Smoked Sausage

Sausage makers in the northern region of Poland (now Lithuania) famously produced smoked sausage that retained its flavor for up to 2 years, even at ambient temperatures. They used only pigs up to 15 months old, fed rye, barley or potatoes — or sometimes only flour. The slaughtering process was also unique. Sausage makers inserted a knife into the pig's heart and plugged the wound with a wooden peg. This prevented blood loss and conferred a deep red color to the meat. To enhance this effect, the carcass was placed stomach down rather than hung. In addition, instead of scalding to remove the hair, which would have softened the meat, the carcass surface was burned and the hair was scraped off with knives.

Portugal

Some types of Portuguese sausages were inspired by Spanish sausages, as is apparent from the similarity of their names: chourico (chorizo) and morcelas (morcilla). Other types include linguiça (a spicy garlic sausage), farinheira (a smoked flour sausage) and alheira (a smoked chicken sausage). Farinheira was created by Portuguese Jews in the 16th century to hang in their smokehouses to feign the consumption of pork. Alheira also traces its origins to this group, but was actually eaten, not just hung for show.

Slovakia

The traditional Slovak sausage, klobása, is made of pork, garlic, paprika, red pepper and caraway seeds. It is prepared as either a fresh sausage or a smoked sausage.

Spain

Three main varieties of traditional Spanish sausages are longaniza, chorizo and sobrasada, but there are numerous recipes within each category. The main difference among the three types is the proportion of paprika and the length of the sausages. They are usually made of pork and contain pimentón, a local paprika that adds a distinctive flavor and dark red color to the sausage. A particularly famous Spanish sausage is

morcilla, their version of blood sausage. Countries throughout the world where Spanish culture was exported, such as Latin America and the Philippines, have added their own distinctive character to Spanish sausages.

Sweden

The Swedish word for "sausage" is *korv*, and a perennial favorite is potatiskorv. This simple sausage consists of beef, pork, potatoes, onion, salt and pepper. Another popular choice is a cooked sausage, falukorv, which contains pork, beef, potato starch and onion.

Thailand

The Thai sausage sai oua (or sai ua) is made of pork and spiced with lemongrass, curry paste, turmeric, sugar, soy, galangal and wild lime leaves. They also make a fermented sausage, sai krok Isan, with a characteristic sour flavor. The sausages are eaten grilled and usually dipped in a variety of sauces.

Turkey

Many types of sausages are popular in Turkey, but the beef sausage, sujuk, is a particular favorite. The meat is coarsely ground, stuffed into beef or sheep casing and either smoked or dried — or sometimes both.

CHAPTER 2
Sausage Science

The science of sausage making begins with an overview of the main ingredient: meat. While meat can include any part of any animal that someone might eat, in meat science circles it refers to the flesh of sheep, pigs and cows. Sausage was created as a way to preserve meat, which is highly perishable and prone to microbial contamination, so that it could be eaten at a future time — perhaps when meat was not plentiful.

Meat Science

One of the reasons for meat's perishability is that its high water content and relatively low acidity make it a welcoming environment for bacteria to grow and multiply. Many people are surprised to learn that some cuts of raw beef are 71% water by weight. But bacteria are also attracted to meat as a source of nutrients. Meat provides ample amounts of the energy all life forms require. The three sources of energy are carbohydrate, protein and fat.

Carbohydrate
Although meat does not contain appreciable amounts of carbohydrate for human consumption, it does contain trace amounts that bacteria can use. We humans have learned to exploit the growth of friendly bacteria as part of the process of making dried sausages (see page 53).

Protein
For humans, one of meat's most important constituents is protein, which makes up 15% to 25% of meat by weight. Not only is meat high in protein, but the protein is of high quality (more on that in Chapter 3).

The protein, or lean part of the meat, consists of the muscles that enabled the animal to move about, its skeletal muscles. Skeletal muscles are made up of muscle fibers. Since most of a cut of lean meat is muscle fibers, that's what gives the meat its structure. The muscle fibers are long and thin and covered by a transparent membrane called a sarcolemma. The sarcolemma contains a jelly-like substance called sarcoplasm.

In some ways, the fibers are similar to the juicy bits of the flesh of citrus fruits, although muscle fibers are much thinner. You can't see the fibers unless you use a microscope, but contained in each are vitamins, minerals, protein and a protein pigment known as myoglobin. Like hemoglobin in our blood, myoglobin's pigment comes from iron, and it gives meat its characteristic reddish color.

Protein and Meat Tenderness
If the butcher freezes a carcass too soon, all the proteins cluster, causing the meat to be extremely tough. When meat is allowed to age, enzymes leak out of the muscle cells and begin to break down the proteins, tenderizing the meat.

Connective Tissue

In addition to protein, muscle also contains connective tissue. The connective tissue surrounds the fibers and unites them in small bundles, and then encompasses the bundles and puts them together in more complex bundles. This bundling eventually builds into muscles, and every muscle is surrounded by more connective tissue.

Connective tissue is formed by a matrix that contains collagen and elastin. The collagen fibers make up tendons, which attach muscle to bone. You've seen this rubbery stuff if you've eaten a chicken drumstick.

Many people who see myoglobin leaking from a package of fresh raw meat mistake it for blood.

If you had a microscope, you could see even tinier structures that make up the thin muscle fibers. These tiny structures are called myofibrils. They appear as alternating light and dark striations (a fancy scientific word for stripes). In turn, the myofibrils are made up of thick and thin myofilaments. The thick myofilaments contain the protein myosin; the thin myofilaments contain the protein actin. After an animal is slaughtered, the actin forms a complex with the myosin called "actomyosin." Actomyosin makes up the protein we get from meat.

The myofilaments are also what allow animals, including humans, to move. Muscle contraction occurs when the thick and thin myofilaments slide over one another in a series of repetitive events to cause mechanical force. This action requires energy, which is supplied by adenosine triphosphate (ATP), the universal energy currency in all organisms. It's a nifty process that converts chemical energy from ATP to mechanical energy, which allows us to contract muscles, which, in turn, allows us to move around.

After death, an animal's blood stops circulating and the muscles use up all the oxygen they were using to make ATP. The muscles don't realize they're dead, so they want to keep making ATP.

But since they no longer have oxygen, they begin a special process to break down glycogen, the muscles' stored carbohydrate, to make ATP. This process is called "anaerobic glycolysis." The breakdown of glycogen releases glucose molecules, which are further broken down to release energy as ATP. This gives the muscles enough energy to contract. It also releases lactic acid, which builds up, leading to the release of calcium, which causes more muscle contraction. Once the glycogen is used up, no more ATP is made, and the actin and myosin get stuck in a permanent contraction known as rigor mortis.

Fat

Fat can range from 5% to 40% of a meat's weight. Just like people, when an animal takes in more energy than it uses up, the extra energy is converted to fat and stored in the connective tissue within the muscle. In meat, fat appears as "marbling" — whitish streaks and globs inside the reddish muscle. Marbling is a desirable characteristic of top-grade beef (as one example) because it tenderizes and flavors the meat during cooking. The fat melts at high cooking temperatures and keeps the meat juicy and tender. Meat without much fat can become dry and tough during cooking. When animals are fed well and have limited exercise, their meat will contain more fat.

What's Science Got to Do with It?

Knowing a bit about meat's components and how it is structured will help you make high-quality, food-safe sausages. In particular, science comes into play in the processes of mixing the meat, fermenting dried sausages and creating emulsified sausages.

Protein and Fat in the Mix

You can see science at work while making your sausages. One of the first things to notice happens during the mixing stage. As you are mixing the ground meat with your other sausage ingredients, you will see thin white strands forming in the mixture. These strands consist of the myosin protein from the muscle fibers of the meat. The protein is released thanks to both the mechanical action of mixing and partial dissolving of the protein by salt, a process called protein extraction.

After the protein molecules are liberated from the tissue, they form crosslinks with each other, giving rise to the visible white strands. At this point, the meat particles begin to stick to each other and hold the mixture together in a stable suspension, a process known as binding. Different meats and cuts of meat vary in binding ability, with skeletal muscle from beef binding the best, followed by lean pork. Generally, non-skeletal meats that are high in fat, such as jowls, hearts and tongue, have low binding ability.

Speaking of fat, ideally the fat molecules in your sausage mixture should be encapsulated by the protein molecules.

But to achieve this ideal, the temperature of the meat, the amount of fat used and the texture of the grind are critical.

Your meat, grinder and bowl should be nicely chilled before you start making sausages (see page 49). And you need to work quickly, so you don't give the fat a chance to warm up. Further, you must be careful not to overmix the ingredients, as this creates too much friction and increases the mixture's temperature. As the temperature rises, the fat will begin to soften and move to the surface in the form of droplets, forming pockets. This will cause the fat to smear on the inside of the casing when you begin to stuff the sausages.

Smearing can also occur if you use too much fat (because there isn't enough protein to encapsulate it) or if you grind the meat too finely (too much fat becomes exposed outside the protein molecules). Other terms for smearing include "greasing out," "fat capping" and "shorting out."

Fermentation

In dried sausage making, fermentation is the process in which bacteria consume nutrients in the meat. Since meat is a nutritious food that's high in water and relatively low in acid, all of which make it an ideal environment for bacteria, the trick is to promote the growth of friendly bacteria (those that don't make us sick) and limit the growth of unfriendly ones.

Early in history, artisan sausage makers figured out that hanging sausages

Over-Salting

You may experience problems with protein extraction if you use too much salt. Excess salt will extract too much protein from the meat and will cut the protein fibers too short, which can cause the sausages to be drier and tougher. Excess salt also adversely affects the taste.

Non-Meat Binders

Other ingredients used in sausages, such as cereal fillers, can add to the meat's binding ability because they absorb water. You can see this principle at work when making meatloaf. Most people use bread crumbs or flour in combination with a raw egg (which provides protein) to bind the ground meat and other ingredients together.

at cool temperatures reduced the amount of water in them — drying them while also protecting them against spoilage. But what's the science behind that? While they are drying, the bacteria in the meat are busily fermenting it. Although there isn't enough carbohydrate in meat to provide any nutritional benefit to humans, there is enough in the form of glucose, the simplest sugar, for bacteria to consume and multiply. In the process, friendly bacteria produce lactic acid, which raises the acid level in the meat, rapidly making the environment hostile to pathogenic bacteria that cause human disease. As the friendly bacteria thrive and reproduce, they also crowd out the pathogenic bacteria by using up the available food and water.

In the modern age, commercial sausage makers have begun to use starter cultures of specific bacteria for more controlled fermentation. Some of the bacteria selected include strains of *Lactobacillus, Pediococcus, Staphylococcus* and *Streptococcus*. The strains are chosen for their lactic-acid-making prowess, ripening flavor and appropriateness for human consumption. Currently, food scientists are exploring the use of specialized starter cultures that will also give sausages a healthy probiotic advantage.

Salt

Certain ingredients are added to sausage meat to help with the fermentation process. The most important of these is salt. This key ingredient has been used since ancient times in food preservation because it promotes drying, inhibits the growth of harmful bacteria and enhances the flavor of the food. Salt exerts its effects by the process of osmosis, which is the movement of water across a cell membrane from a less concentrated solution into a more concentrated one, thereby equalizing the concentrations on each side of the membrane. Bacteria differ in their preferences when it comes to salt concentration; happily, harmful bacteria don't like salt.

Nitrates and Nitrites

Two other compounds that are important in making fermented sausages are nitrates and nitrites. Most people interested in health and diet have heard of nitrates and nitrites, and may have been advised to avoid them. You'll find a review of how nitrates and nitrites relate to health in

The Origin of Dried Sausages

While many historians point to the Mediterranean region as the birthplace of fermented sausages, there's good evidence that traditional products in China and other parts of Asia developed independently at close to the same time. The benefit of dried sausages was clear: they provided a pre-refrigeration way to preserve scarce and costly meat.

A Happy Accident

Nitrates and nitrites were most likely first introduced into fermented sausages by accident when the salt became contaminated with potassium nitrate, also known as "saltpeter." It was only later, in the Middle Ages, that potassium nitrate was added intentionally to preserve meat.

Chapter 3. For now, let's consider their role in preservation.

Nitrates and nitrites promote the drying process and, more importantly, kill and inhibit the growth of harmful bacteria, most notably the dreaded *Clostridium botulinum*, which causes paralysis and death. As a bonus, nitrates and nitrites impart a characteristic flavor to sausages. They also convert the muscle pigment myoglobin into an intense red pigment called nitrosomyoglobin. All this happens in the course of a process known as the curing reaction. The reaction starts with bacteria converting nitrate to nitrite, which is highly reactive. In the presence of acid, supplied by friendly bacteria, nitrite converts to nitrous acid and finally to nitric oxide. Nitric oxide reacts with myoglobin to produce the attractive red color. More importantly, both nitric oxide and nitrous oxide have an antibacterial effect. The mechanism is not yet fully understood, but nitric oxide appears to limit the oxygen available to the bacteria and interfere with the microbes' ability to use energy. This action is more effective in the presence of nitrous acid.

Nitrite's antioxidant action may also impact the flavor of the meat by preventing the breakdown of the fat.

Herbs and Spices

Herbs and spices add more than just flavor to sausages; they also provide antimicrobial protection. In addition, they promote fermentation by stimulating the growth of friendly bacteria. Herbs and spices (and some fruit and vegetables) with antimicrobial effects include the following:

- Allspice
- Basil, sweet
- Bay leaf
- Bergamot
- Caraway
- Cardamom
- Celery
- Cinnamon
- Citronella
- Cloves
- Coriander
- Dill
- Fennel
- Garlic
- Ginger
- Lemon
- Mace
- Marjoram
- Mustard
- Nutmeg
- Onion
- Orange
- Oregano
- Paprika
- Parsley
- Pepper
- Rosemary
- Sage
- Sassafras
- Star anise
- Tarragon
- Thyme
- Turmeric

Emulsions

An emulsion is a mixture of two or more liquids that normally do not blend but

Unique Flavor and Texture

Together, the elements of the drying process — the cool temperature, the production of lactic acid by friendly bacteria and the addition of salt, nitrates and nitrites — create a characteristic flavor and texture and an intense color. Most people describe dried sausages as slightly tangy and chewy.

The Power of Smoke

While the use of salt, nitrates and nitrites preserved the meat much longer than would otherwise have been possible, ancient sausage makers still struggled with rancidity, mold and insect infestations. In Europe during the Middle Ages, smoke was added to extend shelf-life. Native North Americans also used smoke to preserve meat by hanging it over the campfire. We now know that phenols — compounds in wood smoke — are powerful antioxidants and add protection against microbes. As a result, the smoking process is effective in staving off the growth of molds and yeasts. And most people love the smoky flavor.

are held together with an emulsifier. The word comes from a Latin term meaning "to milk" because milk is an emulsion. Milk is made up of water and fat, which separate into two distinct layers. In the days before commercial processing, the fat portion, or cream, would rise to the top of the container. Similarly, when you mix vinegar (which is water-based) with oil (which is a fat), it won't stay blended for very long; you'll soon see two layers begin to form, with the fat rising to the top. But if you add egg yolk, which contains the emulsifying compound lecithin, the oil and vinegar will stay blended. (This is how you make mayonnaise.) For this emulsion to work, you must gradually beat in the oil, so that it divides into small fat droplets. And of course, it only works if you use the correct proportions of each ingredient.

In sausage making, products such as frankfurters and hot dogs are considered emulsions, even though they don't fit the strictest definition of the term. Food scientists call this type of product a meat emulsion. The high-fat meat for these products is finely ground, rather than coarsely ground as with other sausages. The fine grind causes the abundant fat cells to rupture and release the fat. However, fat doesn't dissolve in water, or even mix well with it, so certain steps must be followed to keep it mixed in once liquid is added to the sausage mixture.

Essentially, the process is dependent on protein's ability to form a matrix that encapsulates the tiny fat particles. The process begins when the added salt dissolves and extracts the protein during the mixing phase. Heat generated by the friction of the chopping blades causes the extracted protein to form a film and coagulate, trapping the fat particles in a stable emulsion. The temperature of the meat mixture during this process is critical: it must rise enough to allow the proteins to coagulate, but not beyond 57°F (14°C) or the emulsion will not be stable and the fat will separate. In addition, as with a mayonnaise emulsion, liquids must be added to the sausage mixture gradually to enable the fat particles to form the emulsion.

More Wholesome Than You Think

Interestingly, although emulsified sausages have been the butt of jokes about the parts of the animal they purportedly contain, such as tongues, snouts and lips, these non-skeletal meats actually have very poor binding ability and wouldn't be very useful in making emulsified sausages.

CHAPTER 3
Sausages in a Healthy Diet

The idea that sausages can be part of a healthy diet may seem contrary to what most people think they know about nutrition and health. But as with so many issues in a fast-paced culture that relies on quick sound bites and a tap of the smartphone, nutrition issues can be a bit more complex than people believe. In fact, many aspects of diet that professionals took for granted are coming under increased scientific scrutiny.

What's in a sausage that makes it seem suspect to so many people? The list starts with nitrite and nitrate, and includes fat, saturated fat, salt and even the meat itself. When we sift through these issues with a scientific lens, a clear picture emerges showing that not only have sausages been inaccurately maligned, but they can make a healthful contribution to one's diet.

A Word, or Two, about Science

"Science" is a popular word these days, with debaters on just about every topic claiming to have science on their side. Before we can discuss nutrition and sausages, or indeed nutrition and any food product, we need to address a few points about science and scientific studies.

First, so we're all on the same page, here's *Merriam-Webster's* definition of "science": "knowledge about or study of the natural world based on facts learned through experiments and observation." *Merriam-Webster* further tells us that the word "science" is derived from the Latin word *scientia*, which is "knowledge based on demonstrable and reproducible data." So a key feature of the scientific method, the process that guides scientific study, is that the results of a study must be reproducible. Another important aspect, which we can glean from the definition of science, is that often the answer to a question cannot be definitively "settled." As technology advances, and as analytical equipment, methods and techniques improve, results from later studies may contradict or disprove earlier studies.

Scientific understanding of the variables related to a specific issue can also evolve over time. For example, in the 1990s, researchers learned that blood cholesterol levels vary depending on the season. Prior to the publication of these results, scientists may have incorrectly associated lower cholesterol levels in a particular study with the treatment itself, such as oat bran. Another example is the finding that genetic variation plays an extremely complex role in the development of heart disease. Obviously, genetic variables can profoundly influence study results — a study that includes males and females of various ethnicities may not in fact be measuring the effect of an experimental treatment, but rather individual genetic differences in how the body regulates the processes that lead to heart disease.

Our understanding of diet and health is always changing, because that's the nature of scientific study. Instead of feeling negative about new information, especially when it contradicts earlier information, we need to remember that with each new study comes better understanding.

We do need to be wary, however, of a few recent trends in the study of diet and health. The first problem is the way the media report on health studies, and the second relates to official agencies making recommendations to the public before putting study results into the proper perspective.

Epidemiologic Studies

Most of the studies on diet and health are epidemiologic studies, which compare disease rates among two similar groups of people and look for correlations between disease and diet habits. Journalists who are not trained in the scientific method scan the medical journals, and researchers themselves send out news releases — often before professionals can interpret the full study — and both groups trumpet the results to the public. The headline screams, "Carrots help prevent breast cancer!" but nowhere in the article does the reader get information on the type of study it was.

It was this type of epidemiologic study that led researchers to the link between the Mediterranean diet and a lower risk for heart disease. Epidemiologic studies are useful in pointing to a possible connection between diet and disease, laying the groundwork for further studies. But these studies can show only a statistical association, not cause and effect. In other words, just because a study reports that women who eat lots of carrots tend to get breast cancer less often, the study doesn't prove that carrots prevent the disease. It might be that something else about women who eat lots of carrots is protecting against cancer.

Relative Risk

The second problem — how official agencies make recommendations to the public — is related to the reliance on epidemiologic study results. To understand the problem, we need to understand a statistical term: relative risk. Relative risk, as defined by the University of Michigan School of Public Health, is a "measure of the magnitude of an association between an exposed and non-exposed group. It describes the likelihood of developing disease in an exposed group compared to a non-exposed group."

As an example, let's look at the disease and behavior with the closest association, lung cancer and smoking. Not all smokers will get lung cancer. There are many factors involved in the risk to a particular person: the number of cigarettes he smoked each day, when he started smoking, how many years he smoked, his genetic susceptibility to the disease and many others. If we look at 100 people who smoke, the number who will get lung cancer ranges from 1 to 15, depending on those factors. But those factors are important, so if the 100 smokers were 69 years old and smoked two packs a day for the last 50 years, 15 of them would get lung cancer. But in another group of 100 smokers who were 62 years old and smoked two packs daily for the last 25 years, only 3 would get cancer.

But let's get back to relative risk, which is the metric researchers often use in their studies of diet and disease. A relative risk of 1.0 indicates no increase in risk, while a relative risk of 2.0 is also expressed as 100% and signifies a two-fold, or doubled, increase in risk. Most studies of diet and disease yield relative risks in this gray zone of no risk to double the risk, with most showing relative risks between 1.2 to 1.5, or 20% to 50% increase in risk.

A smoker's relative risk of developing lung cancer compared to a non-smoker is 23. This means that the smoker's risk is 2300% higher.

With that in mind, consider a study telling us that processed meat raises the risk of colon cancer by 21%. This means someone who eats processed meat is 1.21 times more likely to develop colon cancer than his non-processed-meat-eating friend. Recalling all the potential variables that influence a particular person's risk of disease, consider how appropriate it is (or isn't) for an official agency to make a recommendation based on those facts. The U.S. National Cancer Institute stated that recommendations for the public should not be made at relative risks of less than 2.0, or 100%. Yet, the World Cancer Research Fund International and the American Institute for Cancer Research did just that in 2007 and 2011, when they recommended that the public avoid processed meat based on studies showing a relative risk of 1.21, or 21% higher risk, of colorectal cancer with every 50 grams of processed meat eaten daily.

This brings us to the first health issue related to sausages: nitrate and nitrite.

Nitrate and Nitrite

Without a doubt, the biggest slam against sausage — or at least commercial sausages — has been related to the use of nitrite. Although this slam has been repeatedly and definitively debunked by numerous scientific papers, it is still alive and well.

The benefit of making your own sausages, of course, is that you control the ingredients, so your fresh sausages don't have to contain nitrite, although dried sausages do require the use of curing salts, which contain nitrate or both nitrate and nitrate. So that you can continue to enjoy commercial sausages, as well as your homemade dried sausages, let's address this myth.

The Back Story
The negative press on nitrite dates back to studies from the 1950s reporting that many food products contain compounds known as nitrosamines. These food products include vegetables, beer and whiskey. Quite a diverse group! Nitrosamines are a group of compounds, many of which do have the potential to cause cancer. But to get the whole story, we need to start with nitrogen, an element essential for all life on earth. If you hated

What Is Meant By "Processed Meat"?
Processed meats are often not defined by researchers or receive a short description, such as "luncheon meats." However, some researchers are more descriptive, using specific product terms such as "ham, bacon, sausages, cured or preserved meats," and then lump consumption of these products into a single category.

chemistry class, or never took it, you may want to grit your teeth and hang on, because chemistry is the key to getting the facts on nitrites.

Nitrogen is the most abundant gas in the air we breathe. While it's essential to us, we can't use it, and neither can plants or animals, until it's changed to another form. That change takes place in a process known as fixation that happens during the nitrogen cycle. The nitrogen cycle changes plain old nitrogen from the air (N_2) to many other forms, including nitrogen oxides, which, as you may have guessed, include the element oxygen. Bacteria in our environment and inside our bodies play a key role in the cycle by promoting the change from one nitrogen oxide compound to another. You may recognize some of these: nitric oxide (NO), nitrite (NO_2) and nitrate (NO_3). These last two both occur naturally in foods and are added to commercial foods, such as sausages.

In the 1980s, scientific studies and popular talk centered around nitrogen oxide compounds being harmful because nitrate from food accumulates in our saliva and bacteria in the mouth convert it to nitrite; after we swallow, nitrite ends up in the stomach, where stomach acid converts it to nitrosamines, known to potentially cause cancer. Government agencies quickly responded to the concerns by limiting the amount of nitrite that could be used by the food industry and mandating the addition of a form of vitamin C, which inhibits the conversion of nitrite to nitrosamines.

The problem was that these compounds are important in preventing disease-causing bacteria from growing, including deadly types such as botulism. In addition to protecting against deadly bacteria in processed meat, nitrite also is a key ingredient of the cure mix that makes the appetizing pink color in these products and contributes to the characteristic flavor.

Nevertheless, this was the prevailing story on nitrate and nitrite until some pivotal studies in that same decade changed the narrative. The problem is that most people, including health professionals, have not updated their understanding of the issue and adapted what they tell consumers.

The Times They Are A-Changin'

The title of this section is a quote from the editors of the scientific journal *Nitric Oxide*, who in 2010 devoted a considerable number of pages to reporting on more recent articles presenting the potential health *benefits* of nitrogen oxide compounds. In fact, the very name of the journal shows how important nitric oxide has become. It was even recognized as "Molecule of the Year" by the journal *Science* in 1992.

But back to the pivotal studies from the 1980s. Scientists showed that the cells in all mammals crank out lots of nitric oxide using L-arginine, an amino acid, as the starting compound. More importantly, they realized that nitric oxide is a powerful factor in relaxing blood vessels (in scientific terms, it is a potent vasodilator). Why is that important? When blood vessels tighten, or constrict and narrow, high blood pressure can follow, as can heart attack and stroke.

Nitric oxide also plays a crucial role in how platelets (blood clotting cells) function — another key factor in the development of heart attack and stroke — as well as in nerve conduction and immune function.

Studies have also demonstrated that nitrite, independent of its conversion to nitric oxide, increases blood flow, bringing much-needed oxygen to deprived tissues. Researchers have found that Tibetans living at high altitude, where oxygen is low, have high concentrations of nitrite in their blood. Nitrite enhances exercise capacity in people engaged in intense exercise, and promotes blood flow in patients with sickle cell anemia. And in animal studies, nitrite has been shown to prevent damage to the heart, kidney, liver and brain when researchers intentionally harm the cardiovascular system.

So now that we know all of nitric oxide's potential health benefits, why do some professionals continue to slam processed meats? That takes us back to the type of studies — epidemiologic studies — that, along with a consideration of relative risk, helped generate the negative press, much of which came from the World Cancer Research Fund International (WCRF) and the American Institute for Cancer Research (AICR).

The WCRF and the AICR published a document on colorectal cancer that was updated in 2011, the *WCRF/AICR Continuous Update Project* (CUP). The CUP report rated evidence for processed meat at the highest level of "convincing" that these foods increased risk by 21% for a daily intake of 50 grams (just under 2 ounces). (Interestingly, the report also placed adult attained height in this category of "convincing" evidence, stating that every 5 centimeters — about 2 inches — increased the risk by 9%.) Since then, many scientists have challenged the processed meat statement, citing problems with the studies they used in their analysis and epidemiologic studies in general.

A Risk-Benefit Evaluation

Aside from processed meat, what are the other sources of nitrate and nitrite? Fruits and vegetables contain both nitrite and nitrate, which readily converts to nitrite. Some of the highest sources include vegetables, especially superfoods such as spinach, arugula and beets. So does that mean people should stop eating fruits and vegetables?

One of the healthiest diet plans, promoted by many health professionals and government agencies, is the DASH

Nitrate and Nitrite in Saliva

Our body makes nitric oxide in several different ways. One process uses the amino acid L-arginine and molecular oxygen, aided by enzymes, which the body also makes. Through a process of synthesis and recycling, and using dietary sources of nitrite and nitrate, the body maintains a steady supply of nitric oxide and nitrite. The salivary glands extract nitrate, with 25% of the nitrate in saliva coming from our diet, then the bacteria in our mouth convert nitrate to nitrite, and we swallow it. After we swallow it, nitrite is converted to nitric oxide and enters into the recycling process. Scientists say that 90% of the total amount of nitric oxide in our body comes from this process. In fact, dental and oral health researchers report that nitrate and nitrite in saliva, by converting to nitric oxide, play a role in keeping pathogenic bacteria (the "bad" bacteria), from damaging our teeth and oral tissues.

Saltpeter and Nitroglycerin

Over the centuries, nitric oxide has saved countless lives. Nitric oxide was used medically in ancient China as saltpeter (potassium nitrate), with the instruction: "Take a decoction of saltpeter to prolong life." Ancient physicians prescribed saltpeter to treat pain from what we know as angina pectoris, a temporary deprivation of oxygen to the heart. They instructed the patient to place the compound under the tongue for as long as possible and then swallow the saliva. These prescient docs knew this delivery method could save lives, without knowing that bacteria under the tongue convert nitrate to nitrite, thus dilating the blood vessels.

Modern medicine has been using nitroglycerin (glyceryl trinitrate) for decades as an emergency blood vessel dilator for patients with angina to take when experiencing chest pain that signals a heart attack may be striking. A common form of nitroglycerin is the sublingual tablet, from which the compound is quickly converted to nitric oxide, which then causes vasodilation, allowing blood and the oxygen it carries to reach the heart.

Diet (Dietary Approaches to Stop Hypertension), which includes a high intake of fruits and vegetables. One expert calculated that a person who followed the DASH Diet would exceed the recommended level of nitrate set by World Health Organization by 550%. Health professionals may say, "Of course we don't recommend reducing fruit and vegetable intake, just processed meat," suggesting that the nitrate and nitrite from these different foods is somehow different. But according to Dr. Andrew Milkowski, noted biochemist and adjunct professor at the University of Wisconsin, there is no biochemical distinction: "Nitrite is nitrite, nitric oxide is nitric oxide."

Dr. Milkowski has suggested a "risk-benefit evaluation" in how we look at nitric oxide. There's no dispute that the 1992 "Molecule of the Year" is essential to the health of our cardiovascular and immune systems. Indeed, a short supply of this vital compound is a marker for cardiovascular disease. Since the body uses nitrite to generate nitric oxide, Dr. Milkowski has proposed that nitrite may be the backup system for nitric oxide. And since half of our body's nitrite content comes from what we eat, our food intake can play an important role in preventing disease.

The weight of the evidence is that nitrate and nitrite are not harmful in quantities typically consumed through food, including processed meats, in which they serve the valuable function of preventing foodborne illness. In fact, through their conversion to nitric oxide, they may actually help prevent certain chronic diseases. As Dr. Nathan Bryan at the University of Texas Health Science Center states, "Dietary nitrate and nitrite have been shown to reduce inflammation, restore endothelial function, protect from heart attack and stroke, and even improve exercise performance."

Fat

In the 1960s, health agencies and governments around the world began issuing dietary guidelines admonishing everyone to reduce their intake of fat, and especially saturated fat. And starting in the 1980s, the low-fat diet craze hit its peak, with low-fat and nonfat products lining grocery store shelves from one end to the other. Most of today's dietitians and other health professionals were weaned on the belief that saturated fat was public enemy number one in the fight against heart disease. The thinking and teaching went something like this: When blood cholesterol is high, it clogs the blood vessels, cutting off blood (and oxygen) to the heart, and dietary saturated fat, more than dietary cholesterol, is the main driver of high blood cholesterol. This dogma remained unchallenged until the first decade of the 21st century.

Fat in Food and Fat in the Body

Most people think of fat as something to avoid in their diet. But its reputation is largely undeserved. Fat plays an important role in various body functions. The type of fat we eat in foods is the same kind we store in our bodies: triglyceride. As part of the energy-providing nutrient trio (along with carbohydrate and protein), one of fat's most important roles is to save extra energy we get from food for times when we need that energy. Many of us may complain about how fat we are, but if we had to store our energy reserves as carbohydrate, we'd have to buy clothes in a much bigger size!

Body fat acts as insulation against temperature extremes and cushions the organs from injury. On a microscopic level, fat molecules make up the protective membrane surrounding each of the average adult's 37 trillion cells.

As for dietary fat, vitamins A, D, E and K are fat-soluble, which means they need to be eaten with fat to be absorbed and used by the body. People who have diseases that affect their ability to absorb fat, such as Crohn's disease and some disorders of the pancreas and liver, can end up with a deficiency of these vitamins. Dietary fat also helps us absorb phytonutrients, healthy compounds found mostly in plant foods. Moreover, two fatty acids — linoleic acid (an omega-6 fat) and alpha-linolenic acid (an omega-3 fat) — are essential nutrients, meaning the body cannot produce them on its own and must ingest them through diet in order to function normally.

Dietary fat contributes flavor and produces that velvety sensation you experience when you put a piece of dark chocolate in your mouth, which food scientists call mouth feel. Fat also contributes to satiety, a feeling of fullness after a meal, because it's the last nutrient to leave the stomach. This may be one reason why people who eat a diet very low in fat can't seem to get enough food.

Dietary Fat Intake as a Risk Factor for Heart Disease

Even back in the late 1950s, when the American Heart Association first made dietary fat recommendations, they stated, "The ratio between saturated and unsaturated fat may be the basic determinant" in heart disease. Most of

Calories per Gram

Fat takes up roughly half the space, in chemical terms, as carbohydrate or protein. So, at 9 calories per gram, dietary fat has a higher caloric value than carbohydrate and protein, at 4 calories per gram. This is one reason to moderate your intake of fat: it's very easy to take in too many calories, which can lead to weight gain.

the focus was on three general classes of dietary fat, based on an esoteric chemical difference: the number of double bonds between carbon atoms. Saturated fat has no double bonds, monounsaturated fat has one double bond, and polyunsaturated fat has more than one double bond.

American physiologist Ancel Keys first publicized the Mediterranean diet in the 1970s, but the diet didn't gain traction until the 1990s, when it was widely touted as protective against chronic diseases, especially heart disease. Researchers looking at the exact components of the diet quickly realized it was not low in fat. In fact, it contained up to 40% of calories as fat and, in some regions, up to 9% of calories as saturated fat. To put this into perspective, at that time the recommended fat intake was less than 30%, with some famous gurus even promoting a level as low as 10%. As for saturated fat, even now health authorities recommend an intake of less than 7%. The researchers also noted that the Mediterranean diet included more monounsaturated fat, especially in the form of olive oil. But the focus was still on the three major groups of fat.

A few years later, studies started showing that it wasn't as simple as lumping fats into those three major groups. Researchers learned that different fatty acids have different effects on the level of cholesterol in the blood, which they concluded was the real risk factor for heart disease. Further research pointed to how complex the development of heart disease actually is: beyond blood cholesterol levels, the size and number of the particles that carry cholesterol in the blood (high-density lipoprotein, or "good" cholesterol, and low-density lipoprotein, or "bad" cholesterol) is important, as is the process of inflammation and many other variables. Interestingly enough, studies found that reducing saturated fat tends to lower *both* high-density lipoprotein and low-density lipoprotein

cholesterol. Some experts started questioning whether lowering blood cholesterol by changing the diet actually translated into less risk for heart disease.

When it comes right down to it, it's hard to pinpoint what role dietary fat plays in heart disease in real life (as opposed to the test tube). In addition to a mix of many fatty acids, foods contain thousands of other compounds that can influence heart health, some of which are protective. And food is not the only factor involved. Dr. Marion Nestle, nutrition professor at New York University, summed it up nicely: "Diet is one factor that affects heart disease risk among many others: lifestyle, physical activity, cigarette smoking, genetics, etc."

Cousins But Not Clones

We are all different — that seems obvious. But when it comes to nutrition research, genetic differences were not always taken into account. Now scientists tell us that healthy adults differ not only in what they like to eat, but also in how much of each nutrient they need.

You may recall from biology class that we have more than 20,000 genes in the cells of our bodies. These genes serve as blueprints for all the structures and compounds the body has to make. You inherit your genes from your parents, but even though they may both have been tall, you don't have one gene that tells your body to grow to a certain height. Instead, several genes work together with your intake of nutrients and other factors to determine your height. Your body can't choose which genes you get, but it does control which genes are active at a particular point in time. This activation is called gene expression.

Variability in gene expression has ushered in new fields of study that go hand in hand: nutrigenomics and nutrigenetics. Nutrigenomics looks at how your diet affects gene expression, while

Omega-3s and Fetal Brain Development

Studies show that a pregnant woman's intake of omega-3 fatty acids affects brain development and cognitive function in the fetus, probably through gene expression in a specific gene that controls how the body uses fatty acids.

nutrigenetics looks at how your genes make your body respond to changes in your diet. For some people, a high intake of fat, or a specific type of fat, might activate genes that make them susceptible to a certain disease; that's nutrigenomics at work. As for nutrigenetics, some people can eat 14 eggs a week and still have low cholesterol, while for others, consuming even 7 eggs a week can cause their genes to drive up their blood cholesterol levels. (Researchers have actually known for many years that people they call "responders" have an increase in blood cholesterol levels with increased egg intake, while "nonresponders" experience no such effect.)

Researchers need to learn a lot more about the interplay between diet and genes before health professionals can really offer "personalized nutrition." But these new fields do provide a glimpse into the future and help clarify why different studies of dietary fat often have conflicting results, causing a swirl of controversy with experts lined up on opposite sides of the aisle.

The Bottom Line

The old adage "Different strokes for different folks" makes sense when it comes to dietary fat (or any nutrient, for that matter). The total amount of fat that works for most people is in the range of 25% to 35% of total calories, but a bit less or a bit more is probably insignificant. Remember, though, that too high a fat intake can make it hard to manage your weight, because fat provides twice as much energy as protein and carbohydrate. It's easier to ingest too many calories when your fat intake is high. But if you lean toward the lower end of the range, remember that if you eat too little fat you won't optimally absorb fat-soluble vitamins and phytonutrients, and you may feel hungry again sooner.

Most health authorities still recommend reduced intake of saturated fat, especially if you have a history of heart disease, although nutrition experts seem to think there should be less emphasis on this point. If you decide to lower your intake of saturated fat, consider what you are replacing it with. Carbohydrate in the form of sugar or low-fiber starchy desserts may be even worse choices when it comes to heart disease markers.

Another thing to consider when reducing saturated fat is that, while it might lower your "bad" cholesterol, it also might lower your "good" cholesterol.

Lessons from Sardinia

For living proof that sausages can be part of a healthy diet, take a look at the world's longest-lived people, who live on the island of Sardinia, off the coast of Italy. Many Sardinians live to the age of 100. They enjoy a varied diet that includes fish and beans, and they eat meat about once a week. One traditional food is a fresh sausage made with cuts of fatty pork.

And ultimately, as some researchers have pointed out, the level of cholesterol in your blood may not be the most important risk factor for heart disease. A nice summation of these ideas comes from Dr. Tilakavati Karupaiah, Associate Professor and Clinical Coordinator of Health Sciences at the National University of Malaysia: "The best approach is to blend unsaturated and saturated [fat] in one's diet."

Fat in Sausages

One great thing about making sausages at home is that you control the amount and type of fat used. For example, if you are making pork sausage, the typical cut used is pork shoulder blade. If you use this cut without trimming off the cap and outer visible fat, the sausages are still only a medium-fat meat. If you remove the cap and the outer fat, the sausages become a lean meat, providing more than three times as much protein as fat. In our taste tests, we found that the amount of fat panelists preferred was highly subjective, so experiment until you find the right balance to suit your taste preferences and health needs.

Another bonus of making your own sausages is that you don't even have to use meat — you can use fish or beans and cut fat way back. Using fish also provides healthy omega-3 fatty acids, which all experts agree will boost your health, and beans provide lots of fiber and healthy phytonutrients.

But even if you have a sensitive "fat tooth," you can still enjoy traditional sausages that are high in fat and saturated fat, as long as you control the amount you eat and how often you eat them. For example, instead of eating kielbasa as your entrée, cut a small amount into slices or small chunks and mix them with whole grains. You'll find meal suggestions for combination dishes in Part 4.

Salt

Sausages are often criticized for being high in salt. Sodium chloride, the chemical name for table salt, consists of 40% sodium and 60% chloride. Both of these minerals are essential nutrients — we need them to survive. Scientists know the amount we need for survival and have set a dietary reference intake (DRI) level for each. Just about everyone agrees that consuming an amount of sodium far above the DRI is potentially detrimental to overall health. But some health authorities worry that the DRI for sodium is too low; they believe that people striving to lower their sodium to meet this guideline may in fact also be harming their health.

So why is sodium necessary for our survival? In the body, sodium is the main mineral outside the cells, and it controls the amount of water in the blood. It also keeps the blood at the right level of acidity, an important role since small deviations can be deadly. Other key functions include a role in muscle contraction and moving compounds across cell membranes.

Along with sodium, chloride helps us maintain fluid and electrolyte balance. Chloride also forms part of hydrochloric acid in the stomach, helping us digest food. Chloride can be quickly depleted by heavy sweating, chronic vomiting or diarrhea.

The experts that set the DRIs for all essential nutrients have two different categories of recommended intake levels to work from. Knowing the difference between these two categories gives you an idea of how solid the evidence is for the level they set:

- **Recommended dietary allowance (RDA):** The average daily dietary nutrient intake level sufficient to meet the nutrient requirement of nearly all (97% to 98%) of healthy individuals in a particular life stage and gender group.

- **Adequate intake (AI):** The recommended average daily intake level based on observed or experimentally determined approximations or estimates of nutrient intake by a group (or groups) of apparently healthy people. Used when an RDA cannot be determined.

The category used for sodium and chloride is AI, so it is clear that the evidence used to set the DRI is not as compelling as for nutrients that have an RDA.

Here are the current recommendations in North America: adults up to the age of 50 should consume no more than 2300 milligrams of sodium per day. Adults who are over 51, who have African heritage or who have hypertension (high blood pressure), diabetes or kidney disease should consume no more than 1500 milligrams of sodium.

To put those milligrams in perspective, a half teaspoon (2 mL) of salt contains 1200 milligrams. You can see why the recommendations have become controversial: it is very challenging for the average person to meet these guidelines.

Dr. James DiNicolantonio, a researcher in the Department of Preventive Cardiology at Saint Luke's Mid America Heart Institute and one of the authors of the *Open Heart* review on fat recommendations, published an article in that journal in 2015 on the latest salt recommendations. In the article, titled "The Wrong White Crystal," he suggests that sugar, not salt, is the real culprit in hypertension and other diseases. In addition, citing several studies, he points out that "reducing sodium intake could lead to worse health outcomes, such as increased cardiovascular and all-cause mortality in patients with diabetes, and increased hospitalizations and mortality in patients with congestive heart failure."

Dr. DiNicolantonio cites a recent study of over 100,000 patients, reporting that "daily sodium intake between 3000 and 6000 milligrams was associated with a lower risk of death and cardiovascular events compared to either a higher or lower level of intake." In his opinion — and other experts agree with him — "guidelines advising restriction of sodium intake below 3000 milligrams/day may cause harm."

Salt in Sausages

The controversy over sodium intake is ongoing. Nevertheless, people with a very high intake, certain medical conditions or salt sensitivity will benefit from reducing the amount of salt in their diet.

In the past, salt served a vital preservation function in sausages. But now that we have freezers and refrigeration, when you are making fresh or cooked sausages you can easily reduce the salt, or even omit it entirely, and still have a safe product. In these types of sausages, salt is simply a flavoring

An Age-Old Controversy

In some ancient civilizations, salt was considered so valuable it was used as currency. The reason for its exalted status? Its role in food preservation. But in ancient China, doctors cautioned against the use of too much salt, as with this warning, credited to Huang Ti in 2700 BCE: "If too much salt is used in food, the pulse hardens." Who would have guessed that, so many centuries later, the debate about salt would rage on unabated?

Sodium-Potassium Balance

A study published in the *Archives of Internal Medicine* pointed to the importance of the balance of sodium and potassium in the diet for heart and blood pressure health. People with the highest ratio of dietary sodium to potassium had a higher risk for death compared to those with the lowest sodium to potassium dietary intake. The authors suggested increasing intake of fruits and vegetables, which are good sources of potassium and naturally low in sodium. Other experts suggest the use of potassium salt substitutes.

ingredient, and you can compensate somewhat for the loss of flavor through the use of herb and spice combinations.

When making dried sausages, however, you should stick with the amount of salt specified in the recipe, because, as discussed in Chapter 2, salt has important antimicrobial and quality functions that are critical to the safety of these sausages.

If you do decide to omit the salt from your fresh or cooked sausages, you might want to consider replacing it with a sodium-free salt substitute that contains potassium chloride instead of sodium chloride. The added advantage of this product is that it provides potassium, which numerous studies have shown to be protective against hypertension, heart attacks and strokes. (Caution: People with kidney disease must control their intake of potassium, so this product is not for them.) Experiment with the amount of salt substitute you use until you find the flavor balance that suits you.

Protein

Protein is the main constituent of our organs, skeletal muscles and bones. And all of the protein in our body is functional — it performs a job. For example, many of the protein compounds in our blood carry other nutrients or oxygen, and the protein in our muscles allows us to do physical work. So we don't store protein as we do fat. It's not surprising, then, that we need to eat a sufficient amount of protein to help our body keep cranking out the specialized proteins it needs to function.

We get 4 calories from every gram of protein we eat, so along with fat and carbohydrate, protein provides us with energy. But more importantly, when we eat protein, we also get its component building blocks: amino acids. Twenty-one different amino acids are needed to make all of the proteins in the body. The body can make 12 of them on its own, but the remaining 9 must come from dietary protein and are thus considered essential.

The food we eat, whether from plants or animals, contains a combination of amino acids in varying amounts. However, not all protein is created equal, so nutritionists talk about the quality of a protein food. The determining factor in protein quality is the amino acid profile. The protein in animal foods contains all of the essential amino acids. In contrast, plant proteins tend to fall short in one or more essential amino acids. Vegans, who eat no animal products, can still consume adequate protein, but they must be more attentive about including many different plant products in their diet to ensure that deficiencies in essential amino acids in one food are balanced by another.

North Americans typically have no problem getting enough protein. The recommended daily amount for the average adult is 0.8 grams per kilogram of body weight. However, studies now point to the benefit of a higher protein intake for weight loss and maintenance. And for the elderly, evidence suggests that a higher-protein diet preserves muscle. (Caution: People with chronic kidney disease must control or reduce protein in the diet, because the kidneys have difficulty excreting the byproducts of protein digestion.)

Sausages are typically a good source of protein, especially those made with less fat, because this concentrates the protein they contain. Even vegetarian sausages can be a good source of protein if made with tofu or legumes (such as chickpeas or kidney beans).

Nutrition in a Nutshell

No one food in moderate amounts is harmful to health, and no one food is the elixir of good health. To get the most benefit from food, the best approach is one that has been preached for millennia: variety and moderation. Unfortunately, too many people these days promote a way of eating that excludes entire groups of foods. The healthier approach considers that a wide variety of foods contain essential nutrients and health-promoting phytonutrients. Of course, these same foods may also contain compounds we need to consume in moderation.

In a nutshell, a great example is the humble Brazil nut, which you can pick fresh off the tree without any processing, other than removing the shell! This nut provides an ample supply of many essential nutrients and healthy phytonutrients, including protein, essential fatty acids, fiber, vitamin E, thiamin, copper, manganese, magnesium, phosphorus and zinc. Just one Brazil nut contains 100% of the selenium, an essential antioxidant mineral, you need for the entire day. But guess what? Even though selenium is necessary for your survival, it can also be toxic within a very narrow range of intake. So if you eat too many of these nutritious nuts too often, you can develop problems such as abnormal changes in skin and nails, tooth decay, gastrointestinal distress and neurological abnormalities.

Sausages of all types can be a nutritious part of your diet. While meat sausages, especially those made with beef, pork or lamb, can be high in total fat and saturated fat, eaten in moderation they provide valuable essential nutrients such as high-quality protein, vitamins

Nutrient Analysis

We decided not to include nutritional analyses for the recipes after determining that even the most sophisticated analysis software was unable to provide the precision needed. There are many variables that greatly affect the final amount of nutrients in a sausage, and especially total fat, which is the main determinant of calories and saturated fat in the product. For example, in addition to the difficulty in quantifying the amount of fat that is trimmed off the meat, there is wide variation in the amount of fat from one animal to another. In the end, we realized there were far too many variables to allow for accurate nutrient analysis.

Meaty Health Benefits

Red meat, including beef and pork, provides the compound carnitine, which helps in energy production and fights free radicals before they can cause damage. Researchers believe carnitine may help people stay in good cognitive shape and fend off dementia as they age. And in studies of older rats, carnitine improved or reversed the usual decline in mitochondrial functioning in muscle and heart tissue.

Meat also contains iron, another essential nutrient, in its most bioavailable form, which means the body can absorb more of it. In addition, meat contains a compound that improves our absorption of less bioavailable iron from plants.

The mineral zinc is also more bioavailable from meat products than from plants, because plants contain other compounds that reduce our absorption of this essential mineral.

and minerals. Many of the poultry recipes (page 185–210) are lean or even very lean options. And, for variety, as well as important phytonutrients and fiber, you'll also want to try some of the vegetarian sausages.

Including Vegetarian Sausages in Your Meals

Even if you include meat in your diet and don't typically prepare food for vegetarians, there are important nutrition and health reasons to include vegetarian sausages in your diet. Plus, they're a delicious way to add variety to your meal plan!

While meat has many nutritional benefits, when overconsumed it can nudge out other nutritious foods. People who eat a lot of meat often eat fewer whole grains, vegetables, legumes and fruits. And while meat is high in good-quality protein and many vitamins and minerals, it doesn't contain certain essential nutrients. For example, vitamin C protects against oxidative stress, builds collagen and boosts immunity, among many other key functions. And fiber is important for optimal bowel function and feeding the good bacteria that live in the intestinal tract. Meat contains no appreciable

amounts of either vitamin C or fiber.

Vegetarian sausages can also provide another important group of compounds that meat lacks: phytonutrients. These compounds have numerous biologic effects that can help prevent many of the chronic diseases that plague modern humans, including cardiovascular disease, cancer and diabetes.

The majority of vegetarian sausage recipes include some form of legume (beans, peas and lentils), which serves as the protein source. Studies have reported reductions in blood pressure, blood glucose levels and blood cholesterol levels with the addition of just $^1/_2$ cup (125 mL) of legumes per day.

Vegetarian sausages are a terrific addition to your diet, diversifying your health portfolio and increasing your intake of fiber, essential nutrients and phytonutrients.

PART 2

SAUSAGE-MAKING ESSENTIALS

CHAPTER 4
The Right Tools for the Job

When it comes to sausage-making equipment, the choices are endless and the pricing wide-ranging, so it's important to ask yourself a few questions before you head to the store. You can get going on making sausages with just a small monetary investment (though this may make the job a bit more difficult and time-consuming), or you can go all out and purchase an array of top-of-the-line appliances. Some traditionalists still use a hand-crank grinder, while others opt for high-powered machines that can process huge quantities of meat in the blink of an eye.

Essentially, to make sausages, you need a grinder, a mixer and a stuffer. Some sausage-making equipment combines all three in one product; others sell components that can be added to the basic unit to perform the entire job. One example of the latter is a high-end stand mixer. The basic unit comes with a mixing bowl and different types of beater attachments, which is perfect for the mixing component of the process. But you can also purchase meat-grinding and sausage-stuffing attachments that will allow you to make sausages from start to finish.

Aside from how much you want to invest, ask yourself how much sausage you want to make at one time and how often you intend to make sausages. These will be the major determinants in making a good decision about what equipment to purchase.

In addition to grinding, mixing and stuffing equipment, you will also need a kitchen scale and a meat thermometer. If you intend to make smoked sausages, you will need a smoker, and if you intend to make dried sausages, you will need a drying chamber.

Meat Grinder Components

All meat grinders have the same basic parts; a hopper, an auger, blades and grinder plates. Many also come with extruding tubes for stuffing the casings. The auger delivers the meat from the input tube to the blades and then either through the grinder plate (when you're grinding the meat) or into the extruding tube (when you're stuffing the casings).

Hand-Crank Grinder

If you're only going to make sausages infrequently and in small batches, a hand-crank grinder (also called a manual grinder) is the way to go. These grinders, typically made from tin-coated cast iron or plastic, come in a variety of sizes. They usually clamp or bolt to a counter or table, but some have suction cups.

We recommend avoiding the kind with suction cups because they inevitably end up losing their grip, and you'll need to find another way to fasten the grinder to the counter. The type that clamps to the counter will give you the best results.

Hand-crank grinders have a model number associated with them. The higher the number, the more meat per minute you can grind. For example, a #8 grinder will grind 1 to 2 pounds (500 g to 1 kg) of meat per minute, while a #10 grinder will grind 2 to 3 pounds (1 to 1.5 kg) per minute. With each level of increased capacity comes increased hopper size, larger grinder plates and, of course, higher cost.

Electric Grinder

Electric grinders are powered by a motor instead by elbow grease. As with most appliances, their cost varies widely depending on size, the materials the grinder is constructed from and how powerful the motor is. To make cleanup easier, some models have parts that are dishwasher-safe. Keep in mind that machines with aluminum parts cannot be washed in the dishwasher. If you intend to keep your grinder on the countertop, you may want to consider a stainless steel grinder, which is both more attractive and easier to clean than cast-iron or aluminum construction.

The size of the machine plays a role in the cost, but more important is the size of the motor, which is expressed in amps or horsepower. Some machines use plastic parts in the motor, which may fail sooner than a motor that has only metal parts. In the Resources (page 259), you will find the address for an excellent website with reviews on a variety of electric meat grinders.

Heavy-Duty Stand Mixer

Some machines are made to do a host of different jobs. Many heavy-duty stand mixers will accept attachments for grinding meat and stuffing sausages (among many other functions). These machines have a high price tag because they are so versatile, but if you want to purchase a multiuse appliance and you don't plan to make sausages too frequently, a stand mixer might be a good investment.

Even if you decide to purchase a separate meat grinder and sausage stuffer, a stand mixer can come in very handy for mixing the ground meat with the other ingredients. However, the ingredients can also be mixed by hand, so a stand mixer is not a necessity for making sausages.

A Word About Grinder Plates

The grinder plate is the metallic disc through which the meat is extruded after it is cut by the blades of the grinder. There are numerous holes in the plate, and the diameter of those holes determines the coarseness or fineness of the meat particles in the final product. Common hole diameters include $1/8$ inch (3 mm), $5/32$ inch (4 mm), $3/16$ inch (4.5 mm), $1/4$ inch (5 mm) and $3/8$ inch (9.5 mm). Depending on the grinder you purchase, it may include only one plate or as many as six. Our recipes refer to "coarse" and "fine" grinder plates, which, if your grinder comes with only two plates, is likely what they are called. If your plates are named according to the size of their holes, use a $1/8$-inch (3 mm) plate where we say "fine" and a $3/16$-inch (4.5 mm) plate where we say "coarse."

Food Processor

A food processor is indispensable for certain aspects of sausage making. For example, it is the best tool for emulsifying the meat when you are making emulsified sausages such as hot dogs or liverwurst. It is also useful for chopping up non-meat ingredients.

Sausage Stuffer

There are several different types of sausage stuffers, and they all accomplish the same task, though in a slightly different way. The main differences are the mechanisms, the capacity and the speed.

The simplest and cheapest type of stuffer is the sausage funnel. Sausage funnels come in a variety of sizes and materials, but all are about 5 inches (12.5 cm) long — long enough to gather the casings. Although called a funnel, they are not shaped like one: there is very little taper on a sausage funnel. The meat is pushed through the funnel by hand, so it takes quite a while to stuff the casings. If you don't make sausages often and have some time on your hands, this can be a good way to stuff sausages.

Another tool is the push stuffer. These don't have a very large capacity, so they must be reloaded often. It can also be a challenge to push the plunger down when you're making smaller sausages, such as breakfast links, as you are trying to force the meat through a relatively small opening. On the plus side, they're very inexpensive and get the job done nicely.

A popular option is the crank stuffer. If you intend to make a large batch of sausages, this is a good option. Crank stuffers hold anywhere from 3 to 25 pounds (1.5 to 11 kg) of ground meat. They typically have a reducer gear that makes it easier to operate the crank. One person can operate a crank stuffer, but you might want to consider having a helper so one of you can operate the crank while the other guides meat into the casing.

A water stuffer is operated hydraulically and can be run by one person. These are a bit more expensive than other types of stuffers. Some models attach to a garden hose, or you can get adapters to attach them to your kitchen or utility room sink. If you are a regular sausage maker, you might want to consider this type of stuffer.

Sausage Stuffer Attachments

Many meat grinders also come with extruding tubes to allow you to stuff sausages. And if you have a stand mixer, you can purchase a sausage stuffer attachment with extruding tubes. Either way, the tubes may be plastic or stainless steel, and each has advantages and disadvantages. Stainless steel is much more durable than plastic, but it cannot be washed in a dishwasher because this may cause discoloration and corrosion of the metal. In addition, acidic foods can tarnish the finish. If you choose equipment with plastic tubes, make sure they are dishwasher-safe for the easiest cleanup.

Kitchen Scale

Another indispensable piece of equipment is a kitchen scale. A scale will allow you to measure the weight of your meat precisely, so that you end up with the right amount after trimming. If you plan to make dried sausages, you'll also need to weigh a sausage strand right after stuffing it and then periodically as it dries, until it loses 30% of its original weight (which tells you that the sausage is sufficiently dried).

The price of scales varies widely. As long as the tray can hold the largest amount of meat you intend to use, it should be adequate.

Meat Thermometer

An accurate meat thermometer is critical for certain aspects of sausage making. The meat mixture used to make emulsified sausages, for example, must be at a very specific temperature, which you'll need a thermometer to gauge. You'll also need to check the internal temperature when smoking sausages and when cooking fresh sausages, to ensure safe eating.

Purchase a thermometer that measures up to 220°F (104°C). Using the dishwasher to clean a thermometer that has come into contact with meat improves food safety, so look for one that is dishwasher-safe. And make sure to buy one that can be calibrated.

Calibrating Your Thermometer

It's a smart idea to calibrate your meat thermometer periodically, especially before making sausages. The easiest way is to use ice water. Fill a glass with crushed ice topped with cold water. Stir the ice water and let it stand for 3 minutes. Stir again and place the thermometer in the glass for 1 minute, preventing it from touching the sides. If properly calibrated, the thermometer should register 32°F (0°C), plus or minus 2 degrees. If it is off this range, follow the instructions on adjusting the thermometer until it reads the correct temperature. The simple non-digital thermometers have a nut below the head where the adjustment can be made.

Smokers

Smoked meats have been a staple around the world for centuries. There are two basic smoking processes: hot smoking and cold smoking. Hot smoking involves using direct heat to cook the meat to a temperature that makes it safe for consumption while introducing a smoke flavor to the meat. Cold smoking is done at a lower temperature, often with the heat in a separate chamber, and for a shorter time, just to add the smoke flavor before the meat is cured through the drying process. The smoke flavor comes from wood chips that are added to the smoker. Popular wood choices include hardwoods (such as pecan, mesquite, hickory, alder or maple) and fruit woods (such as apple, pear or plum).

There is a dizzying array of smokers available on the market, as well as many plans to build your own. A quick Internet search yields colorful descriptions of using just about anything you can seal up and put smoke and heat inside: terracotta flower pots, garbage cans, old refrigerators, empty metal barrels. We used a commercial smoker, and we recommend you do too because, with makeshift materials, the sausages can become contaminated with various metals and compounds. Another important reason to purchase a smoker is to avoid the guesswork related to maintaining the temperature at the appropriate level, as the better commercial smokers come with a thermostat.

Before making this investment, first ask yourself whether you even enjoy the taste of smoked sausages — many people do not. If you do, and you see yourself making them frequently, there are several considerations that will affect what type of smoker you buy: how many sausages you intend to smoke at one time, what your preferred heat source is and how much money you are willing to spend.

Some barbecue grills are marketed as smokers. While you can smoke sausages using these units, it's not as easy as using a smoker that is specifically designed for sausages. There are several problems. One is that you can't hang the sausages. And because of the design of most grills, the sausage ends up being too close to the heat. Another issue is that there is no thermostat to regulate the internal temperature — you will need to continually monitor the sausages throughout the process, which can take many hours.

One dedicated type of smoker is a kettle smoker, which is similar in appearance to the domed outdoor kettle grills that became popular in the 1990s. These units include a thermometer on the outside of the dome top. You can purchase kettle smokers with different heat sources: charcoal, electric or propane. Our preference is for electric because it doesn't have to be continually monitored. And barring a power outage, the smoker will continue to do its job with less advance preparation and monitoring, which can be a problem if someone forgot to check if the propane tank is full. One minor inconvenience with kettle smokers is that they have smaller capacity and access is only from the top of the unit.

Another type of smoker is a vertical cabinet unit, which offers many advantages. Large cabinet smokers can accommodate large amounts of sausages, but even the smallest will work for a 2-pound (1 kg) batch (or a double batch). If you think you will be smoking sausage in the winter, make sure the smoker has an insulated box. Also check how many racks the unit includes — depending on how many sausages you want to smoke at one time, you'll need enough room to hang them with adequate space between them. (The sausages should be spaced so as not to touch each other or the smoker walls.)

Smokehouses

Really dedicated sausage makers who love the taste of smoked sausages, and intend to make large batches often, might wish to go all out and buy or build a smokehouse. You can easily build your own smokehouse from readily available specifications using brick, wood or metal. Or you can buy a premade smokehouse. The wood pellets intended for burning in a smokehouse are similar in shape to hockey pucks and come in a variety of hardwoods.

Drying Chamber

If you're going to make dried sausages, you'll need a place to dry them that is sufficiently cool and has adequate air movement. When my father used to make sausages, he would dry them in the attic. He hung them on pieces of closet pole, or whatever similar wood pieces he could find, suspended from the rafters by wires tied around nails. It had to be the right time of year, just at the end of winter and the beginning of spring. Every day he would check on them to make sure they didn't freeze or dry improperly.

If you plan to use an attic or basement, aim for a temperature between 36°F and 40°F (2°C and 5°C). If the temperature goes below 28°F (–2°C), the meat will freeze; above 50°F (10°C), bacterial growth is encouraged, and the meat may rot. If your house has gable vents, or continuous soffit vents and a continuous ridge vent, or adequate attic exhaust vents, you should have enough air movement. Make sure everything is sealed up so that animals can't get to the sausages before you do.

Another option is to make your own drying room, like we did. Our room was constructed from a second-hand walk-in cooler, which we set up in the garage and retrofitted with lights, a humidifier and a dehumidifier. Of course, the walk-in cooler already had the cooling unit, which consists of the compressor and evaporator fan. The whole thing is controlled by a thermostat and a humidistat to keep the conditions just right for making dried sausages year-round.

There are two main things to keep in mind when designing your own drying room: the ideal temperature in controlled conditions is between 50°F and 55°F (10°C and 13°C) and the humidity should be about 70%. To get the meat to dry properly and keep it from rotting, you also need a fan to keep the air circulating.

The Humidity Factor

The humidity level is important in attics and basements, too, but it is nearly impossible to control in those locations. We highly recommend constructing your own drying chamber if you want to make dried sausage, to ensure safety and prevent loss of product.

CHAPTER 5

Selecting Your Ingredients

There aren't too many food items that can't be used in sausage making. Ordinarily, we think first of meat sausages, and they are certainly the most common. But you can also make sausages from vegetables, legumes, mushrooms, nuts and grains, or combinations of these healthy foods — just about anything your imagination can conjure up. The ability to create innovative combinations of your favorite ingredients is one of the biggest advantages of making your own sausages.

Sausage Meats

The selection of meats you can use to make sausages is nearly endless: pork, beef, lamb, chicken, turkey, game meats such as venison, elk and moose — even fish. One major decision is whether to buy boneless meat or to bone it yourself. Most people prefer to buy boneless, as it saves a considerable amount of time; however, bone-in meat is less expensive.

Whatever meat you decide to use, it is important to have a clear idea of when you intend to make the sausages, as that will determine when you should buy the meat. For optimal quality, plan to make sausages within 4 days of purchasing fresh meat.

If you are purchasing prepackaged meat, make sure the package has no punctures and is not leaking. There should be minimal or no liquid in the package. Also, check that the package is cool to the touch — a sign that it has been refrigerated at the proper temperature. Look at the "sell by" or "best before" date on the package to make sure it isn't about to expire (unless you intend to freeze it).

Some would argue that where you buy your meat is the most important way to ensure high-quality sausages, and it's hard to disagree. If you've had good success with purchasing meat from a particular grocery store or local butcher, start there. Select your meat just before checking out, and if you live more than a half hour from the store or plan to make a few stops before heading home, place the meat in a cooler full of ice. Once home, either refrigerate the meat immediately or freeze it if you don't plan to make your sausages within the next 4 days.

Pork

A large proportion of the recipes in this book are made with pork, and for good reason: all over the world, pork has long been the most popular meat for sausage making.

The majority of our pork sausages use a boneless pork shoulder blade roast, which is also called pork butt, pork shoulder roast, Boston butt and Boston shoulder roast. It comes from the shoulder of the pig and has a moderate amount of fat on it. But removing the cap, the outer fat and some of the visible internal fat turns it into a lean meat, meaning that it provides more than twice as much protein as fat.

The average pork shoulder roast is about 6 to 10 pounds (2.7 to 4.5 kg), but this cut can also be purchased in multiple portions of as much as 15 pounds (6.8 kg) or more. If you buy a single packaged boneless pork shoulder blade roast at a large grocery store, most of the external fat will have already been trimmed, leaving just the internal fat you'll see when

Lower-Fat Sausages

If you want to reduce the fat content of your sausages, you can either buy a leaner cut of meat or you can trim off as much of the visible fat as possible. Consider adding ingredients that can help compensate for moisture, texture and flavor losses, such as fruits, vegetables or cooked oatmeal or rice. Cheese and nuts, while also improving moisture, texture and flavor, add back fat and therefore calories — but they do contribute valuable nutrients and phytonutrients.

you begin cutting the meat, and will be approximately 85% lean to 15% fat. If you purchase an untrimmed pork shoulder blade roast at the meat counter or a butcher shop, it will likely be about 75% lean meat to 25% fat. Keep in mind, though, that each individual animal of the same species varies in its proportion of lean to fat.

For our pork sausages, we recommend a ratio of 85% lean meat to 15% fat. The majority of our taste testers preferred that ratio, although some preferred fattier sausage and some preferred leaner sausages. In the end, the ratio of lean to fat is really up to you, based on your taste preference. We suggest making the sausages with 85/15 meat the first time you prepare the recipe, then adjust the fat content as desired the next time you make it. (One word of caution: if you remove too much fat, you'll end up with rather dry sausages.)

When you are purchasing an untrimmed pork shoulder blade roast for your first sausage-making attempt, ask a butcher to give you an idea of how much fat you should remove to get an 85% lean to 15% fat ratio. Or, even better, tell the butcher you want 2 pounds (1 kg) of 85/15 meat and have him or her cut the piece and trim it for you. You might want to take pictures of the pork roast before and after trimming, to make it easier to achieve this ratio yourself the next time you make sausages.

When trimming the meat yourself at home, first trim all of the visible fat from the outside of the roast. If you want to remove more fat, make a lengthwise cut into the roast so that you can trim out some fat from the inside of the meat. If you plan to use 85% lean meat to 15% fat, you will need to purchase at least 4 pounds (2 kg) of untrimmed boneless pork shoulder blade roast, depending on the amount of fat on the meat, to end up with the 2 pounds (1 kg) of trimmed meat required for most of the recipes. Any leftover meat can be carefully packed into freezer bags and stored in the freezer for up to 6 months.

Pork Trimmings

Some of the recipes call for pork trimmings. By this, we mean pieces of trimmed fat that still have a bit of meat attached, rather than being pure fat. You can save your trimmings from one sausage-making event and freeze them for another recipe that calls for trimmings. You can also save them to add to meat that is a bit too lean for optimal sausages.

Pork Back Fat

As the name suggests, back fat, also called fatback, comes from the pig's back. Back fat is a hard fat, found just under the animal's skin (as opposed to soft fat, which is contained inside the abdominal cavity). Because it is hard and quite dense, it retains its shape in the sausages and is visible in the final product, whereas soft fat can blend into the meat. This is useful in many classic sausage recipes,

Liver Sausages

For liver sausages, you can use any type of liver, though your local grocery store may be limited in the types available. People use chicken, beef and pork liver for various recipes. Of these, calf's liver is the most prized for its tenderness, but since in the case of sausages the meat will be ground, texture is not critical.

One nutritional consideration is that the liver serves as a filter for toxins in the body, human or animal. The liver from a younger animal, such as a calf, is less likely to have accumulated a high level of undesirable toxins.

such as mortadella, in which the visibility of the fat is considered an appetizing feature.

Most large chain grocery stores do not carry back fat. However, you can find it at some butcher shops and specialty meat markets, especially those that make their own sausages. Back fat can be safely refrigerated for up to 1 week or frozen for up to 6 months.

Pork Skins and Jowls

Many traditional recipes use pork skins and jowls. The jowl, which is popular in Southern U.S. cooking, comes from the jaw area of the pig. It is also the cut from which guanciale, an Italian cured meat, is made. The term "jowl" is sometimes used synonymously with "cheek," although some chefs use the latter more specifically to mean the meat within the hollow of the jowl. The jowl is primarily fat, although it has a layer of meat.

You may be able to find jowls at a large grocery store, but make sure they are raw, not cured, for sausage making. Skins, however, are often not available even at butcher shops. Specialty stores that make their own sausages have access to suppliers from whom they purchase these ingredients, and they are often willing to place an order for you, if you ask nicely.

Beef

The cut of beef we use most in our recipes is the boneless beef shoulder, also known as chuck, clod, clod heart roast or shoulder center roast. The reason for this choice is that it is one of the least expensive cuts of beef because, though flavorful, it is less tender than most cuts. But tenderness isn't a concern for sausage making, since we're going to grind the meat.

Beef shoulder is a large muscular cut with some fat covering the muscle. To achieve the 85% lean to 15% fat ratio that we consider ideal for sausages, you will need to remove some of the fat covering, but not all. Beef shoulder that has been trimmed to 0 inch, as described by the U.S. Department of Agriculture, will be too lean for most people's taste in sausage. If you're just getting started with sausage making, ask the butcher to trim the meat to 85/15 for you until you are experienced enough to eyeball the correct ratio yourself. Another option (which some purists will object to) is to buy 85/15 ground meat the first time you make sausage. This will give you an idea of what ground meat looks like at this ratio.

For 85% lean meat to 15% fat, you will need to purchase at least 4 pounds (2 kg) of untrimmed boneless beef shoulder, depending on the amount of fat covering the meat, to end up with the 2 pounds (1 kg) of trimmed meat required for most of the recipes. As always, you are free to remove more or less fat, to suit your taste. For very lean sausages, remove all of the visible fat covering and whatever amount you can separate when you cut into the meat. Any leftover meat can be carefully packed into freezer bags and stored in the freezer for up to 6 months.

Beef Brisket

The beef brisket is from the breast of a side of beef, with one carcass yielding two whole briskets. It comes with a covering of fat, called a fat cap or nose, which is typically about $\frac{1}{4}$ inch to $\frac{1}{3}$ inch (5 to 8 mm) thick. At grocery stores, however, you are more likely to find a part of the brisket known as the flat; this deep pectoral muscle has more meat and less fat, and has been trimmed to some extent. Another part of the brisket is the deckle, also known as the point, which is higher in fat, but it can usually only be purchased at a butcher shop.

The flat will work well in sausages. It is about 78% lean to 22% fat, with some fat covering. You will need to trim this type of brisket a bit to achieve the 85/15 ratio. A large flat ranges from 6 to 8 pounds (3 to 4 kg), but you can sometimes find smaller cuts. Since you don't have to do much trimming, you would need at least $2\frac{1}{2}$ pounds (1.25 kg) for 2 pounds (2 kg) of trimmed meat.

Corned Beef

Corned beef is usually a beef brisket or round that has been cured in brine, seasoned and slowly simmered until tender. It gets its characteristic pink color from curing salts, and its name from the Old English word *corn*, meaning "large grain," a reference to the large grains of rock salt used in preservation. Corned beef can be purchased raw in seasoned brine inside a pouch and stored unopened in the refrigerator until the "use by" or "best before" date on the label. If you want to store it longer, drain the brine, wrap the beef carefully in freezer paper and freeze it for up to 1 month. Make sure to drain the brine; otherwise, the salt will promote rancidity and undesirable texture changes.

Beef Blood

Many cultures produce traditional blood sausages. For the home sausage enthusiast who is up to the task, it can be difficult to purchase whole blood. If you live near a slaughterhouse or a butcher shop, you may be able to obtain beef blood. Pig's blood cannot be used because it may be contaminated with *Trichinella spiralis*, which causes the infection trichinosis. Some specialty meat shops that make their own sausage can be persuaded to provide beef blood, especially for their regular customers.

Lamb

Leg of lamb is our cut of choice for lamb sausages. It is a bit pricier than other cuts, but the size works well. Although a lamb

What Color Should Beef Be?

Beef's color depends on its packaging. When fresh beef is exposed to oxygen in the air, the myoglobin protein in the muscle reacts with the oxygen to form oxymyoglobin, which has a bright red color. So if you're purchasing beef from a meat case, look for meat that is bright red. Beef that has been vacuum-packed, on the other hand, will be more of a maroon color. For meat in regular plastic packaging (not vacuum-packed), the surface may be bright red while the center is maroon to brown. This is because the plastic wrap is semipermeable, so oxygen reacts on the surface but cannot penetrate the center of the meat.

has four legs, the term "leg of lamb" refers to only the hind legs. It consists of two main parts, sirloin and shank, with sirloin being more tender. The mix of tender, more flavorful meat along with tougher meat is another reason leg of lamb works well for sausages. A typical boneless leg of lamb is about 4 pounds (2 kg), which is enough for a double batch of sausages. Removing some of the visible fat will give you just the right proportion of fat to lean.

Lamb meat should be pinkish to light red and should have what is described as a "velvety texture," but it should not be shiny, which may indicate a high level of bacteria. A dark red color is an indication of less tender meat that is not fresh. Meat that has white flecks of fat throughout the muscle will make for moister sausages.

Chicken and Turkey

Making good chicken or turkey sausages is all about balance: the meat should have an adequate amount of fat to prevent a dry product, but not so much that you lose the lower-calorie advantage of these sausages. After much experimentation, we found that the best results came from a combination of trimmed breasts and untrimmed thighs. If you prefer, you can use all breast meat, but in that case you should use untrimmed breasts; otherwise, the sausages will be too dry by most people's standards, even the most ardent low-fat devotees. With breast meat alone, you'll also lose out on the flavor and

concentrated essential minerals of the darker meat.

You can save a significant amount of money by purchasing a whole chicken or turkey and cutting it up, but that can also be inconvenient and time-consuming. If you decide to use precut chicken and turkey parts instead, you have another option: you can purchase bone-in or boneless meat. If you are fairly handy with a sharp knife, it won't take much time to bone the meat. Boning poultry is a lost art for many of us, but if you plan to make poultry sausage often, it may be worth the cost savings to learn how to quickly cut up and bone a bird.

When selecting packaged poultry, look for meat that is free from bruising or other discoloration and is not shiny, which may indicate bacteria growth. Ice crystals clinging to the meat are a sign that it has been frozen, but it will still work fine in sausages. As long as the meat is still frozen in the center, it can be safely refrozen when you get it home if you don't plan to use it within a day or two.

Game Meats

Any type of game meat can be used to make sausages. To get you started, we've provided recipes for duck, goose, wild turkey, pheasant, venison, elk, moose, bison, bear, bass and lake whitefish sausages. Each recipe provides information about the meat used. If you

Adding Other Meats to Game Sausages

In general, it is a good idea to mix game meat with another type of meat, such as pork (with game mammals) or chicken (with game birds). Doing so can improve the flavor of the sausages and, for very lean game meats, may help you achieve a good ratio of lean meat to fat. Our preference is to use pork as the combination meat for venison, elk, moose, bison and bear sausages because we find that pork fat confers the best flavor. If you don't eat pork, beef is a good choice, but keep in mind that beef fat has a yellow pigmentation that may impart an undesirable color to the sausages.

aren't a hunter and don't have a local source of game meat, you can purchase just about any type of game online.

For venison, elk and moose sausages, it is traditional to use "trim": the meat left over after the steaks and roasts are removed from the animal. But in areas where these meats are difficult to source, you may need to use whatever cut you can find.

When it comes to game meat, it's a good idea to trim off all external fat, as the fat is the source of much of the "gamey" flavor. But experiment with removing different amounts of fat to determine what best suits your taste.

Casings for Meat Sausages

Natural casings come from the intestines of pigs, cows or sheep. The intestines are scraped inside and out, giving the casings an irregular appearance. Natural casings are permeable and somewhat fragile when wet, but are strong and impermeable when dried.

Sheep casings have the smallest diameter and are generally the most fragile, while cow casings are the largest and thickest. The type of casing you use will depend somewhat on the type of sausages you're making, but most of the recipes in this book use hog casing simply because it's the easiest to find and the most versatile.

Natural casings are sold in a brine solution. You probably won't find them at your local grocery store, though it's worth a look just in case. If you don't have luck there, try a local specialty meat market. You can also purchase casings from online sausage-making retailers (see the Resources, page 259). Casings can be safely stored in the refrigerator for up to 1 year.

The recipes all provide a casing size in millimeters, which represents the average diameter of the casing. But unless you purchase casings from a store specializing in sausage-making products, such as a butcher supply store, you may not have a choice. Rest assured that the recipes will work with any casing, although the texture and flavor of the finished product may be slightly different, and you may end up with a different number of links.

The most readily available casing — and the casing used in the majority of our recipes — is 32/35 mm hog casing. Other sizes of hog casings include 30/32 mm (which we use for currywurst and merguez), 35/38 mm (used for larger sausages such as kielbasa and salami) and 39/42 mm (for very large sausages such as Polish smoked sausages).

For smaller sausages, you'll need sheep casing: either 20/22 mm (for breakfast sausages) or 24/26 mm (for hot dogs).

Hog middles are used for specialty sausages such as blood sausages and soppressata. Their diameter is about 60 to 65 mm. They have a strong odor, so make sure to thoroughly rinse these casings before soaking them.

There are three types of beef casings, all of which are inedible and must be peeled off the sausage before eating. Beef bung caps are $4^{1}/_{2}$ to 5 inches (11 to 12.5 cm) in diameter and 18 inches (45 cm) long. They are used for large sausages, such as bologna and mortadella. Beef middles are $2^{1}/_{2}$ inches (6 cm) in diameter and are used for hard salami. Beef rounds, which also come as cut-and-tie rounds (with one end tied and precut to a certain length), are 38 to 46 mm in diameter and form a ring when stuffed. These casings are used for ring bologna and liver sausages.

Collagen Casings

Collagen casings are also a natural product, but they are more highly processed than intestine casings. To make them, collagen from various parts of the animal is formed into a dough-like product that is then extruded to get the proper shape and thickness for various types of sausages. The thinner products can be eaten, but the thicker casings are intended to be peeled from the meat before the sausage is eaten.

Vegetarian Proteins

As noted earlier, you can make vegetarian sausages from just about any plant product: legumes, vegetables, mushrooms, nuts or grains — or any combination of these ingredients. But it makes sense to include legumes and/or nuts, which are important sources of protein for vegetarians. Grains, such as oats or barley, also have protein, though considerably less than legumes. But unless you are following a vegan diet, you can also add protein to your sausages with animal products such as eggs and dairy.

Vegetarian and Vegan Binders

Perhaps the most important component of vegetarian and vegan sausages is the binder, which holds all the other ingredients together. If you don't have a binder, the ingredients will fall out when you cut into the sausage. We have included two sausage binder recipes, one for vegetarian sausages and one for vegan sausages, in the Vegetarian and Vegan Sausages chapter.

Make sure to follow the poaching instructions in the recipes for the best results with your vegetarian sausages. This step causes the sausage binder gums to set up and become firmer.

Cellulose Casing

For our vegetarian and vegan recipes, we used cellulose casing, which is available online. Cellulose is the main component of the cell walls of plants. It is pressed out into a clear and tough casing. Commercial sausage makers use cellulose casing to make many products sold as "skinless" sausages, such as cotto salami and smoked ham, because the casing is removed after the cooking process.

We used Butcher & Packer 30 mm cellulose casing, which comes in

Specialty Vegetarian Casings

We tried several specialty vegetarian casings that were marketed as edible. However, none of them worked for us. Although nothing on the packages indicated that the final sausages should not be heated, the casings we tested melted upon even gentle heating.

compacted 70-foot (21 m) sticks. For each recipe, you'll need about 4 to 5 feet (120 by 150 cm), so you should get about 14 to 17 batches of sausages from each stick. If you have difficulty finding a specific diameter, it will not affect sausage quality, just the number of links.

When you're ready to use the sausages, gently peel off the casing, which is not edible.

Seasonings

The seasonings and other flavorings added to the ground meat are the key to creating unique, mouthwatering sausages. The potential seasonings are as limitless as your imagination, but here we've provided some important details about just a few ingredients that we use regularly in our sausages.

Salt

You can use any type of salt in sausages, including table salt, but many people prefer kosher salt, coarse salt or sea salt. Sea salt, which is more expensive, contains impurities, such as other minerals and chemical compounds. The minerals include magnesium and calcium, and the compounds may include nitrate. If enough nitrate is present, it can give a slight pink coloration to the salt. The various impurities may also impart a bitter flavor.

Coarse salt and kosher salt have a lower density than table salt because of the large crystal size. We used kosher salt in the recipes, so if you decide to use table salt, you will need to adjust the amount by multiplying it by 0.75. Most of the recipes call for 2 teaspoons (10 mL) of kosher salt, so you would use $1\frac{1}{2}$ teaspoons (7 mL) of table salt.

Curing Salts

Dried sausages (such as pepperoni) and emulsified sausages (such as hot dogs) require the addition of curing salts to prevent botulism. As an added bonus, the curing salts add flavor and help the sausages maintain their color. The curing salts, known as cure #1 and cure #2, have different amounts of sodium nitrite and salt. Cure #1 contains *only* sodium nitrite and salt, and is the most widely used throughout the world. Cure #2 contains sodium nitrite, salt and sodium nitrate. The nitrate in cure #2 converts to nitrite by the time the sausages are ready to eat. We used cure #1 curing salts in our recipes. It is important to use the specific curing salt called for in a recipe, as the results will vary with the type used.

Garlic Powder and Garlic Paste

Many of our recipes call for garlic powder, but you can always swap in fresh garlic if you prefer. Make sure to mince the garlic, then press it into a paste for more even distribution. To press minced garlic into paste, press a chef's knife down with both hands and pull it toward you across the garlic. Repeat the motion until you achieve a paste-like consistency. One medium clove of garlic will yield about $\frac{1}{2}$ tsp (2 mL) garlic paste, which will replace $\frac{1}{8}$ tsp (0.5 mL) garlic powder.

We also favor the use of roasted garlic paste in our sausages. You can purchase roasted garlic paste or make your own. To make your own, remove the outer skin from a head of garlic, keeping the head intact, and cut off the tops of the cloves. Place the garlic head on a sheet of foil, drizzle the cloves with 1 tbsp (15 mL) olive oil and gather the foil at the top to enclose the head. Roast in a preheated 400°F (200°C) oven for 45 minutes or until the cloves are fork-tender. Let cool completely. Using a fork, remove the cloves and place them in a bowl. Add the oil pooled in the foil, then mash the cloves with a fork to the desired consistency.

Season to taste with salt and pepper. Store roasted garlic paste in an airtight container in the refrigerator for up to 3 days or freeze it. For convenience, place typical recipe amounts in individual freezer containers.

Basil

Used throughout the world, basil is still most associated with Italian cuisine. This versatile herb is high in essential nutrients, such as vitamins A, C and K, and numerous phytonutrients. Of the many varieties, sweet basil is the best known. It seems to convey an almost meat-like quality to a wide variety of foods, possibly by stimulating the umami taste buds. Fresh basil is by far the most fragrant and provides the most flavor intensity, but frozen basil holds up very well in most recipes. Another great way to add the flavor of basil to sausages is with pesto.

Paprika

Although it's often relegated to a colorful dusting on top of foods, paprika can greatly enhance the flavor of sausages. This versatile spice is made from ground dried red peppers. Different varieties of peppers are used, so the color may range from an intense orange to dark red. Paprikas range from sweet to hot, depending on the variety and the number of seeds ground with the pod. Smoked paprika, which can be either sweet or hot, is, as you would expect, smoked rather than cured in the drying process.

In many grocery stores, sweet paprika is sold simply as "paprika," without any additional descriptors. We use sweet paprika in many of our sausage recipes.

The most famous paprikas hale from Hungary and Spain, although many other countries produce it. Pimentón — Spanish paprika — comes in three different types (sweet, semisweet and hot), and each type comes in three different grades. One well-known paprika, made in La Vera, a county in western Spain, is smoked using oak, which imparts a distinctive flavor and aroma.

Olive Oil

Olive oil has been the main cooking oil in Mediterranean countries for centuries and relatively recently became popular in North America thanks to research on its health benefits. While extra virgin olive oil contains more phytonutrients than olive oil or virgin olive oil, when heated above 350°F (180°C) the unrefined particles in extra virgin olive oil break down, forming polycyclic aromatic hydrocarbons, which cause an off flavor. In addition, some studies suggest possible toxic effects from these compounds. When olive oil is used as an ingredient in fresh sausages, this is not a problem, because the internal temperature of the sausages will not reach this level when they are cooked. If price is a consideration, however, regular olive oil is considerably less expensive than extra virgin.

CHAPTER 6
Let's Make Sausages

Now that you have the equipment and the ingredients, it's time to make sausages. In this chapter, you'll learn how to make fresh, emulsified, smoked and dried sausages, as well as how to safely store and cook your sausages. Once you master the art and science of making your own sausages, you're sure to enjoy both the process and the tasty results!

Making Fresh Sausages

Most of the recipes in this book are for fresh sausages, as they are the most straightforward to make and require less specialized equipment. If you've never made sausages before, these are definitely the ones to start with before trying your hand at more complex sausages. Also wait to try recipes with more unusual ingredients until after you've mastered the basic techniques. Fresh sausages are perhaps the most fun, especially for the novice, because once you've tried making sausages a few times, you can be creative with your own tweaks to the recipes.

For step-by-step instructions on making fresh sausages, with accompanying photographs, see the first photo insert in this book.

Soaking the Casing

About an hour before you plan to make sausages, cut the casing to the length you need — about 4 to 5 feet (120 to 150 cm) for 2 lbs (1 kg) of meat (1 kg) — and rinse it thoroughly. Place the casing in a bowl and add enough warm water to cover. Soak the casing for 1 hour, changing the water several times.

This process will make the casing more pliable and easier to work with, and will remove some of the natural odor, as well as the salt. Some sausage makers like to soak the casings in wine instead of water, as they believe it works better to remove odor.

Store any remaining casing in a brine solution in an airtight container for later use.

Trimming and Chilling the Meat

While the casing is soaking, you can get to work on trimming the meat. Trim off the visible fat until you have a roughly 85/15 ratio of lean meat to fat (or your desired ratio). See Chapter 5 for more information on fat ratios for different

Lower-Fat Sausages

With any type of sausages you make, one of the most critical factors in determining flavor and texture is the ratio of lean meat to fat. As the amount of fat increases, the calories increase, but so does the moisture content. Some people also think higher-fat sausages taste better. If you decide to use less fat and make a leaner and lower-calorie sausage, you can compensate for the loss of moisture — and, to some extent, flavor — by adding grain products (such as rice or barley), fruits or vegetables.

Grinding Chicken and Turkey

When making chicken or turkey sausages, you'll achieve the best texture by grinding the breast and thigh meat separately. Coarsely grinding the breast meat and finely grinding the thigh meat will help compensate for the significant difference in fat content between the two parts. After grinding the parts separately, you can mix them together without further grinding.

types of meat. Discard the trimmed fat, unless otherwise indicated in the recipe, or save it for another use. Use a kitchen scale to weigh out the amount of trimmed meat (and, if applicable, fat and trimmings) you need for the recipe.

Wrap the trimmed meat in plastic wrap and place it in the freezer for 30 minutes to chill. Do not let it start to freeze, as your grinder may not be able to grind frozen pieces. Chilling the meat reduces the potential for smear, which occurs when the fat begins to warm. Smear adversely affects the appearance of the final sausages.

In addition to chilling the meat, many sausage experts recommend chilling the grinder and the mixing bowl. If the ambient temperature and humidity are high, this might be advisable. In normal conditions, it should be sufficient to chill the trimmed meat.

Grinding the Meat

Once the meat is chilled, cut it into pieces small enough to fit in the throat of your grinder. The procedure now varies slightly, depending on which appliance you are using to grind your meat:

- **If using a meat grinder:** Attach the grinding plate specified in the recipe to the meat grinder. Place a large bowl below the end of the grinder head to collect the ground meat.
- **If using a stand mixer:** Attach the mixer bowl and the food grinder attachment to your stand mixer, with the grinding plate specified in the recipe.

When the grinder is ready to go, add the meat pieces to the grinder tray, without overfilling it. Turn the grinder on (if using an electric grinder or stand mixer) or start turning the handle (if using a manual grinder) and use the stomper or food pusher to push the meat into the feed chute. Do not use your hands to push the meat into the chute.

Mixing the Meat

The next step is to mix in the other ingredients, either by hand or with a stand mixer. First, add all of the dry and moist ingredients specified in the recipe, including all seasonings and flavorings. Mix the seasonings into the meat until they are evenly distributed. Then add the liquid ingredients specified in the recipe. Mix until white strands (extracted protein) appear in the mixture and a handful of the mixture holds together. (Mixtures that include vinegar will not hold together, but the white strands will still appear.)

Doing a Taste-Test

Before stuffing the sausages, it's a good idea to sauté a small sample of the meat mixture so you can taste it and make sure you are happy with the seasoning. Sauté the sample in a small skillet, over medium-high heat, until no longer pink or until juices run clear, as instructed in the recipe. Taste the sample. If desired, add additional seasonings to the meat mixture and mix until evenly distributed.

Work as quickly as possible during this step, because the ground meat that's

Surprising Flavor Factors

The casing size you use can make a difference to the flavor of your sausages, even when all of the ingredients in the meat mixture are the same. So, too, can how finely you grind the meat. When you bite into a sausage, your perception of flavor is influenced by the proportion of meat to casing and the particle size of the meat mixture.

waiting to be stuffed is susceptible to microbial contamination in the meantime. Even better, cover the meat mixture and refrigerate it while you perform the taste test.

Stuffing the Sausages and Twisting Links

Once you are satisfied with the flavor of the meat mixture, it's time to stuff sausages! First, you'll need to decide which extruding tube (or funnel or horn) to use. Always use the largest tube on which the casing will fit but still move freely. You should not have to stretch the casing. The user manual that came with your equipment will help you determine the appropriate-size tube for the diameter of casing you are using. If you don't have the manual, use the smallest tube for breakfast sausage. For other sausages, you may need to use trial and error to determine the best tube to use.

Attach the extruding tube to the grinder or stuffer. Pull one end of the casing out of the bowl it is soaking in and open it with your fingers. Scoop a little water from the bowl into the casing so that it will slide on and off the tube easily. Place the open end of the casing over the extruding tube. Slide the full length of the casing onto the tube, then tie a knot in the end of the casing.

Turn the grinder, stuffer or mixer on and, with one hand, slowly and steadily feed the meat mixture into the tray, pushing it down with the stomper or food pusher. With your other hand, hold the casing just beyond the end of the tube to help guide the sausage into the casing. As the meat mixture begins to fill the casing, try to maintain a consistent thickness; the casing should be full, but not to the point of bursting.

Once all of the meat mixture is fed into the casing, cut off any excess casing and tie a knot in the open end. Gently twist the stuffed sausage into the number of links indicated in the recipe — or as desired. How long to make your sausage links is really up to you. Keep in mind that the lengths specified in the recipes are a rough guideline; you may need to adjust the length up or down so that you don't end up with one link smaller than the rest.

A Bit About Bulk Sausage

If you have a recipe that calls for bulk sausage, you can use any of the fresh sausage recipes in this book — just stop short of stuffing the meat mixture into the casing and use it as is. Ground meat is highly perishable, so refrigerate the meat mixture in an airtight container and use it within a day or two. You can also freeze the meat mixture in individual portions. For optimal food safety, thaw the meat in the refrigerator and use it as soon as it has thawed completely.

Making Emulsified Sausages

If you've never made sausages before, emulsified sausages, such as hot dogs and liverwurst, are not the best type to start with. Even seasoned sausage makers have failed at their first attempts, because an emulsion is a delicate mixture that is dependent on precise processing at a specific temperature within a narrow range. You should also skip making emulsified sausages if you are trying to cut the amount of fat in your diet, as they require a relatively high amount of fat to enable the emulsion to form and stabilize.

Emulsified sausages follow the same basic process as for fresh sausages when it comes to soaking the casings and trimming, chilling and grinding the meat (except that the fat ratio is higher and the meat is more finely ground, as indicated in the recipes). However, the mixing process is quite different and requires the use of a food processor and a meat thermometer.

While you are chilling the meat, chill a large bowl and the food processor bowl in the refrigerator for 30 minutes. Grind the meat into the chilled bowl, then transfer it to the chilled food processor bowl and add the seasonings. With the motor running, through the feed tube, gradually add the liquid ingredients, which will include a certain amount of ice or ice water. Continue processing the mixture, carefully monitoring the temperature. As the mixture gets warmer, it will begin to appear pasty, indicating that it is emulsified. When it reaches 57°F (14°C), the mixture should be a uniform consistency and you should stop processing. The mixture must not exceed 57°F (14°C) or the emulsion will break down.

Once a successful emulsion is achieved, the meat mixture is stuffed into the casing as described for fresh sausages. Many emulsified sausages are smoked after they are stuffed.

Making Smoked Sausages

The smoking process imparts flavor, attractive color and some antimicrobial protection, and, in the case of hot smoking, produces cooked sausages. It is important to remember that cold-smoked sausages are not cooked, and they need to be handled accordingly.

Smoked sausages follow all the same steps as for fresh sausages, and then take it a couple steps further. After twisting the sausages into links, let them dry at room temperature for 20 to 30 minutes or until the casings have a slightly tacky feel. With less moisture left on the casings, the smoke will penetrate them more easily. Do not let the sausages stand at room temperature for any longer than 30 minutes.

Smoking Color

The color of smoked sausages indicates the degree of smoking: light smoking produces a yellow color; longer smoking leads to a dark brown color. To a large extent, this is where personal preference determines how long you should smoke for. As long as the sausage is cooked through (for hot-smoking) and handled properly after the smoking process, it will be delicious and safe.

When you are ready to hang the sausages in the smoker, be sure to space them so that they are not touching each other. This will allow the smoke to distribute evenly throughout the chamber and evenly penetrate the sausages. For hot-smoked sausages, smoke at 170°F to 180°F (77°C to 82°C) until a meat thermometer inserted in the center of a sausage link registers 160°F (71°C) for red meat sausages (including pork) or 165°F (74°C) for poultry sausages. If desired, you can continue smoking them past this point, for added smoke flavor.

For cold-smoked sausages, smoke at 80°F to 90°F (25°C to 30°C) until their color indicates that the desired amount of smoke flavor has penetrated the meat (see box, page 52). Monitor the temperature of the smoker throughout the process. As mentioned in Chapter 4, we highly recommend purchasing a smoker with a temperature setting and built-in thermometer.

After removing the sausages from the smoker, let them cool for a short time (no more than 2 hours), then refrigerate or freeze them (see Storing Sausages, below).

Making Dried Sausages

If you want to make dried sausages, first ensure that you have an appropriate drying chamber, as described in Chapter 4. And when you are making the meat mixture, make sure to add curing salts (see page 47) — $\frac{1}{2}$ tsp (2 mL) for 2 lbs (1 kg) of meat. Although this was not done in the past, it is now considered the only safe way to avoid botulism in the finished sausage.

Prepare the sausages as described for fresh sausages, but when filling the casing, start a new strand every 12 inches (30 cm). Strands of this length will be easier to handle and better balanced for hanging. When you have finished filling the sausage strands, twist them into links of the desired length, then lay them flat and, using a pin or a sausage perforator, prick them generously to remove any air bubbles. Air bubbles in dried sausages

can allow bacterial growth.

The sausage strands are now ready to hang in your drying chamber. But before you hang them, weigh one strand and document its weight. (Make sure to keep track of which sausage you weighed.) When hanging the strands, space them 3 to 4 inches (7.5 to 10 cm) apart, so that they don't touch each other, to allow for adequate air circulation.

Check the temperature (and, if possible, the humidity level) of your drying chamber daily. Squeeze any excess moisture out of the sausage strands with your hands. As the drying process continues, occasionally weigh the same strand of sausage you initially weighed. The sausages are ready when that strand has lost 30% of its original weight (based on the reasonable assumption that all of the sausages will dry at the same rate).

Storing Sausages

When storing sausages in the refrigerator, they should be covered to prevent bacteria from settling on the surface. You can use storage wrap or food storage bags for this purpose. Make sure the refrigerator temperature is at the appropriate level — at or below 40°F (4.5°C).

When freezing sausages, give some thought to the portion size(s) you'll want to use and freeze the sausages in those portions. It is best to first wrap each sausage individually in freezer wrap, so they won't stick together. Doing so will make thawing and cooking them much

Thawing in Cold Water

If you have forgotten to take your sausages out of the freezer in time to thaw them in the refrigerator, you can safely thaw them in cold water: Seal them in a food storage bag and submerge it in a clean container filled with cold water. Change the water every 30 minutes and check often to see if the sausages have thawed. As soon as they are thawed, cook them immediately.

easier. After wrapping them individually, place the amount you are likely to use at one time in a freezer bag or airtight container. In this way, you can take out the exact amount you need.

Thawing is best done in the refrigerator, but leaving sausages in the refrigerator too long after they thaw can also lead to foodborne illness. Freezing stops the growth of bacteria, but doesn't kill it. As soon as the food goes in the refrigerator to thaw, the growth begins again. So make sure to use the sausages as soon as they thaw.

Fresh Sausages

Fresh sausages should be refrigerated or frozen as soon as you're done twisting the links. If refrigerated, use fresh sausages within 2 days. Use frozen sausages within 2 months. You should know before you even make the sausages what your plans are for them: store the amount you will use within 2 days in the refrigerator and freeze the rest. For optimal food safety, it's best not to let the sausages sit in the refrigerator for 2 days before you decide to freeze them.

Smoked Sausages

If you plan to use hot-smoked sausages within 4 days, refrigerate them in a single layer in a shallow airtight container. Otherwise, wrap them in freezer wrap, place the wrapped sausages in a freezer bag or airtight container and freeze them for up to 2 months. Store cold-smoked sausages as you would fresh sausages.

Dried Sausages

Although traditionalists may keep dried sausages indefinitely, this is not recommended. The U.S. Department of Agriculture states that an open package of commercial dried sausages should be kept in the refrigerator for no longer than 3 weeks, and it makes sense to apply the same guideline to homemade dried sausages. Keep in mind that dried sausages continue to dry and become quite tough and difficult to chew the longer you store them.

You can slice dried sausages and freeze them by carefully layering the slices between sheets of freezer wrap in a plastic freezer container, but the sausages will lose flavor.

Cooking Sausages

Homemade hot-smoked and dried sausages can be eaten as is, but fresh and cold-smoked sausages must be cooked before you eat them. There are many different ways to cook sausages, though some methods are more traditional for certain types. For example, Italian and Polish sausages are often pan-fried. Vegetarian and vegan sausages are low in fat, so it's best to use at least a small amount of vegetable oil to lightly sauté them.

Whatever cooking method you choose, make sure to cook meat sausages until they reach an internal temperature of

160°F (71°C) for red meat (including pork) or 165°F (74°C) for poultry. Vegetarian sausages made with egg must also be cooked to an internal temperature of 160°F (71°C). Vegan sausages need only be heated through.

How to Pan-Fry Sausages

Place about ½ inch (1 cm) of water in the pan with the sausages. Cover and cook on medium-high heat for about 10 minutes or until the sausages turn gray. Drain the water and add a touch of vegetable oil. Continue cooking, turning the sausages to brown both sides, until they reach an internal temperature of 160°F (71°C) for red meat (including pork) or 165°F (74°C) for poultry.

CHAPTER 7

Think Food Safety First

Whether you're making meat or vegetarian sausages, the ingredients are loaded with nutrients, so bacteria will love your sausages as much as you do. And because the ingredients are ground, the surface area is increased, adding to the susceptibility of your sausage to contamination as bacteria are introduced from your equipment and your hands. To ensure a tasty product that you can safely enjoy, you need to be vigilant and take the proper food safety measures.

Don't Make It Cozy for the Bad Bugs

Bacteria need nutrients to survive and grow, just as we do, which is why they're attracted to the same foods as we are. And like us, they can be picky about their environment. The variables that determine their ability to grow include the presence or absence of oxygen, an adequate water supply, the amount of acid in their environment and the length of time they are exposed to specific temperatures. In general, the bacteria that cause foodborne illness tend to prefer foods with a high level of nutrients, a lot of water and low acidity. The warmer the temperature and the longer the bacteria are at that temperature, the more they grow and the higher the bacterial load becomes in a food item.

Bacteria also like lots of surface area and not too much depth, because it's more difficult to penetrate a thicker food item. A 3-pound (1.5 kg) beef roast is attractive to bacteria because it is loaded with protein, vitamins and minerals, is not too acidic and, depending on fat content, is about 70% water. However, it's not nearly as appealing as beef ground from that roast, which has significantly more surface area and much less depth. Another reason that ground meat is more perishable than a roast is that it is handled by more people and touches more equipment, with each contact increasing the meat's exposure to bacteria.

Government health agencies refer to foods that are bacterial favorites and that support rapid bacterial growth as potentially hazardous foods (PHFs). The higher the bacterial load, the more likely foods will make us sick. The health agencies describe a temperature "danger zone" for PHFs between 41°F and 135°F (5°C and 57°C). After studying the major outbreaks of foodborne illness, the major public health agencies report that the most common cause is not keeping PHFs at the correct temperature, which is above or below the danger zone.

A Food Safety Plan

One way to make sure your sausages are safe to eat is to develop a food safety plan. The food industry uses the hazard analysis critical control points (HACCP) model, which was developed by the Pillsbury Company in the 1960s as part of their work with NASA and the U.S. Army to develop safe food for space flights. It is a systematic approach that reduces the risk of foodborne illness by identifying, evaluating and controlling potential safety hazards. It has become

Bacteria: Friends and Enemies

Some of these little life forms are very beneficial to humans, and some are harmful and even deadly. Fifty-two million North Americans get sick, and well over 3000 die every year, from foodborne illnesses. Of the top ten causes of foodborne illness, eight are bacterial. But some of the bacteria that live in our intestinal tracts, the "friendly bacteria," provide health benefits that range from improving immune system function to reducing the risk of certain chronic diseases. Fermented foods, such as yogurt, tempeh and dried sausages, are a source of these friendly bacteria, and the term "probiotic," which means organisms that provide a beneficial effect, is usually prominently displayed on their labels.

the gold standard, used by virtually every institution responsible for food production and food service, from hospitals to food manufacturers, not just in North America but around the world.

You can easily develop your own HACCP plan to ensure the safety of your sausages by following these five steps:

1. Identify all potential hazards and create measures to control them.
2. Evaluate all process steps and determine the critical control points (CCPs).
3. Establish limits for the CCPs.
4. Monitor the CCPs.
5. Establish corrective actions for deviations from CCP limits.

Step 1

First, identify all of the potential hazards related to sausage making, from the ingredients and equipment themselves to your process for purchasing and storing the ingredients and preparing the recipe. Then figure out how you can control those hazards.

A key hazard in most sausage recipes is the meat. You need to make sure it's fresh when you buy it, so that might mean being picky about where you buy it and checking the date on the package. After you buy it, you must get it home quickly; don't leave it in the car while you run a few more errands, especially if you're shopping in the summer. When you get home, you must decide when you're going to make sausages, so you know whether to refrigerate or freeze the meat.

When you are ready to make sausages, you need to ensure that the meat is at room temperature — in the danger zone — for a minimal amount of time. So have all your equipment set up and ready to go, and all less perishable ingredients measured and prepared. Package the

Cold Doesn't Kill

Bacteria continue to grow in the refrigerator, even when the temperature is set correctly, but the cold does slow the growth of most types of bacteria. One notable exception is the treacherous *Listeria monocytogenes*, which thrives in the refrigerator. Believe it or not, bacteria are not killed in the freezer; freezing just puts growth on hold. As soon as you take the food out of the freezer, the bacteria start to grow and multiply again.

sausages quickly once they're stuffed and determine when you will use them, which in turn will determine whether you should store them in the refrigerator or the freezer.

To control another potential hazard — bacteria on the sausage-making equipment — thoroughly clean all the components of every tool you used after every use. Wash them in hot soapy water and scrub the parts you can. Sanitizing your equipment is a smart move: use a bleach solution of $1/2$ tsp (2 mL) bleach to 1 gallon (4 L) water or rubbing alcohol (60% to 90% isopropyl alcohol is most effective, so don't dilute) and place the equipment parts in the solution for at least 1 minute. Alcohol is more expensive if not diluted, but has the added advantage of drying almost immediately. It is important to allow all the parts to air-dry between uses, to prevent bacteria growth. Before storing the equipment, make sure there is no moisture on any of the components.

Step 2

Map out all the steps in the sausage-making process and identify the critical control points (CCPs) — points in the process at which hazards can occur. Some examples of CCPs include meat purchase, meat storage (both time and temperature),

thawing of frozen meat, storage of sausages and equipment cleaning and sanitizing.

Step 3

Once you've identified the CCPs, you need to establish limits for them. This involves knowing in advance how long you can store fresh meat, and at what temperature, and how long you can safely store your sausages (see table, page 59).

Step 4

This step is just a matter of actually going through the process and writing down all relevant details as you go. If you don't have a refrigerator thermometer, buy one and use it to make sure the temperature in your refrigerator is at or below 40°F (4°C). Keep track of when you bought the meat and when you need to use it by. Carefully label your sausage packages, recording what type of sausages they are and the date you made them.

Step 5

Be willing to discard fresh or thawed meat if you weren't able to achieve the safe limits at any point in the process. And if you don't manage to eat your lovely fresh sausages within 2 days of placing them in the refrigerator, just pitch them.

SAMPLE HACCP PLAN FOR SAUSAGE MAKING

Step 1: Identify potential hazards and create measures to control them.	Potential Hazards	Control Measures
	• Meat • Other sensitive ingredients, such as eggs and fresh cheese • Equipment	1. Purchase fresh meat that isn't about to pass its "sell by" or "best before" date and get it home quickly. 2. Refrigerate or freeze the meat immediately. 3. Prepare sausages quickly and store the finished product immediately. 4. Store other sensitive ingredients properly in the refrigerator. 5. Use clean equipment and properly clean and sanitize between uses.
Step 2: Evaluate all process steps and determine the critical control points (CCPs).	**Process Steps**	**Critical Control Points**
	1. Buy meat. 2. Store meat. 3. Thaw frozen meat. 4. Make sausages. 5. Store sausages. 6. Clean and sanitize equipment.	1. Check date on meat at purchase. Go straight home after purchasing meat. 2. Store meat as soon as you get home. 3. Thaw frozen meat in the refrigerator. 4. Ensure meat is at room temperature for minimal time while making sausages by having equipment set up and ready and all other ingredients prepped and measured. 5. Store the finished sausages immediately. 6. Wash in hot soapy water, sanitize and ensure adequate drying time.
Step 3: Establish limits for the CCPs.	1. Do not buy meat with a "sell by" or "best before" date that is less than 3 days away. If you cannot get home within 30 minutes, place the meat in a cooler full of ice. 2. Decide when you are going to make sausages: if within 4 days, store meat in the refrigerator, at or below 40°F (4°C); if after 4 days, freeze meat at 32°F (0°C) for up to 4 months (food safety is not an issue in freezing, but quality deteriorates past 4 months). 3. Make sure to account for the thawing time when determining your sausage-making date. Use meat within 4 days of transferring it from freezer to refrigerator. 4. Prepare equipment and ingredients in advance to keep sausage preparation time to under 2 hours. 5. If not using fresh sausages within 2 days, freeze them. Use frozen sausages within 2 months. (See page 54 for storage info on other types of sausages.) 6. Use an appropriate sanitizing solution (see page 58). Let equipment dry completely before storing it.	

continued on next page

Step 4: Monitor the CCPs.	**1.** Make sure the package date is appropriate before purchasing the meat. Check the time when you remove the meat from refrigeration at the store and make sure it is in your refrigerator within 30 minutes.
	2. Use a refrigerator thermometer to check the fridge and freezer temperature. Adjust the temperature as needed so that the refrigerator is at or below 40°F (4°C) and the freezer is at 32°F (0°C). Keep track of what date you purchased the meat (save the receipt or write the date on the package) to ensure that you use it within 4 days of refrigerating or 4 months of freezing.
	3. Write down the date when you transfer frozen meat to the refrigerator and use within 4 days.
	4. Note your starting time when you remove the meat from the refrigerator for sausage preparation and work quickly so that you have finished sausages within 2 hours.
	5. Label your packaged sausages with the type of sausages and the date you made them, then refrigerate for up to 2 days or freeze for up to 2 months.
	6. Carefully check equipment to make sure it is completely clean and dry.
Step 5: Establish corrective actions for deviations from CCP limits.	**1.** Discard fresh meat, thawed meat or finished sausages that exceeded any of the established time limits or was stored at a temperature above established limits.
	2. Check equipment carefully before use for signs of inadequate cleaning.

PART 3

SENSATIONAL SAUSAGE RECIPES

Introduction to the Recipes

In the following chapters, you'll find recipes for delectable sausages of all varieties, many of which will appeal to just about everyone. After you purchase your equipment and have learned the basic process, it's time to decide which recipe to make first. The recipes are divided into chapters based on the main ingredient. The notable exception is the first chapter, The Classics Collection, which presents a variety of traditional recipes from around the world.

If you've never made sausages before, we suggest you begin with a main ingredient you are comfortable with, say chicken or pork, and make fresh sausages. Recipes for emulsified, smoked and dried sausages are a bit more complex and are best left until you have the basic techniques mastered. You'll also need additional equipment for these sausages (see Chapter 4).

One final note about nutrition: Most health experts agree that a healthy diet is one that focuses on variety and balance. These recipes provide plenty of variety — from pork to fish to vegetables — and in Part 4 you'll find tips and a sample meal plan to help you work a variety of sausages into your weekly meals.

As discussed in Chapter 3, sausages have a reputation for being high in fat, and though fat is no longer seen as the villain it once was, higher fat content does still increase calorie intake. And that's an important consideration for anyone trying to manage their weight. One advantage of making your own sausages is that you decide exactly how much fat to use. Plus, you know all the other ingredients that went into your sausages and exactly how they were made. You're sure to enjoy the unbeatable flavor and satisfaction of your own homemade sausages!

Nutrient Analysis

We decided not to include nutritional analyses for the recipes after determining that even the most sophisticated analysis software was unable to provide the precision needed. There are many variables that greatly affect the final amount of nutrients in a sausage, and especially total fat, which is the main determinant of calories and saturated fat in the product. For example, in addition to the difficulty in quantifying the amount of fat that is trimmed off the meat, there is wide variation in the amount of fat from one animal to another. In the end, we realized there were far too many variables to allow for accurate nutrient analysis.

The Classics Collection

This chapter includes an international array of recipes that have become sausage favorites many miles from their point of origin. Many of the recipes use similar ingredients, but some country's sausage makers have created products that are unique. The use of pork as the main ingredient is widespread, though it is not used in certain parts of the world for religious reasons. Many of the classic sausages contain pork, some contain beef, and some include a combination of meats. Others contain ingredients that some of today's consumers may feel hesitant about; a good example is blood sausage, made in many countries, which contains blood as the main ingredient. In cases where the traditional recipes called for ingredients that can be hard to find nowadays, we've adapted them to use more readily available ingredients.

The fresh, uncooked sausages in this chapter (from Garlic Sausages through Cajun Boudin Blanc) taste best if they are refrigerated for at least 1 day before they are cooked.

Breakfast Sausage Patties

This breakfast sausage is a highly seasoned ground pork patty, not to be confused with breakfast sausage links, which are stuffed into casing. This is a traditional recipe, although many different seasonings can be used. If you want to make links instead of patties, use the 20/22 mm hog casing.

Tips

To make sure you always have these tasty patties available for a Saturday breakfast, package them individually in plastic sandwich bags. Place packaged patties in three layers in a large plastic food storage container and store in the freezer.

Cooking Breakfast Sausage Patties:

Preheat pan over medium-low heat for 2 minutes. Add patties and cook for 12 to 14 minutes for fresh or refrigerated patties, or up to 18 minutes for frozen. Turn patties often to ensure even browning. Patties are done when temperature at center is 160°F (71°C). Allow cooked patties to rest for 3 minutes to ensure further destruction of harmful bacteria.

2 lbs	trimmed boneless pork shoulder blade roast, chilled (see page 49)	1 kg
2 tsp	kosher salt	10 mL
1 tsp	freshly cracked black pepper	5 mL
1 tsp	finely minced fresh sage	5 mL
1 tsp	finely minced fresh thyme	5 mL
1 tsp	finely minced fresh rosemary	5 mL
1 tsp	garlic powder	5 mL
1 tsp	onion powder	5 mL
½ tsp	dried basil	2 mL
¼ cup	water	60 mL

1. Cut pork into pieces small enough to fit in the throat of your grinder. Using the medium grinder plate, grind pork into a large bowl or stand mixer bowl.

2. Add salt, pepper, sage, thyme, rosemary, garlic powder, onion powder and basil to the ground pork. Using your hands or the stand mixer paddle attachment, mix until seasonings are evenly distributed. Add water and mix until white strands appear in the mixture and a handful of the mixture holds together.

3. In a small skillet, over medium-high heat, sauté a small amount of the sausage mixture until no longer pink. Taste the sample, then adjust seasonings as desired.

4. Form the meat mixture into ten ⅓-inch (0.8 cm) thick patties. Cook immediately or wrap patties individually in plastic wrap or freezer paper and store in the refrigerator for up to 2 days or in the freezer for up to 6 months.

Health Facts

Hippocrates, the Roman physician who lived circa 460 to 370 BCE, wrote about the many therapeutic uses of thyme. It was thought to be especially useful to treat respiratory disorders. Closer to home and in modern times, Canadian researchers reported that one of the herb's constituents, thymol, reduces bacterial resistance to antibiotics such as penicillin.

Garlic Sausages

Perhaps no edible bulb has inspired more medical remedies than garlic, along with both ardent admirers and haters. Roasting garlic caramelizes it, releasing chemicals that create a pleasing caramel flavor and color. These sausages bring the sweetness of roasted garlic together with a heady blend of spices.

<table>
<tr><td>MAKES
6 SAUSAGES</td></tr>
</table>

Tip

Homemade roasted garlic paste, which contains oil, can harbor botulism. The best way to keep leftover garlic paste is to freeze it. For convenience, place typical recipe amounts in individual freezer containers.

2 lbs	trimmed boneless pork shoulder blade roast, chilled (see page 49)	1 kg
2 tbsp	finely minced garlic	30 mL
1 tbsp	roasted garlic paste (see page 47)	15 mL
2 tsp	sweet paprika	10 mL
2 tsp	kosher salt	10 mL
1 tsp	freshly cracked black pepper	5 mL
1 tsp	ground allspice	5 mL
½ tsp	ground coriander	2 mL
¼ cup	white wine	60 mL
1 tbsp	liquid honey	15 mL
4 to 5 feet	32/35 mm hog casing, soaked (see page 49)	120 to 150 cm

1. Cut pork into pieces small enough to fit in the throat of your grinder. Using the coarse grinder plate, grind pork into a large bowl or stand mixer bowl.

2. Add minced garlic, garlic paste, paprika, salt, pepper, allspice and coriander to the ground pork. Using your hands or the stand mixer paddle attachment, mix until seasonings are evenly distributed. Add wine and honey; mix until white strands appear in the mixture and a handful of the mixture holds together.

3. In a small skillet, over medium-high heat, sauté a small amount of the sausage mixture until no longer pink. Taste the sample, then adjust seasonings as desired.

4. Stuff sausage mixture into prepared casing as described on page 51. Twist into 6 links, each about 6 inches (15 cm) in length.

Health Facts

A 2013 study in the journal *Carcinogenesis* reported on the effects of allspice extract, and of a compound in the extract, ericifolin, on prostate cancer cells. Both allspice extract and ericifolin showed significant antitumor activity, leading the authors to suggest a potential for "therapy or for prevention of recurrent prostate cancer."

Bangers

Bangers are a type of sausage that originated in England. They may have developed as a result of meat rationing during wartime, which led to sausage makers using a higher water content. When these sausages were cooked, they would sometimes explode, thereby earning the just moniker of "bangers." Bangers also often contain rusk or other cereal products. A famous dish featuring this sausage is bangers and mash (mashed potatoes).

**MAKES
6 SAUSAGES**

Tips

Although spices don't spoil, they do lose their aroma over time. This is especially true of spices that contain higher levels of essential oils, such as mace. A cool, dark area of the cupboard is the best place to store spices. Rub a small amount between two fingers to find out if the spice is still aromatic enough for use.

If you use your hands to mix the ground meat, have a bowl of water nearby in which to dip your fingers. This will help keep them from getting too sticky.

2 lbs	trimmed boneless pork shoulder blade roast, chilled (see page 49)	1 kg
¼ cup	finely ground rusk or dry bread crumbs	60 mL
2 tsp	kosher salt	10 mL
1 tsp	freshly cracked black pepper	5 mL
1 tsp	ground ginger	5 mL
½ tsp	finely minced fresh sage	2 mL
¼ tsp	ground mace	1 mL
¼ tsp	ground nutmeg	1 mL
¼ cup	water	60 mL
4 to 5 feet	32/35 mm hog casing, soaked (see page 49)	120 to 150 cm

1. Cut pork into pieces small enough to fit in the throat of your grinder. Using the coarse grinder plate, grind pork into a large bowl or stand mixer bowl.

2. Add rusk, salt, pepper, ginger, sage, mace and nutmeg to the ground pork. Using your hands or the stand mixer paddle attachment, mix until seasonings are evenly distributed. Add water and mix until white strands appear in the mixture and a handful of the mixture holds together.

3. In a small skillet, over medium-high heat, sauté a small amount of the sausage mixture until no longer pink. Taste the sample, then adjust seasonings as desired.

4. Stuff sausage mixture into prepared casing as described on page 51. Twist into 6 links, each about 6 inches (15 cm) in length.

Health Facts

Mace comes from the dried covering of the nutmeg seed. It contains essential oils that have antifungal and potentially other biologic activities.

Toulouse Sausages

Toulouse is a city in southern France, between the Mediterranean and the Atlantic. The famed sausage that bears its name has a distinctive flavor, with ingredients such as smoked bacon, wine and garlic. In culinary circles, it is often associated with a cassoulet, a slow-cooked casserole that also originated in the south of France.

**MAKES
4 SAUSAGES**

Tips

Although you can substitute dried parsley for fresh (using one-third the specified amount), always choose fresh when possible. The volatile oils that give this herb its fragrant aroma are greatly diminished in the drying process — a good reason to keep some washed parsley in the freezer.

You'll get the best results with 35/38 mm hog casing in this recipe, but if you cannot find it, 32/35 mm hog casing will work just fine.

How long to make your sausage links is really up to you, although we suggest 8 inches (20 cm) for this recipe. Keep in mind that this is a rough guideline, and that you may have to adjust the length up or down so that you don't end up with one link smaller than the rest.

2	slices thick-sliced applewood-smoked bacon (2 oz/60 g total)	2
2 lbs	trimmed boneless pork shoulder blade roast	1 kg
1 tbsp	finely minced onion	15 mL
1 tbsp	roasted garlic paste (see page 47)	15 mL
1 tbsp	finely minced fresh basil	15 mL
1 tbsp	finely chopped fresh parsley	15 mL
2 tsp	kosher salt	10 mL
1 tsp	freshly cracked black pepper	5 mL
¼ cup	Burgundy wine	60 mL
4 to 5 feet	35/38 mm hog casing, soaked (see page 49)	120 to 150 cm

1. In a small skillet, over medium-high heat, cook bacon until crisp. Let cool completely, then crumble.

2. Meanwhile, chill pork as directed on page 50.

3. Cut pork into pieces small enough to fit in the throat of your grinder. Using the coarse grinder plate, grind pork and bacon into a large bowl or stand mixer bowl.

4. Add onion, garlic paste, basil, parsley, salt and pepper to the ground meat. Using your hands or the stand mixer paddle attachment, mix until seasonings are evenly distributed. Add wine and mix until white strands appear in the mixture and a handful of the mixture holds together.

5. In a small skillet, over medium-high heat, sauté a small amount of the sausage mixture until no longer pink. Taste the sample, then adjust seasonings as desired.

6. Stuff sausage mixture into prepared casing as described on page 51. Twist into 4 links, each about 8 inches (20 cm) in length.

Health Facts

Basil's tender, fragrant leaves are high in vitamins, minerals and phytonutrients. One of the latter is (E)-beta-caryophyllene, which is a powerful anti-inflammatory. Research has shown that it could be effective in fighting diseases in which inflammation drives symptoms, such as arthritis.

Longaniza

Spain's sausages have made a name for themselves across the globe. Longaniza, chorizo and sobrasada are the three main types of Spanish sausage, with many recipes in each group. Spanish sausages tend to contain pork, and many contain a locally grown, sometimes smoked, paprika, known as *pimentón* in Spanish. This special paprika's flavor is quite unique, and it imparts a deep red color to the sausage.

MAKES 6 SAUSAGES

Tips

You can purchase *pimentón* online in three different heat levels, from mild to hot, and either smoked or unsmoked. Hungarian smoked paprika makes a good substitute, and you can add hot pepper flakes for some heat, if you like.

If you decide to use table salt in place of kosher salt, use 1½ tsp (7 mL), as table salt has a higher density.

In any of our sausage recipes, you can swap fresh garlic for the garlic powder. Make sure to mince the garlic, then press it into a paste (see tip, page 92), for more even distribution. One medium clove of garlic will yield about ½ tsp (2 mL) garlic paste, which will replace ⅛ tsp (0.5 mL) garlic powder.

2 lbs	trimmed boneless pork shoulder blade roast, chilled (see page 49)	1 kg
⅓ cup	instant nonfat dry milk (skim milk powder)	75 mL
1 tbsp	Spanish smoked paprika (see tip, at left)	15 mL
2 tsp	garlic powder	10 mL
2 tsp	granulated sugar	10 mL
2 tsp	kosher salt	10 mL
1 tsp	freshly cracked black pepper	5 mL
½ tsp	dried marjoram	2 mL
¼ cup	water	60 mL
1 tbsp	red wine vinegar	15 mL
4 to 5 feet	32/35 mm hog casing, soaked (see page 49)	120 to 150 cm

1. Cut pork into pieces small enough to fit in the throat of your grinder. Using the coarse grinder plate, grind pork into a large bowl or stand mixer bowl.

2. Add dry milk, paprika, garlic powder, sugar, salt, pepper and marjoram to the ground pork, then add water and vinegar. Using your hands or the stand mixer paddle attachment, mix until seasonings are evenly distributed and white strands appear in the mixture.

3. In a small skillet, over medium-high heat, sauté a small amount of the sausage mixture until no longer pink. Taste the sample, then adjust seasonings as desired.

4. Stuff sausage mixture into prepared casing as described on page 51. Twist into 6 links, each about 6 inches (15 cm) in length.

Health Facts

Nonfat dry milk adds protein, calcium, vitamin D and other essential vitamins and minerals to these sausages.

Bratwurst

German sausage makers have exported a wide range of sausages, extending their fame well beyond their borders. As a result, many sausage names contain German words, such as *wurst*, which means "sausage." The *brat* part of "bratwurst" typically denotes a fresh sausage that is intended to be fried. The term "bratwurst" encompasses many different types of sausages that meet those basic criteria.

**MAKES
6 SAUSAGES**

Tip

Nonfat dry milk is an excellent product to have on hand, but it has a limited shelf life that is influenced by exposure to heat and moisture. Keep an unopened package in a cool, dark area of the pantry, and store an opened package in a tightly sealed container in a cool, dark place for up to 3 months.

1¾ lbs	trimmed boneless pork shoulder blade roast, chilled (see page 49)	875 g
4 oz	boneless veal stewing meat, chilled	125 g
½ cup	instant nonfat dry milk (skim milk powder)	125 mL
2 tsp	kosher salt	10 mL
1 tsp	ground nutmeg	5 mL
¼ tsp	ground mace	1 mL
¼ tsp	ground ginger	1 mL
1	large egg, beaten	1
⅓ cup	cold milk	75 mL
4 to 5 feet	32/35 mm hog casing, soaked (see page 49)	120 to 150 cm

1. Cut pork and veal into pieces small enough to fit in the throat of your grinder. Using the coarse grinder plate, grind pork and veal into a large bowl or stand mixer bowl.

2. Add dry milk, salt, nutmeg, mace and ginger to the ground meat. Using your hands or the stand mixer paddle attachment, mix until seasonings are evenly distributed. Add egg and cold milk; mix until white strands appear in the mixture and a handful of the mixture holds together.

3. In a small skillet, over medium-high heat, sauté a small amount of the sausage mixture until no longer pink. Taste the sample, then adjust seasonings as desired.

4. Stuff sausage mixture into prepared casing as described on page 51. Twist into 6 links, each about 6 inches (15 cm) in length.

Health Facts

From a health standpoint, eggs have had a bad reputation for decades. Recently, studies have shown that they contain an important nutrient, choline, which is especially critical for pregnant women.

Sweet Italian Sausages

In North America, the two most familiar Italian sausages are sweet Italian and hot Italian sausages. They are both fresh sausages (*salsiccia fresca* in Italian), and they contain similar ingredients, with one notable exception: hot Italian sausages contain copious amounts of hot pepper flakes.

**MAKES
6 SAUSAGES**

Tips

The easiest way to crack fennel seeds is to place them on a piece of parchment paper on the kitchen counter and roll over them with a heavy rolling pin.

If you use your hands to mix the ground meat, have a bowl of water nearby in which to dip your fingers. This will help keep them from getting too sticky.

2 lbs	trimmed boneless pork shoulder blade roast, chilled (see page 49)	1 kg
1 tbsp	freshly cracked fennel seeds (see tip, at left)	15 mL
2 tsp	kosher salt	10 mL
1 tsp	freshly cracked black pepper	5 mL
1 tsp	sweet paprika	5 mL
1 tsp	garlic powder	5 mL
¼ cup	red wine or water	60 mL
4 to 5 feet	32/35 mm hog casing, soaked (see page 49)	120 to 150 cm

1. Cut pork into pieces small enough to fit in the throat of your grinder. Using the coarse grinder plate, grind pork into a large bowl or stand mixer bowl.

2. Add fennel seeds, salt, pepper, paprika and garlic powder to the ground pork. Using your hands or the stand mixer paddle attachment, mix until seasonings are evenly distributed. Add wine and mix until white strands appear in the mixture and a handful of the mixture holds together.

3. In a small skillet, over medium-high heat, sauté a small amount of the sausage mixture until no longer pink. Taste the sample, then adjust seasonings as desired.

4. Stuff sausage mixture into prepared casing as directed on page 51. Twist into 6 links, each about 6 inches (15 cm) in length.

Health Facts

One of numerous phytonutrients found in fennel seeds is rutin, a compound with powerful antioxidant and anti-inflammatory properties. Oxidative damage and inflammation are both linked to many chronic diseases.

Hot Italian Sausages

Hot Italian sausages are a classic in Italy and are noted abroad for their liberal content of hot and black pepper.

Tip

If you enjoy the flavor of the spice mixture in this recipe, make up a larger batch using 6 tbsp (90 mL) hot pepper flakes and 1 tbsp (15 mL) each freshly cracked black pepper, cayenne pepper, fennel seeds, garlic powder and sweet paprika. It will make a meatless pasta sauce, such as marinara or pomodoro, taste like it has sausage in it.

2 lbs	trimmed boneless pork shoulder blade roast, chilled (see page 49)	1 kg
2 tbsp	hot pepper flakes	30 mL
1 tbsp	finely minced garlic	15 mL
1 tbsp	freshly cracked fennel seeds (see tip, page 70)	15 mL
2 tsp	kosher salt	10 mL
1 tsp	freshly cracked black pepper	5 mL
1 tsp	cayenne pepper	5 mL
1 tsp	sweet paprika	5 mL
1 tsp	garlic powder	5 mL
¼ cup	red wine or water	60 mL
4 to 5 feet	32/35 mm hog casing, soaked (see page 49)	120 to 150 cm

1. Cut pork into pieces small enough to fit in the throat of your grinder. Using the coarse grinder plate, grind pork into a large bowl or stand mixer bowl.

2. Add hot pepper flakes, minced garlic, fennel seeds, salt, black pepper, cayenne, paprika and garlic powder to the ground pork. Using your hands or the stand mixer paddle attachment, mix until seasonings are evenly distributed. Add wine and mix until white strands appear in the mixture and a handful of the mixture holds together.

3. In a small skillet, over medium-high heat, sauté a small amount of the sausage mixture until no longer pink. Taste the sample, then adjust seasonings as desired.

4. Stuff sausage mixture into prepared casing as directed on page 51. Twist into 6 links, each about 6 inches (15 cm) in length.

Health Facts

Piperine is a phytonutrient contained in black pepper. Recent studies have shown that it may prevent new fat cells from forming, although to date the only studies have been conducted in animal cells.

Swedish Sausages

The Swedish word for "sausage" is *korv*. Among the various types of *korv*, a traditional recipe is *potatis korv*, made with potatoes. This recipe here, which uses both beef and pork, makes a hearty centerpiece to a warming meal on a chilly winter day.

Tips

If you decide to use table salt in place of kosher salt, use 1½ tsp (7 mL), as table salt has a higher density.

If you use your hands to mix the ground meat, have a bowl of water nearby in which to dip your fingers. This will help keep them from getting too sticky.

Health Facts

Of the numerous phytonutrients in garlic, one intriguing compound is allicin. Allicin has dozens of biologic activities, including inhibiting the formation of blood cells that form clots. Clot formation can lead to both heart attacks and strokes.

1 lb	85/15 boneless beef shoulder, chilled (see page 49)	500 g
1 lb	trimmed boneless pork shoulder blade roast, chilled	500 g
5 oz	russet potato (about 1 small), peeled and sliced lengthwise	150 g
¼ cup	finely minced onion	60 mL
2 tsp	finely minced fresh rosemary	10 mL
2 tsp	garlic powder	10 mL
2 tsp	kosher salt	10 mL
1 tsp	freshly cracked black pepper	5 mL
½ tsp	ground allspice	2 mL
1 tbsp	pickle relish	15 mL
¼ cup	heavy or whipping (35%) cream	60 mL
4 to 5 feet	32/35 mm hog casing, soaked (see page 49)	120 to 150 cm

1. Cut beef and pork into pieces small enough to fit in the throat of your grinder. Using the fine grinder plate, grind beef into a medium bowl. Add pork and potatoes to the ground beef and grind again into a large bowl or stand mixer bowl, this time using the coarse grinder plate.

2. Add onion, rosemary, garlic powder, salt, pepper, allspice and relish to the ground meat mixture. Using your hands or the stand mixer paddle attachment, mix until seasonings are evenly distributed. Add cream and mix until white strands appear in the mixture and a handful of the mixture holds together.

3. In a small skillet, over medium-high heat, sauté a small amount of the sausage mixture until no longer pink. Taste the sample, then adjust seasonings as desired.

4. Stuff sausage mixture into prepared casing as directed on page 51. Twist into 8 links, each about 6 inches (15 cm) in length.

Variation

For an even richer taste, try sautéing the potatoes in olive oil before grinding them.

Ryynimakkara

In Finnish, *makkara* is the word for "sausage." It is often preceded by another word that denotes the specific type of sausage. For example, *mustamakkara* is blood sausage. *Ryynimakkara* contains groats, the hulled kernels of almost any cereal grain, including oat, wheat and rye. Finnish sausages tend to be mild and are usually eaten with condiments, such as mustard and ketchup.

**MAKES
8 SAUSAGES**

Tip

Groats are readily available at some grocery stores, natural food stores and online. Buckwheat or rye groats would make an interesting substitution when you try this recipe again.

Health Facts

As a whole grain, groats are nutrient-dense because they include the vitamin-rich germ and fiber-rich bran. The germ contains both fat-soluble vitamins, such as vitamin E, and essential fatty acids, such as alpha-linolenic acid (ALA). ALA is a plant-based omega-3 fatty acid that may protect against cardiovascular disease.

½ cup	oat groats	125 mL
	Boiling water	
2 lbs	trimmed boneless pork shoulder blade roast	1 kg
2 tsp	granulated sugar	10 mL
2 tsp	onion powder	10 mL
2 tsp	kosher salt	10 mL
1 tsp	freshly cracked black pepper	5 mL
½ tsp	ground nutmeg	2 mL
½ tsp	ground allspice	2 mL
4 to 5 feet	32/35 mm hog casing, soaked (see page 49)	120 to 150 cm

1. Place groats in a bowl and add enough boiling water to just cover; soak for 1 hour. Drain groats, reserving any remaining soaking liquid. Add enough water to the liquid to make ¼ cup (60 mL).

2. Meanwhile, chill pork as directed on page 50.

3. Cut pork into pieces small enough to fit in the throat of your grinder. Using the coarse grinder plate, grind pork into a large bowl or stand mixer bowl.

4. Add soaked groats, sugar, onion powder, salt, pepper, nutmeg and allspice to the ground pork. Using your hands or the stand mixer paddle attachment, mix until seasonings are evenly distributed. Add the reserved soaking water and mix until white strands appear in the mixture and a handful of the mixture holds together.

5. In a small skillet, over medium-high heat, sauté a small amount of the sausage mixture until no longer pink. Taste the sample, then adjust seasonings as desired.

6. Stuff sausage mixture into prepared casing as directed on page 51. Twist into 8 links, each about 6 inches (15 cm) in length.

Kielbasa

Many sausages go by the name of kielbasa, the Polish word for "sausage." Kielbasa may contain pork, beef or a combination of these meats in varying proportions. The modern kielbasa descended from an 18th-century long, dark sausage that was heavily smoked. This recipe is for a fresh kielbasa.

MAKES 4 SAUSAGES

Tips

While garlic is healthy and tasty, it can leave a persistent odor on your hands. Try this: pour some baking soda on your hands and rub them together for at least 10 seconds, then rinse with water. You can also try rubbing your fingers with a stainless steel spoon to rid them of garlic odor.

You'll get the best results with 35/38 mm hog casing in this recipe, but if you cannot find it, 32/35 mm hog casing will work just fine.

2 lbs	trimmed boneless pork shoulder blade roast, chilled (see page 49)	1 kg
6	large cloves garlic, finely minced	6
2 tsp	kosher salt	10 mL
1 tsp	freshly cracked black pepper	5 mL
1 tsp	dried marjoram	5 mL
½ tsp	dried thyme	2 mL
½ tsp	sweet paprika	2 mL
¼ cup	water	60 mL
4 to 5 feet	35/38 mm hog casing, soaked (see page 49)	120 to 150 cm

1. Cut pork into pieces small enough to fit in the throat of your grinder. Using the coarse grinder plate, grind pork into a large bowl or stand mixer bowl.

2. Add garlic, salt, pepper, marjoram, thyme and paprika to the ground pork. Using your hands or the stand mixer paddle attachment, mix until seasonings are evenly distributed. Add water and mix until white strands appear in the mixture and a handful of the mixture holds together.

3. In a small skillet, over medium-high heat, sauté a small amount of the sausage mixture until no longer pink. Taste the sample, then adjust seasonings as desired.

4. Stuff sausage mixture into prepared casing as directed on page 51. Twist into 4 links, each about 8 inches (20 cm) in length.

Health Facts

Cymene, one of the phytonutrients in marjoram, is a potent antioxidant. A 2015 study reported that cymene acted as a neuroprotective agent in the brain cells of mice.

Slovak Sausages

Slovak sausage making has a long history. This traditional fresh sausage includes ingredients that typify the sausages of this region — and it's spicy!

**MAKES
6 SAUSAGES**

Tip
Adjust the spiciness of this sausage up or down to your preference. For a spicier version, use hot paprika and add 1 tsp (5 mL) or more cayenne pepper. For a milder version, decrease or omit the hot pepper flakes.

2 lbs	trimmed boneless pork shoulder blade roast, chilled (see page 49)	1 kg
1 tbsp	finely minced garlic	15 mL
1 tbsp	granulated sugar	15 mL
1 tbsp	sweet paprika	15 mL
1 tbsp	hot pepper flakes	15 mL
2 tsp	kosher salt	10 mL
1 tsp	freshly cracked black pepper	5 mL
¼ cup	water	60 mL
4 to 5 feet	32/35 mm hog casing, soaked (see page 49)	120 to 150 cm

1. Cut pork into pieces small enough to fit in the throat of your grinder. Using the coarse grinder plate, grind pork into a large bowl or stand mixer bowl.

2. Add garlic, sugar, paprika, hot pepper flakes, salt and black pepper to the ground pork. Using your hands or the stand mixer paddle attachment, mix until seasonings are evenly distributed. Add water and mix until white strands appear in the mixture and a handful of the mixture holds together.

3. In a small skillet, over medium-high heat, sauté a small amount of the sausage mixture until no longer pink. Taste the sample, then adjust seasonings as desired.

4. Stuff sausage mixture into prepared casing as directed on page 51. Twist into 6 links, each about 6 inches (15 cm) in length.

Health Facts
Garlic is in the allium family of vegetables, along with onions and leeks. A panel of experts with the American Institute for Cancer Research reviewed over 7000 studies related to cancer and found that the allium group was protective against seven different types of cancer.

Russian Dill Sausages

Dill and caraway seeds give these sausages their characteristic Russian flavor. Caraway is native to Asia and was traditionally used to treat digestive problems (although, paradoxically, it can cause digestive problems at high doses). It was also thought to maintain a lover's interest. While these latter uses may not stand up to close scrutiny, the seeds are loaded with healthy phytonutrients and essential nutrients.

Tips

The two main parsley varieties are flat-leaf (also known as Italian) and curly-leaf. They are basically interchangeable in recipes, but curly-leaf has a more bitter flavor.

If you use your hands to mix the ground meat, have a bowl of water nearby in which to dip your fingers. This will help keep them from getting too sticky.

2 tsp	onion flakes	10 mL
2 tbsp	warm water	30 mL
2 lbs	trimmed boneless pork shoulder blade roast, chilled (see page 49)	1 kg
3 tbsp	finely chopped fresh dill	45 mL
1 tbsp	finely chopped fresh parsley	15 mL
1 tbsp	garlic powder	15 mL
2 tsp	kosher salt	10 mL
1 tsp	freshly cracked black pepper	5 mL
¼ tsp	ground caraway seeds	1 mL
2 tbsp	water	30 mL
4 to 5 feet	32/35 mm hog casing, soaked (see page 49)	120 to 150 cm

1. In a small bowl, combine onion flakes and warm water. Let stand for about 20 minutes or until softened.

2. Meanwhile, cut pork into pieces small enough to fit in the throat of your grinder. Using the coarse grinder plate, grind pork into a large bowl or stand mixer bowl.

3. Add dill, parsley, garlic powder, onion flakes mixture, salt, pepper and caraway to the ground pork. Using your hands or the stand mixer paddle attachment, mix until seasonings are evenly distributed. Add 2 tbsp (30 mL) water and mix until white strands appear in the mixture and a handful of the mixture holds together.

4. In a small skillet, over medium-high heat, sauté a small amount of the sausage mixture until no longer pink. Taste the sample, then adjust seasonings as desired.

5. Stuff sausage mixture into prepared casing as directed on page 51. Twist into 6 links, each about 6 inches (15 cm) in length.

Health Facts

Although most people consider parsley only a garnish, it is loaded with essential nutrients and phytonutrients. It is a rich source of vitamins A, C and K, folate and minerals including iron, calcium and magnesium. So use it often — and throw in a bit extra!

Red Sujuk Sausages

Sujuk (or sucuck) is a semi-dried sausage that likely originated in Turkey but it is made throughout the Balkans and Mediterranean, and into parts of Asia. It may contain a variety of meats, but beef is typically used, as is pork in non-Muslim countries. The two main varieties are red sujuk and black sujuk, with the difference being the inclusion of paprika and red wine in red sujuk. Although this is a fresh sausage, the use of beef and traditional seasonings evoke the sujuk from these regions.

**MAKES
6 SAUSAGES**

Tips

You can customize your own paprika by combining the different types, hot, sweet and smoked, in various proportions. Paprika will stay fresh for up to 4 years if kept in a dry, cool cupboard.

If you decide to use table salt in place of kosher salt, use 1½ tsp (7 mL), as table salt has a higher density.

2 lbs	85/15 beef brisket, chilled (see page 49)	1 kg
2 tbsp	finely minced garlic	30 mL
1 tbsp	sweet smoked paprika	15 mL
1 tbsp	sweet paprika	15 mL
2 tsp	ground fenugreek seeds	10 mL
2 tsp	ground cumin	10 mL
2 tsp	kosher salt	10 mL
1 tsp	freshly cracked black pepper	5 mL
¼ cup	red wine	60 mL
4 to 5 feet	32/35 mm hog casing, soaked (see page 49)	120 to 150 cm

1. Cut beef into pieces small enough to fit in the throat of your grinder. Using the coarse grinder plate, grind beef into a large bowl or stand mixer bowl.

2. Add garlic, smoked paprika, sweet paprika, fenugreek, cumin, salt and pepper to the ground beef. Using your hands or the stand mixer paddle attachment, mix until seasonings are evenly distributed. Add wine and mix until white strands appear in the mixture and a handful of the mixture holds together.

3. In a small skillet, over medium-high heat, sauté a small amount of the sausage mixture until no longer pink. Taste the sample, then adjust seasonings as desired.

4. Stuff sausage mixture into prepared casing as directed on page 51. Twist into 6 links, each about 6 inches (15 cm) in length.

Health Facts

Fenugreek and fennel are often confused, but they're from different plants. Both have been used as medicinal herbs throughout history. In a 2014 study of 88 males, fenugreek improved blood levels of the hormone adiponectin, which is important in body weight regulation.

Merguez

Merguez hails from North Africa and is made with beef or lamb, or sometimes a combination, traditionally in lamb casing. Harissa, a hot sauce made with chile peppers, gives the sausage a fiery flavor. This fresh sausage is typically grilled and enjoyed either as an entrée or tucked into a sandwich.

MAKES 6 SAUSAGES

Tips

Toasted seeds are a great addition to many recipes. Make an extra batch and store them in an airtight container in the refrigerator for up to 3 weeks. Grind them just before use.

You'll get the best results with 30/32 mm hog casing in this recipe, but if you cannot find it, 32/35 mm hog casing will work just fine.

1 tsp	olive oil	5 mL
1 tsp	cumin seeds	5 mL
1 tsp	coriander seeds	5 mL
1 tsp	fennel seeds	5 mL
2 lbs	85/15 boneless beef shoulder, chilled (see page 49)	1 kg
2 tbsp	finely minced fresh parsley	30 mL
1 tbsp	hot pepper flakes	15 mL
2 tsp	garlic powder	10 mL
2 tsp	kosher salt	10 mL
1 tsp	freshly cracked black pepper	5 mL
1 tbsp	harissa	15 mL
¼ cup	water	60 mL
4 to 5 feet	30/32 mm hog casing, soaked (see page 49)	120 to 150 cm

1. In a small skillet, heat oil over medium heat. Add cumin, coriander and fennel seeds; toast for 2 minutes or until fragrant and lightly browned. Let cool for a few minutes, then grind with a spice grinder or mortar and pestle.

2. Cut beef into pieces small enough to fit in the throat of your grinder. Using the coarse grinder plate, grind beef into a large bowl or stand mixer bowl.

3. Add ground seeds, parsley, hot pepper flakes, garlic powder, salt, black pepper and harissa to the ground beef. Using your hands or the stand mixer paddle attachment, mix until seasonings are evenly distributed. Add water and mix until white strands appear in the mixture and a handful of the mixture holds together.

How long to make your sausage links is really up to you, although we suggest 6 inches (15 cm) for this recipe. Keep in mind that this is a rough guideline, and that you may have to adjust the length up or down so that you don't end up with one link smaller than the rest.

4. In a small skillet, over medium-high heat, sauté a small amount of the sausage mixture until no longer pink. Taste the sample, then adjust seasonings as desired.

5. Stuff sausage mixture into prepared casing as directed on page 51. Twist into 6 links, each about 6 inches (15 cm) in length.

Health Facts

Parsley contains many phytonutrients, one of which is apigenin. This flavonoid is associated with a reduced risk of heart problems, neurological conditions and several types of cancer. A 2015 study of a plant extract containing apigenin reported that it prevented DNA damage.

Fresh Chorizo

Unlike traditional Spanish chorizo, which is usually dry-fermented and smoked, Mexican chorizo is a fresh sausage, usually made with pork, though it may also use beef. It is sold both loose and in casings. If stuffed into casing, the casing is typically removed before the meat is added to tacos and other Mexican dishes.

MAKES 6 SAUSAGES

Tips

Instead of removing the casing, slice this sausage for use in your favorite taco recipe.

For recipes that call for seasoned sausage meat, use the ground pork mixture without stuffing it into casing.

2 lbs	trimmed boneless pork shoulder blade roast, chilled (see page 49)	1 kg
1 tbsp	finely minced garlic	15 mL
1 tbsp	sweet paprika	15 mL
1 tbsp	cayenne pepper	15 mL
2 tsp	freshly cracked black pepper	10 mL
2 tsp	kosher salt	10 mL
2 tsp	chili powder	10 mL
2 tsp	dried oregano	10 mL
1 tsp	dried thyme	5 mL
¼ cup	water	60 mL
3 tbsp	apple cider vinegar	45 mL
4 to 5 feet	32/35 mm hog casing, soaked (see page 49)	120 to 150 cm

1. Cut pork into pieces small enough to fit in the throat of your grinder. Using the coarse grinder plate, grind pork into a large bowl or stand mixer bowl.

2. Add garlic, paprika, cayenne, black pepper, salt, chili powder, oregano and thyme to the ground pork. Using your hands or the stand mixer paddle attachment, mix until seasonings are evenly distributed. Add water and vinegar; mix until white strands appear in the mixture.

3. In a small skillet, over medium-high heat, sauté a small amount of the sausage mixture until no longer pink. Taste the sample, then adjust seasonings as desired.

4. Stuff sausage mixture into prepared casing as described on page 51. Twist into 6 links, each about 6 inches (15 cm) in length.

Health Facts

Vinegar has been shown to help lower blood glucose levels. Research from Arizona State University suggests that vinegar may partially block the digestion of starch.

Green Chorizo

Green chorizo hails from Toluca, Mexico, and has a truly unique color and flavor profile. Its deep green color makes a stark contrast to the more common Mexican chorizo, which is a deep reddish color. The inclusion of leafy greens and herbs makes it a nutrient-packed entrée sausage that goes well with any meal.

MAKES 8 SAUSAGES

Tips

You can use ½ cup (125 mL) frozen spinach instead of fresh, but first let it thaw completely, then press out excess liquid.

If you use your hands to mix the ground meat, have a bowl of water nearby in which to dip your fingers. This will help keep them from getting too sticky.

Health Facts

Spinach has moved well beyond being the favorite food of a cartoon sailor. It is rich in several essential nutrients, as well as the phytonutrient betaine, which has cardioprotective effects.

- **Blender**

¼ cup	water	60 mL
3 oz	flat-leaf spinach, trimmed	90 g
2	serrano chile peppers, seeded and minced	2
½ cup	packed fresh cilantro leaves	125 mL
½ cup	packed fresh parsley leaves	125 mL
3 tbsp	green pumpkin seeds (pepitas)	45 mL
1 tbsp	minced fresh oregano	15 mL
2 tsp	garlic powder	10 mL
2 tsp	kosher salt	10 mL
1½ tsp	freshly cracked black pepper	7 mL
½ tsp	ground cumin	2 mL
¼ cup	cold water	60 mL
2 lbs	trimmed boneless pork shoulder blade roast, chilled (see page 49)	1 kg
4 to 5 feet	32/35 mm hog casing, soaked (see page 49)	120 to 150 cm

1. In a large saucepan, bring water to a boil over medium-high heat. Add spinach and boil for 15 seconds or until wilted. Drain and squeeze out liquid, then let cool completely.

2. In blender, combine spinach, chiles, cilantro, parsley, pumpkin seeds, oregano, garlic powder, salt, pepper, cumin and cold water; purée until smooth. Set aside.

3. Cut pork into pieces small enough to fit in the throat of your grinder. Using the coarse grinder plate, grind pork into a large bowl or stand mixer bowl.

4. Add spinach purée to the ground pork. Using your hands or the stand mixer paddle attachment, mix until purée is evenly distributed, white strands appear in the mixture and a handful of the mixture holds together.

5. In a small skillet, over medium-high heat, sauté a small amount of the sausage mixture until no longer pink. Taste the sample, then adjust seasonings as desired.

6. Stuff sausage mixture into prepared casing as described on page 51. Twist into 8 links, each about 6 inches (15 cm) in length.

Cajun Boudin Blanc

This sausage gets its name from the Old French words *boudin*, meaning "sausage," and *blanc*, meaning "white." This is a Cajun take on the traditional French recipe, so it's quite spicy.

Tips

The various types of liver are equivalent from a nutritional standpoint, but calves' liver is more tender. If price is a consideration, you can substitute beef or pork liver.

If you decide to use table salt in place of kosher salt, use 3¾ tsp (18 mL), as table salt has a higher density. Use 2¼ tsp (11 mL) in step 1 and the remainder in step 3.

1⅓ lbs	trimmed boneless pork shoulder blade roast	700 g
10 oz	calves' liver	300 g
1	sprig fresh thyme	1
1	stalk celery, diced	1
½	red bell pepper, finely chopped	½
½	onion, finely chopped	½
5 tsp	kosher salt, divided	25 mL
2 tsp	freshly cracked black pepper	10 mL
1½ cups	cooked long-grain white rice	375 mL
¼ cup	finely chopped fresh chives	60 mL
2 tsp	finely chopped fresh thyme	10 mL
2 tsp	garlic powder	10 mL
2 tsp	onion powder	10 mL
2 tsp	hot pepper flakes	10 mL
1 tsp	freshly ground black pepper	5 mL
1 tsp	cayenne pepper	5 mL
1 tsp	sweet paprika	5 mL
1 tsp	dried oregano	5 mL
4 to 5 feet	32/35 mm hog casing, soaked (see page 49)	120 to 150 cm

1. Cut pork and liver into 1-inch (2.5 cm) cubes. Place meat in a stockpot and add enough water to cover. Add thyme sprig, celery, red pepper, onion, 3 tsp (15 mL) salt and cracked black pepper; bring to a boil over high heat. Reduce heat and simmer for about 75 minutes or until meat is tender and falls apart easily. Using a slotted spoon, transfer meat to a plate. Reserve ¼ cup (60 mL) of the liquid and discard remaining liquid and vegetables. Let meat and liquid cool.

2. Using the coarse grinder plate, grind pork and liver into a large bowl or stand mixer bowl.

3. Add rice, chives, chopped thyme, garlic powder, onion powder, the remaining salt, hot pepper flakes, ground black pepper, cayenne, paprika and oregano to the ground meat. Using your hands or the stand mixer paddle attachment, mix until seasonings are evenly distributed. Add the reserved liquid and mix until mixture has a thick custard-like consistency.

4. In a small skillet, over medium-high heat, sauté a small amount of the sausage mixture until no longer pink. Taste the sample, then adjust seasonings as desired.

5. Stuff sausage mixture into prepared casing as described on page 51. Twist into 9 links, each about 6 inches (15 cm) in length.

Health Facts

Celery contains antioxidants, phenolic acids, flavonols and phytosterols, as well as phthalides, which researchers believe help lower blood pressure by relaxing the tissues of the artery walls to increase blood flow.

Boudin Noir

Boudin noir means "black sausage" in Old French. It's one of the oldest French sausages, dating back at least 2000 years. The dark color comes from its blood content. Traditionally, the pig was bled by continuously moving one of the forelegs, which promoted drainage and prevented clot formation. Children were often drafted to stir the warm blood, to keep it from coagulating. French sausage makers now remove the blood using a vacuum system and centrifuge it to prevent coagulation. We modified the traditional recipe for modern sensibilities, but it still takes a stout heart to make these sausages!

MAKES 11 SAUSAGES

Tips

When dicing the pork fat, keep the size of the dice to just under ⅕ inch (5 mm). This will help you achieve the traditional texture.

Extra fat and lean pork can be carefully packed into freezer bags and stored in the freezer for up to 6 months.

- Cheesecloth

1½ lbs	boneless pork shoulder blade roast	750 g
1½ tbsp	vegetable oil	22 mL
1 lb	onions, finely chopped	500 g
1 tbsp	kosher salt	15 mL
1 tsp	freshly ground black pepper	5 mL
½ tsp	cayenne pepper	2 mL
½ tsp	ground cinnamon	2 mL
3 oz	jowl bacon	90 g
1 lb	beef blood	500 g
1 cup	dry bread crumbs	250 mL
2	large eggs, beaten	2
¼ cup	heavy or whipping (35%) cream	60 mL
4 to 5 feet	32/35 mm hog casing, soaked (see page 49)	120 to 150 cm

1. Cut off the fat from the pork roast, trimming it down to lean meat as much as possible. Weigh out 8 oz (250 g) pork fat and finely dice to just under ⅕ inch (5 mm). Weigh out 6 oz (175 g) lean pork. Reserve any extra fat and lean pork for another use.

2. In a medium skillet, heat oil over medium-high heat. Add onions and cook, stirring, for about 8 minutes or until translucent.

3. In a pot of hot water (up to 200°F/93°C), blanch pork fat for 5 minutes, gently stirring to immerse the fat, to seal the surface and prevent discoloration when added to blood. Drain and let cool completely.

4. In a large bowl, combine onions, pork fat, salt, black pepper, cayenne and cinnamon.

5. Using the fine grinder plate, grind lean pork and bacon into a large bowl or stand mixer bowl.

Tip

If you don't have two large shallow pans, you can poach the sausages one batch at a time. Refrigerate the second batch until the first batch is done.

6. Stir beef blood to ensure a smooth texture and filter it through cheesecloth to remove any clots. Carefully pour half the blood over the onion mixture. Add ground pork, bread crumbs, eggs and cream. Add the remaining blood and mix until color is uniform.

7. In a small skillet, over medium-high heat, sauté a small amount of the sausage mixture until no longer pink. Taste the sample, then adjust seasonings as desired.

8. Stuff sausage mixture into prepared casing as described on page 51. Twist into 11 links, each about 6 inches (15 cm) in length.

9. Divide sausages into two batches. In two large shallow pans of simmering (180°F/82°C) water (see tip, at left), poach sausages for 1 hour, topping up water if level dips, until just beginning to firm up. Drain sausages, transfer to a bowl and let rest for 5 minutes, then chill in cold water, refreshing water often, until completely cool. Wipe dry with paper towels and refrigerate for up to 2 days or freeze.

Health Facts

Cinnamon contains many antioxidant compounds. One study that compared the antioxidant activity of 26 herbs and spices reported that cinnamon's antioxidant activity beat out all the others.

Traditional Polish Blood Sausages

Blood sausage has a long tradition in many sausage-making countries, with pig's blood the most often used. The sausage usually also includes a filler, which can be animal fat, meat, a grain or bread. We've made some modifications to the ingredients and process, but be warned that this type of sausage making is not for the faint of heart.

MAKES 1 LARGE SAUSAGE

Tips

Some blood sausage recipes call for a larger quantity of blood; the amount in this recipe is based on our taste and color preference.

If you decide to use table salt in place of kosher salt, use 1½ tsp (7 mL), as table salt has a higher density.

1 lb	well-marbled boneless pork shoulder blade roast	500 g
8 oz	pork skins	250 g
4 oz	pork jowl	125 g
4 oz	pork liver	125 g
½ cup	pearl barley	125 mL
1	onion, quartered	1
2 tsp	kosher salt	10 mL
1 tsp	freshly ground black pepper	5 mL
1 tsp	dried marjoram	5 mL
¼ cup	beef blood	60 mL
4 to 5 feet	cut-and-tie beef rounds, soaked (see page 49)	120 to 150 cm

1. Place pork meat, skins and jowl in a large stockpot and add enough water to cover the meat by at least 6 inches (15 cm) to allow for some boil-off. Bring to a boil over high heat. Boil for about 75 minutes, or until meat starts to become tender. Add liver and boil until meat is fork-tender. Using a slotted spoon, transfer meat to a plate and let cool completely. Tear any large chunks into pieces small enough to fit in the throat of your grinder.

2. Add barley to the water remaining in the stockpot and boil gently for 40 minutes or until tender. Drain, reserving 2 cups (500 mL) water, and let barley cool completely.

3. Using the fine grinder plate, grind cooled meat and onion into a large bowl or stand mixer bowl.

4. Add salt, pepper and marjoram to the ground pork. Using your hands or the stand mixer paddle attachment, mix until seasonings are evenly distributed. Add the reserved cooking water and mix until well combined. Add cooled barley and mix until well combined. Taste a small sample and adjust seasonings as desired.

5. Carefully pour beef blood into the ground pork mixture and mix until color is even.

Tip

If you use your hands to mix the ground meat, have a bowl of water nearby in which to dip your fingers. This will help keep them from getting too sticky.

6. Stuff sausage mixture into prepared casing as directed on page 51 and tie off the open end with a double knot.

7. In a large shallow pan of gently simmering water (175°F/80°C), poach sausage for 45 minutes, topping up water if level dips, until just beginning to firm up. Drain sausage, transfer to a bowl and let rest for 5 minutes, then chill in cold water, refreshing water often, until completely cool. Wipe dry with paper towels and refrigerate for up to 2 days or freeze.

Health Facts

Barley is high in fiber and many other nutrients and phytonutrients. A 2010 Dutch study reported that men who ate barley instead of wheat at dinner had 30% better insulin sensitivity the next morning after a high-glycemic-index breakfast.

Liverwurst

Liverwurst — or *leberwurst* in German — is, unsurprisingly, made with liver. As with other German sausages, it often appears with another name before it, denoting the specific type of liver sausage. For example, *Frankfurter leberwurst* hails from the city of Frankfurt.

**MAKES
1 LARGE
SAUSAGE**

Tip

Calves' liver is considered to be the best in culinary circles, but lamb and beef liver are similar and less expensive. Beef liver is considerably tougher, although in making sausage, this is not an issue.

- **Large bowl, chilled in the refrigerator for 30 minutes**
- **Food processor, bowl chilled in the refrigerator for 30 minutes**
- **Meat thermometer**

1⅓ lbs	trimmed boneless pork shoulder blade roast, chilled (see page 49)	700 g
10 oz	calves' liver, chilled	300 g
1½ tsp	kosher salt	7 mL
1 tsp	freshly ground white pepper	5 mL
1 tsp	ground allspice	5 mL
1 tsp	dried marjoram	5 mL
½ tsp	dried sage	2 mL
¼ cup	puréed onion (see tip, at right)	60 mL
2 tbsp	puréed garlic (see tip, at right)	30 mL
¾ cup	ice water	175 mL
4 to 5 feet	cut-and-tie beef rounds, soaked (see page 49)	120 to 150 cm

1. Cut pork and liver into pieces small enough to fit in the throat of your grinder. Using the fine grinder plate, grind pork and liver into chilled large bowl.

2. Transfer ground meat to chilled food processor bowl and add salt, pepper, allspice, marjoram and sage. With the motor running, through the feed tube, gradually add puréed onion, puréed garlic and ice water. Continue processing the mixture, carefully monitoring the temperature. As the mixture gets warmer, it will begin to appear pasty, indicating that it is emulsified. When it reaches 57°F (14°C), the mixture should be a uniform consistency and you should stop processing. The mixture must not exceed 57°F (14°C) or the emulsion will break down.

3. In a small skillet, over medium-high heat, sauté a small amount of the sausage mixture until no longer pink. Taste the sample, then adjust seasonings as desired.

4. Stuff sausage mixture into prepared casing as directed on page 51 and tie off the open end with a double knot.

To make ¼ cup (60 mL) puréed onion, roughly chop 1 small onion. In a mini chopper, combine onion and 1 tbsp (15 mL) water; process until smooth.

To make 2 tbsp (30 mL) puréed garlic, roughly chop 5 cloves of garlic. In a mini chopper, combine garlic and ½ tsp (2 mL) olive oil; process to a paste-like consistency.

5. In a large shallow pan of gently simmering water (175°F/80°C), poach sausage for 45 minutes, topping up water if level dips, until just beginning to firm up. Drain sausage, transfer to a bowl and let rest for 5 minutes, then chill in cold water, refreshing water often, until completely cool. Wipe dry with paper towels and refrigerate for up to 2 days or freeze.

Health Facts

Liverwurst is high in calories, fat and saturated fat, but is a source of essential vitamins and minerals. It is especially high in vitamin A and iron.

Variation

Smoked Liverwurst: Add ½ tsp (2 mL) cure #1 curing salts with the salt in step 2. Instead of poaching the sausage, let it dry at room temperature for 20 to 30 minutes or until casing has a slightly tacky feel. Meanwhile, prepare a fire in your smoker. Smoke sausage at 170°F to 180°F (77°C to 82°C) for 3 to 4 hours or until a meat thermometer inserted in the center of a sausage link registers 160°F (71°C). Let cool completely, then refrigerate.

Currywurst

Currywurst derives its name from the fact that it's topped with a curry ketchup. Our version includes curry powder in the sausage itself, and we've included a Curry Ketchup recipe (opposite) to slather on top.

Tips

Extra fat and lean pork can be carefully packed into freezer bags and stored in the freezer for up to 6 months.

You'll get the best results with 30/32 mm hog casing in this recipe, but if you cannot find it, 32/35 mm hog casing will work just fine.

How long to make your sausage links is really up to you, although we suggest 5 inches (12.5 cm) for this recipe. Keep in mind that this is a rough guideline, and that you may have to adjust the length up or down so that you don't end up with one link smaller than the rest.

- Large bowl, chilled in the refrigerator for 30 minutes
- Food processor, bowl chilled in the refrigerator for 30 minutes
- Meat thermometer

2 lbs	boneless pork shoulder blade roast	1 kg
7 oz	pork back fat	210 g
1½ tbsp	yellow curry powder	22 mL
1½ tsp	kosher salt	7 mL
¼ tsp	freshly ground white pepper	1 mL
¼ tsp	ground nutmeg	1 mL
¼ tsp	ground cardamom	1 mL
¼ tsp	ground ginger	1 mL
⅛ tsp	ground coriander	0.5 mL
2	cloves garlic, minced and pressed into paste (see tip, page 92)	2
2 tbsp	cold water	30 mL
2 tbsp	crushed ice	30 mL
4 to 5 feet	30/32 mm hog casing, soaked (see page 49)	120 to 150 cm

1. Cut off the fat from the pork roast, trimming it down to lean meat as much as possible. Weigh out 1¼ lbs (625 g) lean pork and 7 oz (210 g) pork trimmings (fat with a little meat attached). Chill lean pork, trimmings and back fat as directed on page 50. Reserve any extra lean pork and trimmings for another use.

2. Cut lean pork, trimmings and fat into pieces small enough to fit in the throat of your grinder. Using the fine grinder plate, grind lean pork, fat and trimmings into chilled large bowl.

3. Transfer ground meat to chilled food processor bowl and add curry powder, salt, pepper, nutmeg, cardamom, ginger and coriander. With the motor running, through the feed tube, gradually add garlic paste, water and ice. Continue processing the mixture, carefully monitoring the temperature. As the mixture gets warmer, it will begin to appear pasty, indicating that it is emulsified. When it reaches 57°F (14°C), the mixture should be a uniform consistency and you should stop processing. The mixture must not exceed 57°F (14°C) or the emulsion will break down.

4. In a small skillet, over medium-high heat, sauté a small amount of the sausage mixture until no longer pink. Taste the sample, then adjust seasonings as desired.

Health Facts

One of the main ingredients in curry powder is turmeric, which contains the compound curcumin. Studies have shown that curcumin's anti-inflammatory effects may be comparable to drugs such as corticosteroids and ibuprofen.

MAKES ABOUT 4½ CUPS (1.05 ML)

You'll enjoy this curry ketchup on many foods, not just sausages. It's a natural pairing for Currywurst (opposite), but try it on any mild sausage that is not highly seasoned.

Tip

This ketchup can be stored in an airtight container in the refrigerator for up to 1 month or in the freezer for up to 4 months.

5. Stuff sausage mixture into prepared casing as directed on page 51. Twist into 7 links, each about 5 inches (12.5 cm) in length. Refrigerate immediately.

Variation

Smoked Currywurst: Add ½ tsp (2 mL) cure #1 curing salts with the salt in step 3. After twisting the sausages into links, let them dry at room temperature for 20 to 30 minutes or until casings have a slightly tacky feel. Meanwhile, prepare a fire in your smoker. Smoke sausage at 170°F to 180°F (77°C to 82°C) for 2 to 3 hours or until a meat thermometer inserted in the center of a sausage link registers 160°F (71°C). Let cool completely, then refrigerate.

Curry Ketchup

* Blender

2 tbsp	olive oil	30 mL
1	sweet onion, finely chopped	1
4	cloves garlic, finely minced	4
1 tbsp	yellow curry powder	15 mL
1 tsp	dry mustard	5 mL
1 tsp	kosher salt	5 mL
½ tsp	hot pepper flakes	2 mL
½ tsp	sweet smoked paprika	2 mL
¼ tsp	ground allspice	1 mL
⅛ tsp	ground cloves	0.5 mL
1 tbsp	tomato paste	15 mL
1	can (28 oz/796 mL) crushed tomatoes	1
⅓ cup	packed brown sugar	75 mL
¼ cup	apple cider vinegar	60 mL

1. In a medium saucepan, heat oil over medium heat. Add onion and cook, stirring for 6 to 8 minutes or until softened and beginning to brown. Add garlic and cook, stirring, for 1 minute. Add curry powder, mustard, salt, hot pepper flakes, paprika, allspice, cloves and tomato paste, stirring until all ingredients are well distributed; cook, stirring, for 1 minute.

2. Stir in tomatoes, brown sugar and vinegar; bring to a gentle boil. Reduce heat and simmer, stirring occasionally, for 45 minutes or until reduced and thickened. Remove from heat and let cool.

3. Transfer tomato mixture to blender and purée until smooth. Taste and adjust seasonings as desired. If a smoother consistency is desired, strain the purée.

American Hot Dogs

The modern hot dog descended from the German wienerwurst, whose creators brought the sausage when they immigrated to North America in the 1800s. The sausage became a popular fixture, and commercial production began soon after. Commercial hot dog production also brought many changes to the recipe and process, creating a milder skinless sausage. Making skinless hot dogs is best left to commercial producers, as specialized casings are used in the cooking and packaging process. However, this recipe brings together the familiar flavors of an American classic for the home sausage maker.

MAKES 8 SAUSAGES

Tips

To press minced garlic into paste, press a chef's knife down with both hands and pull it toward you across the garlic. Repeat the motion until you achieve a paste-like consistency.

You'll get the best results with 24/26 mm sheep casing in this recipe, but if you cannot find it, 32/35 mm hog casing will work just fine, though your hot dogs will be more sausage-shaped.

- Large bowl, chilled in the refrigerator for 30 minutes
- Food processor, bowl chilled in the refrigerator for 30 minutes
- Meat thermometer
- Smoker

2 lbs	boneless pork shoulder blade roast	1 kg
7 oz	pork back fat	210 g
2 tsp	kosher salt	10 mL
1 tsp	freshly ground white pepper	5 mL
1 tsp	sweet paprika	5 mL
1 tsp	dry mustard	5 mL
½ tsp	cure #1 curing salts	2 mL
¼ tsp	ground mace	1 mL
¼ tsp	dried marjoram	1 mL
1	large egg white	1
2	cloves garlic, minced and pressed into paste (see tip, at left)	2
2 tbsp	crushed ice	30 mL
2 tbsp	cold water	30 mL
4 to 5 feet	24/26 mm sheep casing, soaked (see page 49)	120 to 150 cm

1. Cut off the fat from the pork roast, trimming it down to lean meat as much as possible. Weigh out 1¼ lbs (625 g) lean pork and 7 oz (210 g) pork trimmings (fat with a little meat attached). Chill lean pork, trimmings and back fat as directed on page 50. Reserve any extra lean pork and trimmings for another use.

2. Cut lean pork, trimmings and fat into pieces small enough to fit in the throat of your grinder. Using the fine grinder plate, grind lean pork, fat and trimmings into chilled large bowl.

Tip

If you use your hands to mix the ground meat, have a bowl of water nearby in which to dip your fingers. This will help keep them from getting too sticky.

3. Transfer ground meat to chilled food processor bowl and add salt, pepper, paprika, mustard, curing salts, mace, marjoram and egg white. With the motor running, through the feed tube, gradually add garlic paste, ice and cold water. Continue processing the mixture, carefully monitoring the temperature. As the mixture gets warmer, it will begin to appear pasty, indicating that it is emulsified. When it reaches 57°F (14°C), the mixture should be a uniform consistency and you should stop processing. The mixture must not exceed 57°F (14°C) or the emulsion will break down.

4. In a small skillet, over medium-high heat, sauté a small amount of the sausage mixture until juices run clear. Taste the sample, then adjust seasonings as desired.

5. Stuff sausage mixture into prepared casing as directed on page 51. Twist into 8 links, each about 6 inches (15 cm) in length. Let dry at room temperature for 20 to 30 minutes or until casings have a slightly tacky feel.

6. Meanwhile, prepare a fire in your smoker. Smoke sausages at 170°F to 180°F (77°C to 82°C) for 2 to 3 hours or until a meat thermometer inserted in the center of a sausage link registers 160°F (71°C). Let cool completely, then refrigerate.

Health Facts

As with all traditional hot dog recipes, these sausages are high in calories and fat, so you may want to lighten up for the rest of the day when you treat yourself to this classic.

Frankfurters

The German frankfurter is usually considered to be the same sausage as the hot dog. Some food encyclopedias distinguish between the two, however, saying the frankfurter is "slightly more elongated than a regular hot dog and may be in a thin casing."

Tips

If you decide to use table salt in place of kosher salt, use 1½ tsp (7 mL), as table salt has a higher density.

You'll get the best results with 24/26 mm sheep casing in this recipe, but if you cannot find it, 32/35 mm hog casing will work just fine, though your frankfurters will be more sausage-shaped.

- Large bowl, chilled in the refrigerator for 30 minutes
- Food processor, bowl chilled in the refrigerator for 30 minutes
- Meat thermometer
- Smoker

1¼ lbs	80/20 boneless beef shoulder, chilled (see page 49)	625 g
8 oz	pork back fat, chilled	250 g
4 oz	boneless pork loin chop, chilled	125 g
2 tsp	kosher salt	10 mL
1 tsp	freshly ground white pepper	5 mL
1 tsp	sweet paprika	5 mL
1 tsp	onion powder	5 mL
½ tsp	cure #1 curing salts	2 mL
½ tsp	dry mustard	2 mL
¼ tsp	ground mace	1 mL
¼ tsp	dried marjoram	1 mL
1	large egg white	1
2 tbsp	crushed ice	30 mL
2 tbsp	cold water	30 mL
4 to 5 feet	24/26 mm sheep casing, soaked (see page 49)	120 to 150 cm

1. Cut beef, pork fat and pork meat into pieces small enough to fit in the throat of your grinder. Using the fine grinder plate, grind beef, pork fat and pork meat into chilled large bowl.

2. Transfer ground meat to chilled food processor bowl and add salt, pepper, paprika, onion powder, curing salts, mustard, mace, marjoram and egg white. With the motor running, through the feed tube, gradually add ice and cold water. Continue processing the mixture, carefully monitoring the temperature. As the mixture gets warmer, it will begin to appear pasty, indicating that it is emulsified. When it reaches 57°F (14°C), the mixture should be a uniform consistency and you should stop processing. The mixture must not exceed 57°F (14°C) or the emulsion will break down.

Tip

How long to make your sausage links is really up to you, although we suggest 6 inches (15 cm) for this recipe. Keep in mind that this is a rough guideline, and that you may have to adjust the length up or down so that you don't end up with one link smaller than the rest.

3. In a small skillet, over medium-high heat, sauté a small amount of the sausage mixture until juices run clear. Taste the sample, then adjust seasonings as desired.

4. Stuff sausage mixture into prepared casing as directed on page 51. Twist into 8 links, each about 6 inches (15 cm) in length. Let dry at room temperature for 20 to 30 minutes or until casings have a slightly tacky feel.

5. Meanwhile, prepare a fire in your smoker. Smoke sausages at 170°F to 180°F (77°C to 82°C) for 2 to 3 hours or until a meat thermometer inserted in the center of a sausage link registers 160°F (71°C). Let cool completely, then refrigerate.

Health Facts

These franks are a definite diet buster, so they should be eaten only as a rare treat. You would need to run up stairs for 20 minutes to burn off the calories in one of these sausages. Here's a handy website for calculating the amount of exercise needed to burn off a specific number of calories: www.healthstatus.com/calculate/cbc.

Andouille

Andouille is a pork sausage created in France in the 1600s. The name is most likely derived from the Latin *inductilia*, which means "to load in," as with loading filling into a casing. Andouille traditionally included tripe, but our recipe is geared more to modern sensibilities. Andouille differs only in diameter from its smaller cousin, andouillette.

Tips

To save time for your next sausage-making endeavor, cut up larger amounts of meat and freeze the portion sizes you'll need. The recipes in this book are all based on 2 lbs (1 kg) of meat, so that's a handy portion size. When you're ready to make sausage, place the meat in the refrigerator and let it partially thaw.

You'll get the best results with 35/38 mm hog casing in this recipe, but if you cannot find it, 32/35 mm hog casing will work just fine.

Health Facts

Of marjoram's many phytonutrients, several have been shown to reduce tumor formation and help prevent cancer. These nutrients include carvone, alpha-humulene and caffeic acid.

- Smoker
- Meat thermometer

2 lbs	boneless pork shoulder blade roast	1 kg
1 tbsp	sweet paprika	15 mL
1 tbsp	garlic powder	15 mL
2 tsp	dried thyme	10 mL
2 tsp	freshly cracked black pepper	10 mL
1 tsp	kosher salt	5 mL
1 tsp	dried marjoram	5 mL
½ tsp	cure #1 curing salts	2 mL
¼ cup	water	60 mL
4 to 5 feet	35/38 mm hog casing, soaked (see page 49)	120 to 150 cm

1. Cut off the visible fat from the pork roast. Chill lean pork and fat as directed on page 50.

2. Cut lean pork and fat into pieces small enough to fit in the throat of your grinder, keeping them separate. Using the fine grinder plate, grind fat into a medium bowl. Add pork meat to the ground fat and grind again into a large bowl or stand mixer bowl.

3. Add paprika, garlic powder, thyme, pepper, salt, marjoram and curing salts to the ground meat. Using your hands or the stand mixer paddle attachment, mix until seasonings are evenly distributed. Add water and mix until white strands appear in the mixture and a handful of the mixture holds together.

4. In a small skillet, over medium-high heat, sauté a small amount of the sausage mixture until juices run clear. Taste the sample, then adjust seasonings as desired.

5. Stuff sausage mixture into prepared casing as described on page 51. Twist into 4 links, each about 8 inches (20 cm) in length. Let dry at room temperature for 20 to 30 minutes or until casings have a slightly tacky feel.

6. Meanwhile, prepare a fire in your smoker. Smoke sausages at 170°F to 180°F (77°C to 82°C) for about 3 hours or until a meat thermometer inserted in the center of a sausage link registers 160°F (71°C). Let cool completely, then refrigerate.

Louisiana Andouille

Louisiana andouille (also known as Cajun andouille) is a spicier version of its French ancestor (see page 96). Cajun cuisine is characterized by a heavy hand on the hot spices and a combination of French and Spanish influences. This tasty sausage is an important ingredient in two other Cajun specialties: gumbo and jambalaya.

**MAKES
4 SAUSAGES**

Tips

When adding curing salts, be careful to use the exact amount called for.

You'll get the best results with 35/38 mm hog casing in this recipe, but if you cannot find it, 32/35 mm hog casing will work just fine.

Health Facts

Thyme demonstrates high antioxidant and antimicrobial activity. In a study of the herb's use in fighting acne, researchers at Leeds University reported that thyme preparations may be more effective than prescription acne creams.

- Smoker
- Meat thermometer

2 lbs	trimmed boneless pork shoulder blade roast, chilled (see page 49)	1 kg
2 tsp	dried thyme	10 mL
2 tsp	garlic powder	10 mL
2 tsp	cayenne pepper	10 mL
2 tsp	freshly cracked black pepper	10 mL
1 tsp	hot pepper flakes	5 mL
1 tsp	kosher salt	5 mL
1 tsp	dried marjoram	5 mL
½ tsp	cure #1 curing salts	2 mL
¼ cup	water	60 mL
4 to 5 feet	35/38 mm hog casing, soaked (see page 49)	120 to 150 cm

1. Cut pork into pieces small enough to fit in the throat of your grinder. Using the coarse grinder plate, grind pork into a large bowl or stand mixer bowl.

2. Add thyme, garlic powder, cayenne, black pepper, hot pepper flakes, salt, marjoram and curing salts to the ground pork. Using your hands or the stand mixer paddle attachment, mix until seasonings are evenly distributed. Add water and mix until white strands appear in the mixture and a handful of the mixture holds together.

3. In a small skillet, over medium-high heat, sauté a small amount of the sausage mixture until juices run clear. Taste the sample, then adjust seasonings as desired.

4. Stuff sausage mixture into prepared casing as described on page 51. Twist into 4 links, each about 8 inches (20 cm) in length. Let dry at room temperature for 20 to 30 minutes or until casings have a slightly tacky feel.

5. Meanwhile, prepare a fire in your smoker. Smoke sausages at 170°F to 180°F (77°C to 82°C) for about 3 hours or until a meat thermometer inserted in the center of a sausage link registers 160°F (71°C). Let cool completely, then refrigerate.

Polish Smoked Sausages

The phrase "Polish sausage" is a generic term, but in North America, most people use it to mean a smoked sausage that contains pork or beef, or a combination. According to the USDA, Polish sausage has been "cured, cooked, and usually smoked; an uncured (fresh) uncooked variety with no more than 3% water also exists." This is a traditional Polish smoked sausage, which requires smoking.

**MAKES
4 SAUSAGES**

Tip

Always make sure the sausage casing is dry before placing in the smoker, because the smoke doesn't effectively penetrate the casing when it's wet. The sausage will feel slightly tacky to the touch when it's sufficiently dry and ready for the smoker.

Health Facts

The mustard plant is in the Brassica family, along with other cruciferous plants. These foods contain many phytonutrients, most notably glucosinolates, which break down into isothiocyanates. Studies have shown that isothiocyanates have anticancer effects, especially against cancers of the intestinal tract.

- Smoker
- Meat thermometer

2 lbs	trimmed boneless pork shoulder blade roast, chilled (see page 49)	1 kg
6	cloves garlic, finely minced	6
1 tbsp	mustard seeds	15 mL
1 tsp	dried marjoram	5 mL
1 tsp	kosher salt	5 mL
1 tsp	freshly ground black pepper	5 mL
½ tsp	cure #1 curing salts	2 mL
¼ cup	ice water	60 mL
4 to 5 feet	39/42 mm hog casing, soaked (see page 49)	120 to 150 cm

1. Cut pork into pieces small enough to fit in the throat of your grinder. Using the coarse grinder plate, grind pork into a large bowl or stand mixer bowl.

2. Add garlic, mustard seeds, marjoram, salt, pepper and curing salts to the ground pork. Using your hands or the stand mixer paddle attachment, mix until seasonings are evenly distributed. Add ice water and mix until white strands appear in the mixture and a handful of the mixture holds together.

3. In a small skillet, over medium-high heat, sauté a small amount of the sausage mixture until juices run clear. Taste the sample, then adjust seasonings as desired.

4. Stuff sausage mixture into prepared casing as described on page 51. Twist into 4 links, each about 8 inches (20 cm) in length. Let dry at room temperature for 20 to 30 minutes or until casings have a slightly tacky feel.

5. Meanwhile, prepare a fire in your smoker. Smoke sausages at 170°F to 180°F (77°C to 82°C) for about 3 hours or until a meat thermometer inserted in the center of a sausage link registers 160°F (71°C). Let cool completely, then refrigerate.

Soppressata

The name of this dried Italian sausage is derived from the process used to make it: in Italian, *pressare* means "to press." There are many different versions from various parts of Italy; this recipe, which includes small chunks of back fat, is from the Abruzzo region. Soppressata shares similarities with salami (see page 102) but has a coarser grind, and its devotees are legion.

MAKES 1 LARGE SAUSAGE

Tips

Back fat retains its shape in the sausage, whereas fat from other parts can blend into the meat. When you cut into the finished sausage, you should see small cubes of fat surrounded by lean meat.

If you prefer, you can just use 2 lbs (1 kg) boneless pork shoulder blade roast and skip the back fat.

Don't stuff the sausage to full capacity; you need room in the casing to allow for the flattening step.

Health Facts

Soppressata is a high-fat product. When you treat yourself to this sausage, make sure to stick to a small portion and lighten up on your fat intake for the rest of the day.

• Drying chamber

1³⁄₄ lbs	trimmed boneless pork shoulder blade roast, chilled (see page 49)	875 g
4 oz	pork back fat, chilled	125 g
1 tbsp	kosher salt	15 mL
1 tbsp	freshly cracked black pepper	15 mL
2 tsp	garlic powder	10 mL
1 tsp	ground cloves	5 mL
½ tsp	cure #1 curing salts	2 mL
¼ cup	water	60 mL
4 to 5 feet	hog middles casing, soaked (see page 49)	120 to 150 cm

1. Cut pork into pieces small enough to fit in the throat of your grinder. Cut the back fat into ¼-inch (0.5 cm) cubes. Using the coarse grinder plate, grind pork meat and fat into a large bowl or stand mixer bowl.

2. Add salt, pepper, garlic powder, cloves and curing salts to the ground pork. Using your hands or the stand mixer paddle attachment, mix until seasonings are evenly distributed. Add water and mix until white strands appear in the mixture and a handful of the mixture holds together.

3. In a small skillet, over medium-high heat, sauté a small amount of the sausage mixture until juices run clear. Taste the sample, then adjust seasonings as desired.

4. Stuff sausage mixture into prepared casing as described on page 51, using butcher's twine to tie the knots at the ends of the casing and filling casing only to 80% capacity. Lay sausage flat and prick generously to remove air bubbles. Weigh the sausage and document its weight.

5. In your drying chamber, place sausage between two large cutting boards. Place a 10-lb (4.5 kg) weight on top to flatten the sausage and let stand for 3 days.

6. After 3 days, hang sausage in the drying chamber until it has lost 30% of its original weight.

Landjäger

Landjäger (or landjaeger) is a smoked German sausage. Its name comes from the German word for "hunter," probably because this sausage is very portable, with no need for refrigeration. It may include pork, beef and other meats, as well as various spices. During the fermentation process, the sausage is flattened to take on a rectangular appearance.

Tips

Keeping the strands to two links makes them easier to manage through the various steps of the process.

To grind caraway seeds, you can use a spice grinder, a clean coffee grinder or a mortar and pestle. For small quantities, the mortar and pestle works best.

- Drying chamber
- Cold smoker

1 lb	trimmed boneless pork shoulder blade roast, chilled (see page 49)	500 g
1 lb	85/15 boneless beef shoulder, chilled	500 g
1 tbsp	kosher salt	15 mL
2 tsp	ground caraway seeds (see tip, at left)	10 mL
1½ tsp	freshly ground black pepper	7 mL
1 tsp	granulated sugar	5 mL
1 tsp	ground cumin	5 mL
½ tsp	cure #1 curing salts	2 mL
¼ cup	water	60 mL
4 to 5 feet	32/35 mm hog casing, soaked (see page 49)	120 to 150 cm

1. Cut pork and beef into pieces small enough to fit in the throat of your grinder. Using the coarse grinder plate, grind pork and beef into a large bowl or stand mixer bowl.

2. Add salt, caraway, pepper, sugar, cumin and curing salts to the ground meat. Using your hands or the stand mixer paddle attachment, mix until seasonings are evenly distributed. Add water and mix until white strands appear in the mixture and a handful of the mixture holds together.

3. In a small skillet, over medium-high heat, sauté a small amount of the sausage mixture until juices run clear. Taste the sample, then adjust seasonings as desired.

4. Stuff sausage mixture into prepared casing as described on page 51, filling casing only to 80% capacity and starting a new strand every 12 inches (30 cm). Twist each strand into two 6-inch (15 cm) links. Lay sausage strands flat and prick generously to remove air bubbles. Weigh a sausage strand and document its weight.

If you use your hands to mix the ground meat, have a bowl of water nearby in which to dip your fingers. This will help keep them from getting too sticky.

5. In your drying chamber, place all sausage strands between two large cutting boards. Place a 10-lb (4.5 kg) weight on top to flatten the sausages and let stand for 3 days.

6. Prepare a fire in your cold smoker and place a pan of ice on top of the cold plate. Smoke sausages at 80°F to 90°F (25°C to 30°C) for 20 hours (fair warning: this takes continual monitoring to keep the wood burning and the temperature from rising past 90°F/30°C).

7. Hang sausage strands in the drying chamber until the strand you weighed has lost 30% of its original weight.

Health Facts

Cumin has a long history of medicinal use, including as a digestive aid. Recent research bears this use out, reporting that cumin stimulates the release of pancreatic enzymes, which are needed for nutrient digestion and absorption.

Salami

Salami comes in many different forms and with varying ingredients. Some salami is dried sausage with a distinctive covering of white mold; others have no mold. Another type, cotto salami, consists of cooked and cured sausage with visible whole peppercorns. The recipe here is a dried sausage with a smaller diameter than what most people are familiar with, but the casing is edible, unlike many salamis. As is more traditional in the central regions of Italy, it is not heavily spiced.

Tip

You'll get the best results with 35/38 mm hog casing in this recipe, but if you cannot find it, 32/35 mm hog casing will work just fine.

Health Facts

Dried sausage is a fermented product, which means that friendly bacteria begin to grow and prevent the growth of harmful bacteria, also known as pathogenic bacteria. Although researchers don't yet know all the health benefits of all nonpathogenic bacteria, fermented foods have a long history in the human diet and may provide benefits beyond crowding out pathogens.

- **Drying chamber**

1¾ lbs	trimmed boneless pork shoulder blade roast, chilled (see page 49)	875 g
4 oz	pork trimmings (fat with a little meat attached), chilled	125 g
1 tbsp	kosher salt	15 mL
1 tsp	freshly cracked black pepper	5 mL
1 tsp	mustard seeds	5 mL
¾ tsp	sweet paprika	3 mL
½ tsp	cure #1 curing salts	2 mL
½ tsp	granulated sugar	2 mL
½ tsp	garlic powder	2 mL
¼ cup	water	60 mL
4 to 5 feet	35/38 hog casing, soaked (see page 49)	120 to 150 cm

1. Cut pork meat and trimmings into pieces small enough to fit in the throat of your grinder. Using the coarse grinder plate, grind pork meat and trimmings into a large bowl or stand mixer bowl.

2. Add salt, pepper, mustard seeds, paprika, curing salts, sugar and garlic powder to the ground pork. Using your hands or the stand mixer paddle attachment, mix until seasonings are evenly distributed. Add water and mix until white strands appear in the mixture and a handful of the mixture holds together.

3. In a small skillet, over medium-high heat, sauté a small amount of the sausage mixture until juices run clear. Taste the sample, then adjust seasonings as desired.

4. Stuff sausage mixture into prepared casing as described on page 51, starting a new strand every 12 inches (30 cm). Twist each strand into two 6-inch (15 cm) links. Lay sausage strands flat and prick generously to remove air bubbles. Weigh a sausage strand and document its weight.

5. Hang sausage strands in your drying chamber until the strand you weighed has lost 30% of its original weight.

Pepperoni

Although pepperoni shares some characteristics with spicy Italian salami, it is an American invention. Food historians believe it was created in the early 1900s in response to the pizza craze. Food writer John Mariani says, "This air-dried somewhat spicy sausage has a few very distinctive characteristics: fine-grained, lightly smoky, bright red and relatively soft." Even its name is not quite Italian, as *peperoni* is the plural form for large peppers.

MAKES
6 SAUSAGES

Tips

The 32/35 mm hog casing will give you a sausage that will make nice-sized slices for topping pizza. But you can also try this recipe with 20/22 mm sheep casing for a smaller-diameter sausage that will be more like a snack stick.

If you use your hands to mix the ground meat, have a bowl of water nearby in which to dip your fingers. This will help keep them from getting too sticky.

Health Facts

Allspice contains numerous antioxidant, anti-inflammatory and anticancer phytonutrients.

- Drying chamber

1 lb	85/15 boneless beef shoulder, chilled (see page 49)	500 g
1 lb	trimmed boneless pork shoulder blade roast, chilled	500 g
1 tbsp	hot pepper flakes	15 mL
2 tsp	freshly cracked fennel seeds	10 mL
2 tsp	kosher salt	10 mL
1 tsp	freshly cracked black pepper	5 mL
1 tsp	ground allspice	5 mL
1 tsp	granulated sugar	5 mL
½ tsp	cure #1 curing salts	2 mL
¼ cup	water	60 mL
4 to 5 feet	32/35 mm hog casing, soaked (see page 49)	120 to 150 cm

1. Cut beef and pork into pieces small enough to fit in the throat of your grinder. Using the coarse grinder plate, grind beef and pork into a large bowl or stand mixer bowl.

2. Add hot pepper flakes, fennel seeds, salt, black pepper, allspice, sugar and curing salts to the ground meat. Using your hands or the stand mixer paddle attachment, mix until seasonings are evenly distributed. Add water and mix until white strands appear in the mixture and a handful of the mixture holds together.

3. In a small skillet, over medium-high heat, sauté a small amount of the sausage mixture until juices run clear. Taste the sample, then adjust seasonings as desired.

4. Stuff sausage mixture into prepared casing as described on page 51, starting a new strand every 12 inches (30 cm). Twist each strand into two 6-inch (15 cm) links. Lay sausage strands flat and prick generously to remove air bubbles. Weigh a sausage strand and document its weight.

5. Hang sausage strands in your drying chamber until the strand you weighed has lost 30% of its original weight.

Traditional Dried Pork Sausages d'Abruzzi

These dry fermented sausages have been made for centuries throughout Italy. The addition of curing salts is important for food safety, although traditionalists continue to omit this crucial ingredient. Many also continue to hang sausages to dry in an attic in the winter months, eschewing the modern use of temperature- and humidity-controlled drying chambers. The method used in this recipe will ensure optimal food safety.

MAKES 6 SAUSAGES

Tips

During the drying process, check periodically for signs of spoilage, which appear as gray to black areas of meat.

The calories and fat content of dried sausage depend on the amount of fat trimmed in preparing the meat. A high fat content can impede the drying process. However, trimming away too much fat makes the final product tougher.

• Drying chamber

2 lbs	trimmed boneless pork shoulder blade roast, chilled (see page 49)	1 kg
5 tsp	kosher salt	25 mL
1½ tsp	freshly cracked black pepper	7 mL
½ tsp	cure #1 curing salts	2 mL
¼ cup	water	60 mL
4 to 5 feet	32/35 mm hog casing, soaked (see page 49)	120 to 150 cm

1. Cut pork into pieces small enough to fit in the throat of your grinder. Using the coarse grinder plate, grind pork into a large bowl or stand mixer bowl.

2. Add salt, pepper and curing salts to the ground pork. Using your hands or the stand mixer paddle attachment, mix until seasonings are evenly distributed. Add water and mix until white strands appear in the mixture and a handful of the mixture holds together.

3. In a small skillet, over medium-high heat, sauté a small amount of the sausage mixture until no longer pink. Taste the sample, then adjust seasonings as desired.

4. Stuff sausage mixture into prepared casing as described on page 51, starting a new strand every 12 inches (30 cm). Twist each strand into two 6-inch (15 cm) links. Lay sausage strands flat and prick generously to remove air bubbles. Weigh a sausage strand and document its weight.

5. Hang sausage strands in your drying chamber until the strand you weighed has lost 30% of its original weight.

Health Facts

Black pepper belongs to the Piperaceae family and has long been used as a food preservative. A 2015 study showed that pepper extract reduced bacterial cells' ability to produce energy, thus triggering bacterial cell death.

Pork Sausages

Throughout history and continuing to the present day, more sausage has contained pork than any other type of meat. The reason for this is not entirely clear, although certainly pigs have been more plentiful, are not picky eaters, and don't provide milk or wool. Pork also contains a sufficient amount of fat for making sausage, and many people consider it a tasty meat selection. If you count yourself among this group, you're in luck with the recipes you'll find here!

All of the sausages in this chapter taste best if they are refrigerated for at least 1 day before they are cooked.

Oatmeal Raisin Breakfast Sausages

This recipe is a virtual one-stop breakfast, covering three food groups. The addition of grains to the sausage mixture not only provides added nutrients, but also lowers the fat content.

1 cup	steel-cut oats	250 mL
	Hot water	
2 lbs	trimmed boneless pork shoulder blade roast, chilled (see page 49)	1 kg
1 cup	finely chopped raisins	250 mL
1 tbsp	packed dark brown sugar	15 mL
2 tsp	ground cinnamon	10 mL
2 tsp	kosher salt	10 mL
1 tsp	freshly cracked black pepper	5 mL
1 tsp	garlic powder	5 mL
1 tsp	onion powder	5 mL
½ tsp	hot pepper flakes	2 mL
½ tsp	ground sage	2 mL
¼ cup	water	60 mL
4 to 5 feet	20/22 mm sheep casing, soaked (see page 49)	120 to 150 cm

MAKES 26 SAUSAGES

Tips

Any type of oats can be used here, but I prefer steel-cut because they provide a bit of chewiness.

If you can't find 20/22mm sheep casing, you can use the more common 32/35 mm hog casing. Make short links of 2½ inches (6 cm) for a more suitable breakfast portion.

Health Facts

Oats contain a healthy dose of soluble fiber, which researchers tell us helps lower blood cholesterol levels and feeds health-promoting bacteria in the intestines. In addition, oats contain a moderate amount of protein and essential minerals such as iron, magnesium, zinc and copper. Both oats and cinnamon contain phytonutrients that fight free radicals and inflammation. Cinnamon has been shown to help regulate blood glucose levels.

1. Place oats in a bowl and add enough hot water to just cover; soak for 30 minutes. Drain oats, reserving any remaining soaking liquid. Add enough water to the liquid to make ¼ cup (60 mL).

2. Cut pork into pieces small enough to fit in the throat of your grinder. Using the coarse grinder plate, grind pork into a large bowl or stand mixer bowl.

3. Add soaked oats, raisins, brown sugar, cinnamon, salt, black pepper, garlic powder, onion powder, hot pepper flakes and sage to the ground pork. Using your hands or the stand mixer paddle attachment, mix until seasonings are evenly distributed. Add water and mix until white strands appear in the mixture and a handful of the mixture holds together.

4. In a small skillet, over medium-high heat, sauté a small amount of the sausage mixture until no longer pink. Taste the sample, then adjust seasonings as desired.

5. Stuff sausage mixture into prepared casing as described on page 51. Twist into 26 links, each about 4 inches (10 cm) in length.

Apple Cinnamon Breakfast Sausages

Apples and cinnamon are the perfect pair for a crisp autumn morning, and this sausage adds the flavors of sage, marjoram, garlic and onion for savory perfection. In addition to great taste, the apples and spices provide healthy phytonutrients.

MAKES 23 SAUSAGES

Tips

Any apples will work in this recipe, so experiment with different varieties. If you prefer a sweeter taste, good choices include Gala, Honeycrisp, Pink Lady or Delicious. For a tart flavor, try Fuji or Granny Smith.

Use a box grater to shred the apples.

If you can't find 20/22 mm sheep casing, you can use the more common 32/35 mm hog casing. Make short links of 2½ inches (6 cm) for a more suitable breakfast portion.

2 lbs	trimmed boneless pork shoulder blade roast, chilled (see page 49)	1 kg
2	apples, peeled and shredded (see tips, at left)	2
1 tbsp	raw cane sugar	15 mL
2 tsp	ground cinnamon	10 mL
2 tsp	kosher salt	10 mL
1 tsp	freshly cracked black pepper	5 mL
1 tsp	ground sage	5 mL
½ tsp	garlic powder	2 mL
½ tsp	onion powder	2 mL
½ tsp	dried marjoram	2 mL
¼ cup	cinnamon-flavored liqueur	60 mL
4 to 5 feet	20/22 mm sheep casing, soaked (see page 49)	120 to 150 cm

1. Cut pork into pieces small enough to fit in the throat of your grinder. Using the coarse grinder plate, grind pork into a large bowl or stand mixer bowl.

2. Add apples, sugar, cinnamon, salt, pepper, sage, garlic powder, onion powder and marjoram to the ground pork. Using your hands or the stand mixer paddle attachment, mix until seasonings are evenly distributed. Add liqueur and mix until white strands appear in the mixture and a handful of the mixture holds together.

3. In a small skillet, over medium-high heat, sauté a small amount of the sausage mixture until no longer pink. Taste the sample, then adjust seasonings as desired.

4. Stuff sausage mixture into prepared casing as described on page 51. Twist into 23 links, each about 4 inches (10 cm) in length.

Health Facts

Recent studies have shown that apples contain many phytonutrients with antioxidant and other beneficial effects. Some of its flavonoids include quercetin, procyanidin and epicatechin, which may help fight cancer.

Blueberry Breakfast Sausages

These delightful breakfast sausages include several ingredients that make them a perfect start to the day, especially antioxidant-rich blueberries.

MAKES 20 SAUSAGES

Tips

In place of the dried blueberries, try using a mixture of dried blueberries, cranberries and cherries.

If you can't find 20/22 mm sheep casing, you can use the more common 32/35 mm hog casing. Make short links of 2½ inches (6 cm) for a more suitable breakfast portion.

2 lbs	trimmed boneless pork shoulder blade roast, chilled (see page 49)	1 kg
1 cup	finely chopped dried blueberries	250 mL
2 tsp	dried sage	10 mL
2 tsp	kosher salt	10 mL
1 tsp	freshly cracked black pepper	5 mL
1 tsp	ground cinnamon	5 mL
⅛ tsp	ground nutmeg	0.5 mL
2 tbsp	pure maple syrup	30 mL
1 tsp	vanilla extract	5 mL
¼ cup	water	60 mL
4 to 5 feet	20/22 mm sheep casing, soaked (see page 49)	120 to 150 cm

1. Cut pork into pieces small enough to fit in the throat of your grinder. Using the coarse grinder plate, grind pork into a large bowl or stand mixer bowl.

2. Add blueberries, sage, salt, pepper, cinnamon, nutmeg, maple syrup and vanilla to the ground pork. Using your hands or the stand mixer paddle attachment, mix until seasonings are evenly distributed. Add water and mix until white strands appear in the mixture and a handful of the mixture holds together.

3. In a small skillet, over medium-high heat, sauté a small amount of the sausage mixture until juices run clear. Taste the sample, then adjust seasonings as desired.

4. Stuff sausage mixture into prepared casing as described on page 51. Twist into 20 links, each about 4 inches (10 cm) in length.

Health Facts

A 2012 study reported that people who ate just ½ cup (125 mL) each of blueberries and strawberries every week had a lower risk for developing dementia. It may be because the flavonoids in these berries fight stress and inflammation — processes linked to dementia.

Breakfast Hash Sausages

These sausages pay homage to the dish known as breakfast hash, typically a corned beef hash served with a side of eggs, potatoes and toast.

Tips

Cooked potatoes don't normally freeze well, as the water in the potato separates from the starch molecules, causing a grainy texture. However, in sausage this graininess is unlikely to be detectable, so sausage-making is a good use for leftover potatoes that you have frozen.

If you can't find 20/22 mm sheep casing, you can use the more common 32/35 mm hog casing. Make short links of 2½ inches (6 cm) for a more suitable breakfast portion.

8 oz	finely diced potatoes	250 g
1 lb	trimmed boneless pork shoulder blade roast, chilled (see page 49)	500 g
1 lb	corned beef, chilled	500 g
¼ cup	finely chopped onion	60 mL
¼ cup	minced red bell pepper	60 mL
3 tbsp	finely diced cooked smoked bacon	45 mL
2 tsp	kosher salt	10 mL
1 tsp	freshly cracked black pepper	5 mL
1 tsp	minced fresh sage	5 mL
1 tsp	minced fresh thyme	5 mL
1 tsp	minced fresh rosemary	5 mL
1 tsp	garlic powder	5 mL
¼ cup	water	60 mL
4 to 5 feet	20/22 mm sheep casing, soaked (see page 49)	120 to 150 cm

1. Add potatoes to a saucepan of cold water and bring to a boil over medium-high heat. Boil for about 10 minutes or until tender. Drain and let cool completely.

2. Cut pork and beef into pieces small enough to fit in the throat of your grinder. Using the coarse grinder plate, grind pork and beef into a large bowl or stand mixer bowl.

3. Add potatoes, onion, red pepper, bacon, salt, pepper, sage, thyme, rosemary and garlic powder to the ground meat. Using your hands or the stand mixer paddle attachment, mix until seasonings are evenly distributed. Add water and mix until white strands appear in the mixture and a handful of the mixture holds together.

4. In a small skillet, over medium-high heat, sauté a small amount of the sausage mixture until no longer pink. Taste the sample, then adjust seasonings as desired.

5. Stuff sausage mixture into prepared casing as described on page 51. Twist into 22 links, each about 4 inches (10 cm) in length.

Health Facts

A medium potato with skin on provides 45% of the daily value for vitamin C and more potassium than a banana. Leave the skin to get the most nutrients.

European Potato Breakfast Sausages

The inclusion of potatoes in sausage has long been common throughout Europe. One historical reason was that it extended the meat, which was often a prized commodity, but it also imparts wonderful texture to the sausage. This recipe includes a combination of spices and herbs that make it the perfect accompaniment to eggs.

**MAKES
10 SAUSAGES**

Tips

Depending on the fat content, 1 slice of bacon will yield about 1 tbsp (15 mL) crumbled cooked bacon. For this recipe, you'll need about 16 slices.

When cooking up a batch of these sausages, make a few extra and slice up a few links. Divide the slices into portions, freeze them in freezer bags and thaw them to top your favorite quiche or breakfast casserole.

2 tsp	onion flakes	10 mL
2 tbsp	warm water	30 mL
2 lbs	trimmed boneless pork shoulder blade roast, chilled (see page 49)	1 kg
1 lb	russet potatoes, grated	500 g
1 cup	crumbled cooked bacon	250 mL
2 tsp	kosher salt	10 mL
1 tsp	freshly cracked black pepper	5 mL
1 tsp	garlic powder	5 mL
1 tsp	dried marjoram	5 mL
2 tbsp	water	30 mL
2 tbsp	butter, softened	30 mL
4 to 5 feet	32/35 mm hog casing, soaked (see page 49)	120 to 150 cm

1. In a small bowl, combine onion flakes and warm water. Let stand for about 20 minutes or until softened.

2. Meanwhile, cut pork into pieces small enough to fit in the throat of your grinder. Using the coarse grinder plate, grind pork into a large bowl or stand mixer bowl.

3. Add potatoes, bacon, onion flakes mixture, salt, pepper, garlic powder and marjoram to the ground pork. Using your hands or the stand mixer paddle attachment, mix until seasonings are evenly distributed. Add 2 tbsp (30 mL) water and butter; mix until white strands appear in the mixture and a handful of the mixture holds together.

4. In a small skillet, over medium-high heat, sauté a small amount of the sausage mixture until no longer pink. Taste the sample, then adjust seasonings as desired.

5. Stuff sausage mixture into prepared casing as described on page 51. Twist into 10 links, each about 6 inches (15 cm) in length.

Health Facts

Researchers have shown that marjoram contains several antibacterial and anti-inflammatory compounds, such as eugenol, cymene and terpinolene.

Eggs Benedict Sausages

Many chefs and cities take credit for the creation of eggs Benedict, but food historians believe it dates to the 1890s in New York City. A 2007 article in *The New York Times* suggests it was the creation of Lemuel Benedict, a "dashing ladies' man" and a chef from the Waldorf Astoria. This iconic recipe finds a perfect fit nestled inside a breakfast sausage.

MAKES 8 SAUSAGES

Tip

To make perfect hard-cooked eggs, place cold eggs in a single layer in a pan with enough cold water to cover by 1 inch (2.5 cm). Bring water to a boil over high heat, then cover the pan and remove it from the heat. Let stand for 12 minutes (for large eggs) or 15 minutes (for extra-large eggs). Transfer eggs to a bowl of cold water and let cool to room temperature, adding more cold water as needed. It's easiest to peel the eggs when they reach room temperature, rather than allowing them to cool further.

2 lbs	trimmed boneless pork shoulder blade roast, chilled (see page 49)	1 kg
3	large eggs, hard-cooked (see tip, at left) and roughly chopped	3
1½ cups	diced Canadian bacon	375 mL
1 tbsp	finely chopped fresh parsley	15 mL
2 tsp	finely minced fresh tarragon	10 mL
2 tsp	sweet paprika	10 mL
2 tsp	garlic powder	10 mL
2 tsp	kosher salt	10 mL
1 tsp	freshly cracked black pepper	5 mL
1 tsp	onion powder	5 mL
2 tbsp	white vinegar	30 mL
2 tbsp	water	30 mL
2 tbsp	melted butter	30 mL
4 to 5 feet	32/35 mm hog casing, soaked (see page 49)	120 to 150 cm

1. Cut pork into pieces small enough to fit in the throat of your grinder. Using the coarse grinder plate, grind pork into a large bowl or stand mixer bowl.

2. Add eggs, bacon, parsley, tarragon, paprika, garlic powder, salt, pepper and onion powder to the ground pork. Using your hands or the stand mixer paddle attachment, mix until seasonings are evenly distributed. Add vinegar, water and butter; mix until white strands appear in the mixture.

3. In a small skillet, over medium-high heat, sauté a small amount of the sausage mixture until no longer pink. Taste the sample, then adjust seasonings as desired.

4. Stuff sausage mixture into prepared casing as described on page 51. Twist into 8 links, each about 6 inches (15 cm) in length.

Health Facts

Tarragon is an underused herb that adds flavor and a healthy mix of phytonutrients. One of these beneficial compounds, naringenin, has been shown to have antimicrobial, antioxidant, anticancer and anti-inflammatory effects.

Irish Whiskey Sausages

The addition of liqueur to sausage turns an everyday food item into a holiday specialty. In these sausages, steel-cut oats — also known as Irish oats — and Irish whiskey cream liqueur lend a Gaelic flair and mellow flavor perfect for any occasion.

Tip

In addition to a pleasant effect on the sausage's texture, the oats help bind the ingredients. To add more oats to your diet, you can use them in this same role in almost any recipe that includes bread crumbs, such as meatloaf or tuna patties.

Health Facts

Oats contain several antioxidant compounds, and one group of them, avenanthramides, is unique to oats. A Tufts University study reported that these compounds prevented free radicals from damaging low-density lipoprotein (LDL) cholesterol (the "good" cholesterol), an effect that could help protect against heart attack.

1 cup	steel-cut oats	250 mL
	Hot water	
2 lbs	trimmed boneless pork shoulder blade roast, chilled (see page 49)	1 kg
2 tsp	kosher salt	10 mL
1 tsp	freshly cracked black pepper	5 mL
1 tsp	onion powder	5 mL
1 tsp	dried sage	5 mL
1 tsp	ground cinnamon	5 mL
1 tsp	ground coriander	5 mL
1/4 tsp	ground nutmeg	1 mL
1/4 cup	Irish cream liqueur	60 mL
4 to 5 feet	32/35 mm hog casing, soaked (see page 49)	120 to 150 cm

1. Place oats in a bowl and add enough hot water to just cover; soak for 30 minutes. Drain oats, reserving any remaining soaking liquid. Add enough water to the liquid to make 1/4 cup (60 mL).

2. Cut pork into pieces small enough to fit in the throat of your grinder. Using the coarse grinder plate, grind pork into a large bowl or stand mixer bowl.

3. Add soaked oats, salt, pepper, onion powder, sage, cinnamon, coriander and nutmeg to the ground pork. Using your hands or the stand mixer paddle attachment, mix until seasonings are evenly distributed. Add reserved water and liqueur; mix until white strands appear in the mixture and a handful of the mixture holds together.

4. In a small skillet, over medium-high heat, sauté a small amount of the sausage mixture until no longer pink. Taste the sample, then adjust seasonings as desired.

5. Stuff sausage mixture into prepared casing as described on page 51. Twist into 8 links, each about 6 inches (15 cm) in length.

Yorkie Sausages

Inspired by the Yorkshire sausages of Britain, these sausages include rusk, which continues to be a popular ingredient in that locale's recipes. Rusk can be either a dry biscuit or a piece of bread that has been baked twice, often used for babies who are teething. In sausage making, it serves as a binding agent and a meat extender.

**MAKES
6 SAUSAGES**

Tips

If you don't have rusk, you can grind up crisp unseasoned croutons to use in its place.

If you use your hands to mix the ground meat, have a bowl of water nearby in which to dip your fingers. This will help keep them from getting too sticky.

2 lbs	trimmed boneless pork shoulder blade roast, chilled (see page 49)	1 kg
¼ cup	finely ground rusk or dry bread crumbs	60 mL
2 tsp	dried parsley	10 mL
2 tsp	kosher salt	10 mL
1 tsp	freshly ground white pepper	5 mL
½ tsp	ground coriander	2 mL
¼ tsp	ground mace	1 mL
⅛ tsp	ground nutmeg	0.5 mL
¼ cup	water	60 mL
4 to 5 feet	32/35 mm hog casing, soaked (see page 49)	120 to 150 cm

1. Cut pork into pieces small enough to fit in the throat of your grinder. Using the coarse grinder plate, grind pork into a large bowl or stand mixer bowl.

2. Add rusk, parsley, salt, pepper, coriander, mace and nutmeg to the ground pork. Using your hands or the stand mixer paddle attachment, mix until seasonings are evenly distributed. Add water and mix until white strands appear in the mixture and a handful of the mixture holds together.

3. In a small skillet, over medium-high heat, sauté a small amount of the sausage mixture until no longer pink. Taste the sample, then adjust seasonings as desired.

4. Stuff sausage mixture into prepared casing as described on page 51. Twist into 6 links, each about 6 inches (15 cm) in length.

Health Facts

Parsley contains the flavonoid chrysoeriol, which has several biologic activities that may help fight disease. Chrysoeriol is an antioxidant and an antiviral, and some studies have shown that it may help prevent cancer. A 2015 study reported that it might also be useful in treating respiratory disorders such as asthma and those causing chronic cough.

Sage Potato Sausages

In these sausages, thyme's lemony nuances complement the extra-peppery flavor contributed by sage and cracked black pepper. These days, sage is best known as a seasoning for stuffing, but German and British sausage makers know it's a wonderful addition to sausage, too!

**MAKES
7 SAUSAGES**

Tips

Dried herbs lose their potency within about a year. Many of us tuck the container up in the cupboard and forget about it until we need it. When you first open the container, write the date on it. If a year passes and you haven't used it up, smell the dried herb and discard it if it's no longer fragrant.

If you decide to use table salt in place of kosher salt, use 1½ tsp (7 mL), as table salt has a higher density.

1 tsp	onion flakes	5 mL
1 tbsp	warm water	15 mL
2 lbs	trimmed boneless pork shoulder blade roast, chilled (see page 49)	1 kg
5 oz	russet potatoes, peeled, cut lengthwise	150 g
1 tsp	finely chopped fresh sage	5 mL
2 tsp	dried thyme	10 mL
2 tsp	garlic powder	10 mL
2 tsp	kosher salt	10 mL
1 tsp	freshly cracked black pepper	5 mL
2 tbsp	water	30 mL
4 to 5 feet	32/35 mm hog casing, soaked (see page 49)	120 to 150 cm

1. In a small bowl, combine onion flakes and warm water. Let stand for about 20 minutes or until softened.

2. Meanwhile, cut pork into pieces small enough to fit in the throat of your grinder. Using the fine grinder plate, grind pork into a medium bowl. Add potatoes to the ground pork and grind again into a large bowl or stand mixer bowl, this time using the coarse grinder plate.

3. Add sage, thyme, garlic powder, salt, pepper and onion flakes mixture to the ground pork mixture. Using your hands or the stand mixer paddle attachment, mix until seasonings are evenly distributed. Add 2 tbsp (30 mL) water and mix until white strands appear in the mixture and a handful of the mixture holds together.

4. In a small skillet, over medium-high heat, sauté a small amount of the sausage mixture until no longer pink. Taste the sample, then adjust seasonings as desired.

5. Stuff sausage mixture into prepared casing as described on page 51. Twist into 7 links, each about 6 inches (15 cm) in length.

Health Facts

Several medical studies have shown sage to be a potent antioxidant and bacteria-killer. It appears to inhibit the growth of the deadly methicillin-resistant *Staphylococcus aureus* (MRSA) bacterium that has made headlines in recent years.

Madeira Sausages

Portuguese seafarers discovered Madeira wine in the 1400s while making their way around Africa to the East Indies. The inhabitants of the island of Madeira were renowned for their wine-making skills, touted by the many sailors who enjoyed this port of call. In these sausages, the fortified sweet wine adds depth to the flavor of the herbs.

**MAKES
6 SAUSAGES**

Tips

The easiest way to remove thyme from the stem is to slide your thumb and index figure along the stem in a downward motion while holding the top of the stem with your other hand.

Madeira wines range from dry to sweet, and sweet works best in this sausage. This wine has a distinctive flavor, so don't be tempted to substitute a port or sherry.

2 lbs	trimmed boneless pork shoulder blade roast, chilled (see page 49)	1 kg
1½ tsp	finely chopped fresh parsley	7 mL
1 tsp	finely chopped fresh thyme	5 mL
2 tsp	kosher salt	10 mL
1 tsp	freshly cracked black pepper	5 mL
1 tsp	onion powder	5 mL
1 tsp	mustard seeds	5 mL
½ tsp	dried basil	2 mL
1	large egg, beaten	1
¼ cup	sweet Madeira wine	60 mL
¼ cup	water	60 mL
4 to 5 feet	32/35 mm hog casing, soaked (see page 49)	120 to 150 cm

1. Cut pork into pieces small enough to fit in the throat of your grinder. Using the coarse grinder plate, grind pork into a large bowl or stand mixer bowl.

2. Add parsley, thyme, salt, pepper, onion powder, mustard seeds, basil and egg to the ground pork. Using your hands or the stand mixer paddle attachment, mix until seasonings are evenly distributed. Add wine and water; mix until white strands appear in the mixture and a handful of the mixture holds together.

3. In a small skillet, over medium-high heat, sauté a small amount of the sausage mixture until no longer pink. Taste the sample, then adjust seasonings as desired.

4. Stuff sausage mixture into prepared casing as described on page 51. Twist into 6 links, each about 6 inches (15 cm) in length.

Health Facts

Mustard seeds have been used medicinally throughout history. The Ancient Romans made a paste from them, which Hippocrates, often called the father of medicine, relied on as a treatment for numerous ailments. Researchers have reported that intake of isothiocyanates, a compound found in mustard seeds, not only inhibits the growth of existing cancer cells but also protects against their development.

Spanish Sausages

These sausages have a distinctive flavor thanks to the manchego cheese, a creamy, flavorful Spanish cheese made from the milk of manchega sheep. Saffron adds its own delightful contribution to the characteristic Spanish flair.

Tip

There are several high-quality grades of Spanish saffron: coupe, superior, La Mancha and Rio, with coupe being the priciest. For a sausage recipe, top-grade isn't necessary; unless your curiosity gets the best of you, the other grades will work. Avoid ground saffron, which is often cut with other, cheaper spices. The saffron should appear as tiny reddish-orange threads.

4	threads saffron, crushed	4
¼ cup	water	60 mL
2 lbs	trimmed boneless pork shoulder blade roast, chilled (see page 49)	1 kg
½ cup	shredded manchego cheese	125 mL
2 tbsp	finely minced drained green olives	30 mL
1½ tsp	kosher salt	7 mL
1 tsp	freshly cracked black pepper	5 mL
4 to 5 feet	32/35 mm hog casing, soaked (see page 49)	120 to 150 cm

1. In a small bowl, combine saffron and water; set aside.

2. Cut pork into pieces small enough to fit in the throat of your grinder. Using the coarse grinder plate, grind pork into a large bowl or stand mixer bowl.

3. Add cheese, olives, salt and pepper to the ground pork. Using your hands or the stand mixer paddle attachment, mix until seasonings are evenly distributed. Add saffron water and mix until white strands appear in the mixture and a handful of the mixture holds together.

4. In a small skillet, over medium-high heat, sauté a small amount of the sausage mixture until no longer pink. Taste the sample, then adjust seasonings as desired.

5. Stuff sausage mixture into prepared casing as described on page 51. Twist into 6 links, each about 6 inches (15 cm) in length.

Health Facts

Saffron's medicinal history is legendary, and research is ongoing. Two 2015 reviews reported on its potential health benefits. The first found that saffron may improve the symptoms of depression, premenstrual syndrome, sexual dysfunction and excessive snacking behaviors. The second concluded that several studies have demonstrated saffron's antitumor and cancer-preventive activities.

Cheese and Wine Sausages

Cheese and wine are both ingredients that have found a place in sausage making. In this recipe, the Italian flavor palette gets an unusual boost from the addition of coriander, which adds a touch of the exotic to the more familiar ingredients.

**MAKES
6 SAUSAGES**

Tip

Like many spices that are commonly purchased already ground, ground coriander will lose its flavor more quickly than the seeds. To determine whether a ground spice is still aromatic and flavorful, rub a small amount in your hand and taste it. Most will lose their aroma after 1 year.

2 lbs	trimmed boneless pork shoulder blade roast, chilled (see page 49)	1 kg
¼ cup	grated Pecorino Romano cheese	60 mL
2 tbsp	finely minced fresh rosemary	30 mL
2 tbsp	roasted garlic paste (see page 47)	30 mL
2 tbsp	finely minced drained green olives	30 mL
2 tsp	kosher salt	10 mL
1 tsp	freshly cracked black pepper	5 mL
1 tsp	ground coriander	5 mL
¼ cup	sweet sherry	60 mL
4 to 5 feet	32/35 mm hog casing, soaked (see page 49)	120 to 150 cm

1. Cut pork into pieces small enough to fit in the throat of your grinder. Using the coarse grinder plate, grind pork into a large bowl or stand mixer bowl.

2. Add cheese, rosemary, garlic paste, olives, salt, pepper and coriander to the ground pork. Using your hands or the stand mixer paddle attachment, mix until seasonings are evenly distributed. Add sherry and mix until white strands appear in the mixture and a handful of the mixture holds together.

3. In a small skillet, over medium-high heat, sauté a small amount of the sausage mixture until no longer pink. Taste the sample, then adjust seasonings as desired.

4. Stuff sausage mixture into prepared casing as described on page 51. Twist into 6 links, each about 6 inches (15 cm) in length.

Health Facts

Ancient healers believed anything with a strong odor had potent attributes, so it was likely coriander's pungent aroma that led them to use it as a medicine. A 2014 study backs up one potential medical use: it reported that coriander extract shows antidiabetic properties.

Pesto Pork Sausages

Pesto can be made with just about any herbs and nuts, but the most famous recipe combines basil, pine nuts, garlic, Parmesan cheese and olive oil. It originated in Genoa, Italy, which is also famous for its salami. This Mediterranean-inspired sausage takes its name from the inclusion of many of these traditional pesto ingredients.

MAKES
6 SAUSAGES

Tip

A quick way to toast pine nuts is on the stovetop. Heat a small skillet over medium heat for 2 minutes (no oil), then add the pine nuts. Toast for up to 45 seconds, toss or flip with a spatula, then toast for another 30 seconds. They are done when they just start to brown; remove them from the pan quickly.

Health Facts

Pine nuts, also known as pignoli, are the seeds of pine trees. They provide many of the same nutrients and antioxidants as other seeds and nuts, but they also contain a fatty acid, pinolenic acid, which stimulates the release of a gut hormone that suppresses appetite. Some researchers have suggested that pinolenic acid might aid in weight loss.

1 tsp	onion flakes	5 mL
1 tbsp	warm water	15 mL
2 lbs	trimmed boneless pork shoulder blade roast, chilled (see page 49)	1 kg
¼ cup	coarsely chopped toasted pine nuts (see tip, at left)	60 mL
¼ cup	finely chopped fresh basil	60 mL
1 tbsp	finely chopped fresh parsley	15 mL
1 tbsp	roasted garlic paste (see page 47)	15 mL
2 tsp	kosher salt	10 mL
1 tsp	freshly cracked black pepper	5 mL
1 tbsp	olive oil	15 mL
1 tbsp	water	15 mL
4 to 5 feet	32/35 mm hog casing, soaked (see page 49)	120 to 150 cm

1. In a small bowl, combine onion flakes and warm water. Let stand for about 20 minutes or until softened.

2. Meanwhile, cut pork into pieces small enough to fit in the throat of your grinder. Using the coarse grinder plate, grind pork into a large bowl or stand mixer bowl.

3. Add pine nuts, basil, parsley, garlic paste, salt, pepper and onion flakes mixture to the ground pork. Using your hands or the stand mixer paddle attachment, mix until seasonings are evenly distributed. Add oil and 1 tbsp (15 mL) water; mix until white strands appear in the mixture and a handful of the mixture holds together.

4. In a small skillet, over medium-high heat, sauté a small amount of the sausage mixture until no longer pink. Taste the sample, then adjust seasonings as desired.

5. Stuff sausage mixture into prepared casing as described on page 51. Twist into 6 links, each about 6 inches (15 cm) in length.

Pizza Sausages

Although many ancient cultures lay claim to eating a form of pizza — flatbread topped with cheese — the more modern version didn't appear until well after Spanish and Portuguese explorers brought tomatoes to Europe in the 16th century. Two centuries later, diners in Naples, Italy, embraced the creation of pizza margherita. These savory sausages will make you wonder why it took people so long to bring these delicious ingredients together.

Tips

Customize your pizza sausages by adding your favorite pizza toppings, such as finely chopped green bell peppers, mushrooms or ham. You can add up to ¼ cup (60 mL) of each without adversely affecting sausage texture.

How long to make your sausage links is really up to you, although we suggest 6 inches (15 cm) for this recipe. Keep in mind that this is a rough guideline, and that you may have to adjust the length up or down so that you don't end up with one link smaller than the rest.

2 lbs	trimmed boneless pork shoulder blade roast, chilled (see page 49)	1 kg
1 cup	shredded mozzarella cheese	250 mL
¼ cup	finely minced onion	60 mL
2 tbsp	tomato paste	30 mL
2 tsp	garlic powder	10 mL
2 tsp	kosher salt	10 mL
1 tsp	freshly cracked black pepper	5 mL
1 tsp	dried oregano	5 mL
¼ cup	water	60 mL
4 to 5 feet	32/35 mm hog casing, soaked (see page 49)	120 to 150 cm

1. Cut pork into pieces small enough to fit in the throat of your grinder. Using the coarse grinder plate, grind pork into a large bowl or stand mixer bowl.

2. Add mozzarella, onion, tomato paste, garlic powder, salt, pepper and oregano to the ground pork. Using your hands or the stand mixer paddle attachment, mix until seasonings are evenly distributed. Add water and mix until white strands appear in the mixture and a handful of the mixture holds together.

3. In a small skillet, over medium-high heat, sauté a small amount of the sausage mixture until juices run clear. Taste the sample, then adjust seasonings as desired.

4. Stuff sausage mixture into prepared casing as described on page 51. Twist into 7 links, each about 6 inches (15 cm) in length.

Health Facts

The potential synergism of various antioxidants is an intriguing area of study. In a 2007 study, researchers developed a special bread containing tomatoes, oregano, green tea and soy for the experimental group among a group of smokers. The group who ate the special bread had lower blood levels of markers of oxidative stress, which is associated with smoking, than the smokers who ate plain bread.

Bandiera Sausages

Bandiera sausages are inspired by a dish known as "flag pasta" — the Italian word for "flag" is *bandiera*. The savory sausages bring together several favorite regional ingredients that stimulate the umami taste sensors, including anchovy paste, basil, capers, tomato paste and garlic.

**MAKES
7 SAUSAGES**

Tips

Anchovy paste is available in a tube, and it lasts longer than paste in a jar. You can keep an opened tube in the refrigerator for up to 6 weeks.

If you decide to use table salt in place of kosher salt, use ¾ tsp (3 mL), as table salt has a higher density.

2 lbs	trimmed boneless pork shoulder blade roast, chilled (see page 49)	1 kg
¼ cup	grated Pecorino Romano cheese	60 mL
¼ cup	finely chopped fresh basil	60 mL
¼ cup	tomato paste	60 mL
2 tbsp	roasted garlic paste (see page 47)	30 mL
1 tbsp	anchovy paste	15 mL
1 tbsp	finely minced drained capers	15 mL
2 tsp	granulated sugar	10 mL
1½ tsp	kosher salt	7 mL
1 tsp	freshly cracked black pepper	5 mL
¼ cup	water	60 mL
4 to 5 feet	32/35 mm hog casing, soaked (see page 49)	120 to 150 cm

1. Cut pork into pieces small enough to fit in the throat of your grinder. Using the coarse grinder plate, grind pork into a large bowl or stand mixer bowl.

2. Add cheese, basil, tomato paste, garlic paste, anchovy paste, capers, sugar, salt and pepper to the ground pork. Using your hands or the stand mixer paddle attachment, mix until seasonings are evenly distributed. Add water and mix until white strands appear in the mixture and a handful of the mixture holds together.

3. In a small skillet, over medium-high heat, sauté a small amount of the sausage mixture until juices run clear. Taste the sample, then adjust seasonings as desired.

4. Stuff sausage mixture into prepared casing as described on page 51. Twist into 7 links, each about 6 inches (15 cm) in length.

Health Facts

Anchovies contain omega-3 fatty acids. The list of chronic diseases that these fats may help prevent — and in some cases even treat — grows by the year. Most recently, large epidemiological studies have pointed to omega-3s protecting cognitive function in aging.

Calabrian Sausages

Calabria is a region in southern Italy usually described as the "toe of the boot." It has a long history of sausage making, especially preserved meats such as soppressata. In ancient times, when Greeks colonized this area, wine-making was another important tradition. This recipe brings Calabria's traditions together into a delicious blend of spices and wine. But be prepared: they are spicy. If you want less heat, cut back on the cayenne pepper.

MAKES 6 SAUSAGES

Tips

Any type of red table wine will work, but consider a more full-bodied variety, such as Burgundy. The deeper flavor will enhance those of the oregano and hot pepper.

If you use your hands to mix the ground meat, have a bowl of water nearby in which to dip your fingers. This will help keep them from getting too sticky.

2 lbs	trimmed boneless pork shoulder blade roast, chilled (see page 49)	1 kg
1 tbsp	finely chopped fresh oregano	15 mL
2 tsp	kosher salt	10 mL
2 tsp	freshly cracked black pepper	10 mL
2 tsp	hot pepper flakes	10 mL
2 tsp	cayenne pepper	10 mL
2 tsp	garlic powder	10 mL
1 tsp	fennel seeds	5 mL
¼ cup	red wine (see tip, at left)	60 mL
4 to 5 feet	32/35 mm hog casing, soaked (see page 49)	120 to 150 cm

1. Cut pork into pieces small enough to fit in the throat of your grinder. Using the coarse grinder plate, grind pork into a large bowl or stand mixer bowl.

2. Add oregano, salt, black pepper, hot pepper flakes, cayenne, garlic powder and fennel seeds to the ground pork. Using your hands or the stand mixer paddle attachment, mix until seasonings are evenly distributed. Add wine and mix until white strands appear in the mixture and a handful of the mixture holds together.

3. In a small skillet, over medium-high heat, sauté a small amount of the sausage mixture until no longer pink. Taste the sample, then adjust seasonings as desired.

4. Stuff sausage mixture into prepared casing as described on page 51. Twist into 6 links, each about 6 inches (15 cm) in length.

Health Facts

One of the phytonutrients in oregano, among many with biologic activity, is thymol. Studies have shown thymol's potent action as an antioxidant, anti-inflammatory and antimicrobial. A 2015 study reported that thymol induced apoptosis (cell suicide) in stomach cancer cells. The authors concluded that their results suggest thymol may be a "tentative agent in the future to treat cancer."

Piedmont Sausages

Northwestern Italy is home to the Piedmont region. One of its specialties is Barbaresco wine, made from the Nebbiolo grape and characterized by a sweet flavor owing to the late-October harvesting of the grapes. Another is Saras del Fen, a ripened ricotta cheese. In combination with other regional ingredients, such as cream and basil, these sausages bring Piedmont's culinary delights to your table.

Tip

If you've only tasted ricotta cheese in packaged form from the dairy aisle of the grocery store, you've missed out on its true flavor. Purchase this delicate cheese at an Italian specialty store, and make sure it's fresh. You'll notice that it's not just the flavor that is different — and amazing — but also the texture: it's soft and creamy, rather than grainy.

2 lbs	trimmed boneless pork shoulder blade roast, chilled (see page 49)	1 kg
½ cup	ricotta cheese	125 mL
¼ cup	finely chopped fresh basil	60 mL
1 tbsp	roasted garlic paste (see page 47)	15 mL
2 tsp	kosher salt	10 mL
1 tsp	freshly cracked black pepper	5 mL
¼ cup	Barbaresco wine	60 mL
2 tbsp	heavy or whipping (35%) cream	30 mL
4 to 5 feet	32/35 mm hog casing, soaked (see page 49)	120 to 150 cm

1. Cut pork into pieces small enough to fit in the throat of your grinder. Using the coarse grinder plate, grind pork into a large bowl or stand mixer bowl.

2. Add cheese, basil, garlic paste, salt and pepper to the ground pork. Using your hands or the stand mixer paddle attachment, mix until seasonings are evenly distributed. Add wine and cream; mix until white strands appear in the mixture and a handful of the mixture holds together.

3. In a small skillet, over medium-high heat, sauté a small amount of the sausage mixture until no longer pink. Taste the sample, then adjust seasonings as desired.

4. Stuff sausage mixture into prepared casing as described on page 51. Twist into 7 links, each about 6 inches (15 cm) in length.

Health Facts

Ricotta cheese is high in many nutrients, and its main protein is whey, which has been touted for health benefits ranging from improved weight loss and reductions in blood pressure and cholesterol to reduction of blood glucose levels in people with type 2 diabetes after a high-glycemic meal. You can purchase ricotta made from whole or part-skim milk, and even fat-free ricotta, although texture and flavor suffer with removal of all of the fat.

San Giovanni Sausages

San Giovanni is a town in southern Italy, situated at the tip of the boot, near Sicily. Its culinary influences are similar to those of Sicily. These sausages contain ingredients with intense umami flavors, for a savory meat that goes well with pasta.

**MAKES
6 SAUSAGES**

Tip

Capers are one of those food items that people know very little about, which is unfortunate. They are the tiny buds from the caper bush, which is indigenous to the Mediterranean region. Try adding them to more of your recipes. Their piquant flavor adds zest and depth to sauces, pasta and salads. You can keep an opened jar of capers in the refrigerator for up to 1 year.

2 lbs	trimmed boneless pork shoulder blade roast, chilled (see page 49)	1 kg
¼ cup	finely minced drained capers	60 mL
2 tbsp	finely minced fresh basil	30 mL
2 tsp	garlic powder	10 mL
1½ tsp	kosher salt	7 mL
1 tsp	freshly cracked black pepper	5 mL
1 tsp	anchovy paste	5 mL
¼ cup	water	60 mL
4 to 5 feet	32/35 mm hog casing, soaked (see page 49)	120 to 150 cm

1. Cut pork into pieces small enough to fit in the throat of your grinder. Using the coarse grinder plate, grind pork into a large bowl or stand mixer bowl.

2. Add capers, basil, garlic powder, salt, pepper and anchovy paste to the ground pork. Using your hands or the stand mixer paddle attachment, mix until seasonings are evenly distributed. Add water and mix until white strands appear in the mixture and a handful of the mixture holds together.

3. In a small skillet, over medium-high heat, sauté a small amount of the sausage mixture until no longer pink. Taste the sample, then adjust seasonings as desired.

4. Stuff sausage mixture into prepared casing as described on page 51. Twist into 6 links, each about 6 inches (15 cm) in length.

Health Facts

Capers are high in the flavonoids rutin and quercetin, which convey many health benefits, including antioxidant, anti-inflammatory and analgesic (pain-relieving) activities.

Spicy Sicilian Sausages

Although fennel is widely used in the cuisines of many countries, it is associated most often with Italian sausages. Its distinctive licorice flavor is due to the aromatic compound anethole. These spicy sausages include all the traditional herbs and spices of traditional Sicilian sausages, along with some added heat.

**MAKES
6 SAUSAGES**

Tips

You can store fennel seeds in an airtight container in a cool, dry cupboard, where they'll remain fresh for up to 6 months. But the refrigerator is even better — in that case, the storage time can be almost doubled.

The easiest way to crack fennel seeds is to place them on a piece of parchment paper on the kitchen counter and roll over them with a heavy rolling pin.

2 lbs	trimmed boneless pork shoulder blade roast, chilled (see page 49)	1 kg
¼ cup	finely chopped fresh basil	60 mL
2 tbsp	roasted garlic paste (see page 47)	30 mL
2 tbsp	hot pepper flakes	30 mL
1 tbsp	freshly cracked fennel seeds (see tips, at left)	15 mL
2 tsp	kosher salt	10 mL
1 tsp	freshly cracked black pepper	5 mL
1 tsp	sweet paprika	5 mL
1 tsp	dried oregano	5 mL
¼ cup	red wine	60 mL
4 to 5 feet	32/35 mm hog casing, soaked (see page 49)	120 to 150 cm

1. Cut pork into pieces small enough to fit in the throat of your grinder. Using the coarse grinder plate, grind pork into a large bowl or stand mixer bowl.

2. Add basil, garlic paste, hot pepper flakes, fennel seeds, salt, black pepper, paprika and oregano to the ground pork. Using your hands or the stand mixer paddle attachment, mix until seasonings are evenly distributed. Add wine and mix until white strands appear in the mixture and a handful of the mixture holds together.

3. In a small skillet, over medium-high heat, sauté a small amount of the sausage mixture until no longer pink. Taste the sample, then adjust seasonings as desired.

4. Stuff sausage mixture into prepared casing as described on page 51. Twist into 6 links, each about 6 inches (15 cm) in length.

Health Facts

In India, fennel seeds are believed to aid in digestion and are often chewed after a meal. Fennel seeds also contain several important phytonutrients, such as rutin, quercetin, kaempferol and anethole. These compounds have been shown to possess antioxidant activity. Studies of anethole have reported that it may reduce the risk of heart disease and cancer.

Spicy Fresh Kielbasa

Here, a few spicy ingredients are added to traditional fresh Polish sausages, for a heat sensation that's sure to please the more adventurous diner.

Tip

Herbs are easy to grow in the summer and dry for use in the winter. The time-honored method of twining the stems together and hanging them upside down is useful, but only if done properly. While the hanging herbs offer an attractive focal point for your kitchen, they dry more effectively in a well-ventilated, warm and dry location away from direct light. Under the right conditions, they should dry within 2 weeks.

2 lbs	trimmed boneless pork shoulder blade roast, chilled (see page 49)	1 kg
¼ cup	finely minced garlic	60 mL
2 tsp	hot paprika	10 mL
2 tsp	onion powder	10 mL
2 tsp	cayenne pepper	10 mL
2 tsp	kosher salt	10 mL
1 tsp	freshly cracked black pepper	5 mL
1 tsp	dried marjoram	5 mL
½ tsp	dried thyme	2 mL
¼ cup	water	60 mL
4 to 5 feet	32/35 mm hog casing, soaked (see page 49)	120 to 150 cm

1. Cut pork into pieces small enough to fit in the throat of your grinder. Using the coarse grinder plate, grind pork into a large bowl or stand mixer bowl.

2. Add garlic, paprika, onion powder, cayenne, salt, black pepper, marjoram and thyme to the ground pork. Using your hands or the stand mixer paddle attachment, mix until seasonings are evenly distributed. Add water and mix until white strands appear in the mixture and a handful of the mixture holds together.

3. In a small skillet, over medium-high heat, sauté a small amount of the sausage mixture until no longer pink. Taste the sample, then adjust seasonings as desired.

4. Stuff sausage mixture into prepared casing as described on page 51. Twist into 6 links, each about 6 inches (15 cm) in length.

Health Facts

Paprika is a spice made from dried peppers, which can be either sweet or hot. All peppers are rich in essential nutrients and phytonutrients, and peppers with red pigmentation contain high levels of lycopene, a powerful antioxidant.

Romanian Sausages

Romania's cuisine reflects that of its neighbors, including Greece, Bulgaria and Turkey. The residents of these countries also share a love of sausages. Romanian sausages, or *mititei*, are often enjoyed grilled, which makes them the perfect summer supper entrée.

MAKES 6 SAUSAGES

Tips

Toast caraway seeds in a small skillet over medium heat, without using oil. Shake the pan often and toast for up to 2 minutes, until aromatic and lightly browned.

If you use your hands to mix the ground meat, have a bowl of water nearby in which to dip your fingers. This will help keep them from getting too sticky.

2 lbs	trimmed boneless pork shoulder blade roast, chilled (see page 49)	1 kg
2 tbsp	finely minced garlic	30 mL
2 tbsp	mustard seeds	30 mL
2 tsp	toasted caraway seeds (see tip, at left)	10 mL
2 tsp	hot paprika	10 mL
2 tsp	kosher salt	10 mL
1 tsp	freshly cracked black pepper	5 mL
1 tsp	dried thyme	5 mL
2 tbsp	water	30 mL
4 to 5 feet	32/35 mm hog casing, soaked (see page 49)	120 to 150 cm

1. Cut pork into pieces small enough to fit in the throat of your grinder. Using the coarse grinder plate, grind pork into a large bowl or stand mixer bowl.

2. Add garlic, mustard seeds, caraway seeds, paprika, salt, pepper and thyme to the ground pork. Using your hands or the stand mixer paddle attachment, mix until seasonings are evenly distributed. Add water and mix until white strands appear in the mixture and a handful of the mixture holds together.

3. In a small skillet, over medium-high heat, sauté a small amount of the sausage mixture until no longer pink. Taste the sample, then adjust seasonings as desired.

4. Stuff sausage mixture into prepared casing as described on page 51. Twist into 6 links, each about 6 inches (15 cm) in length.

Health Facts

Caraway seeds have a long tradition of medical use in treating autoimmune diseases, such as asthma. A 2015 study found that the immune function of mice was stimulated by an extract of caraway seeds, showing that compounds in caraway may indeed have a positive effect on the immune system.

Macedonian Sausages

Macedonia's cuisine combines Balkan and Mediterranean elements, with a heavy Turkish influence from centuries of Ottoman rule. It includes a bounty of tomatoes, carrots, red peppers, parsley, onions, and garlic, which are used in many savory recipes. These sausages feature the Macedonian specialty of ajvar, a relish of eggplant, roasted red bell peppers, paprika and garlic.

**MAKES
6 SAUSAGES**

Tip

Depending on the brand of ajvar and its specific ingredients, it may develop mold once opened and refrigerated. To protect this somewhat expensive but savory relish, divide it into small portions and freeze them.

2 lbs	trimmed boneless pork shoulder blade roast, chilled (see page 49)	1 kg
¼ cup	spicy ajvar	60 mL
2 tbsp	finely minced garlic	30 mL
2 tsp	hot paprika	10 mL
2 tsp	kosher salt	10 mL
1 tsp	freshly cracked black pepper	5 mL
1 tsp	ground cumin	5 mL
2 tbsp	water	30 mL
4 to 5 feet	32/35 mm hog casing, soaked (see page 49)	120 to 150 cm

1. Cut pork into pieces small enough to fit in the throat of your grinder. Using the coarse grinder plate, grind pork into a large bowl or stand mixer bowl.

2. Add ajvar, garlic, paprika, salt, pepper and cumin to the ground pork. Using your hands or the stand mixer paddle attachment, mix until seasonings are evenly distributed. Add water and mix until white strands appear in the mixture and a handful of the mixture holds together.

3. In a small skillet, over medium-high heat, sauté a small amount of the sausage mixture until juices run clear. Taste the sample, then adjust seasonings as desired.

4. Stuff sausage mixture into prepared casing as described on page 51. Twist into 6 links, each about 6 inches (15 cm) in length.

Health Facts

Ajvar contains roasted red peppers, which are an excellent source of the carotenoid lycopene. Lycopene's protective role in cancer, especially prostate cancer, is well known. But a 2015 study reported that this carotenoid also protected kidney cells from the inflammation and oxidative damage that occurs in diabetes.

Greek Sausages

These sausages bring together all the traditional ingredients from Greek cuisine. You can complete the menu with Greek rice pilaf and a fresh spinach salad topped with sliced beets.

Tip

You can use either oil-packed or dry-packed sun-dried tomatoes. If you use oil-packed, drain well before mincing and measuring. An opened container of oil-packed tomatoes will remain fresh in the refrigerator for up to 6 months. The oil will turn into a white solid, but it will liquefy in 30 minutes at room temperature. To store dry-packed tomatoes, squeeze any air out of the bag before sealing it; this will keep them fresh for about a year in the refrigerator.

2 lbs	trimmed boneless pork shoulder blade roast, chilled (see page 49)	1 kg
8	drained kalamata olives, roughly chopped	8
½ cup	crumbled feta cheese	125 mL
¼ cup	finely chopped fresh basil	60 mL
2 tbsp	finely chopped fresh mint	30 mL
2 tbsp	finely minced onion	30 mL
2 tbsp	finely minced sun-dried tomatoes (see tip, at left)	30 mL
2 tbsp	roasted garlic paste (see page 47)	30 mL
1 tbsp	grated lemon zest	15 mL
1½ tsp	kosher salt	7 mL
1 tsp	freshly cracked black pepper	5 mL
2 tbsp	water	30 mL
4 to 5 feet	32/35 mm hog casing, soaked (see page 49)	120 to 150 cm

1. Cut pork into pieces small enough to fit in the throat of your grinder. Using the coarse grinder plate, grind pork into a large bowl or stand mixer bowl.

2. Add olives, cheese, basil, mint, onion, sun-dried tomatoes, garlic paste, lemon zest, salt and pepper to the ground pork. Using your hands or the stand mixer paddle attachment, mix until seasonings are evenly distributed. Add water and mix until white strands appear in the mixture and a handful of the mixture holds together.

3. In a small skillet, over medium-high heat, sauté a small amount of the sausage mixture until no longer pink. Taste the sample, then adjust seasonings as desired.

4. Stuff sausage mixture into prepared casing as described on page 51. Twist into 7 links, each about 6 inches (15 cm) in length.

Health Facts

Feta cheese is available with varying levels of fat, including fat-free. When the fat is either partially or completely removed, the protein content increases, as does the calcium content. Sausage recipes tend to be quite forgiving if you use a lower-fat variety, since the meat provides ample fat. If you want to reduce the calories and fat in these sausages, use a lower-fat or fat-free feta.

Preparing the Casing and Meat

Cut the casing to the length you need — about 4 to 5 feet (120 to 150 cm) for 2 lbs (1 kg) of meat (1 kg) — and rinse it thoroughly.

Place the casing in a bowl and add enough warm water to cover. Soak for 1 hour, changing the water several times.

Meanwhile, trim the visible fat off the meat until you have a roughly 85/15 ratio of lean meat to fat (or your desired ratio). Discard the trimmed fat, unless otherwise indicated in the recipe, or save it for another use.

Use a kitchen scale to weigh out the amount of meat (and, if applicable, fat and trimmings) you need for the recipe.

Wrap the trimmed meat in plastic wrap and place it in the freezer for 30 minutes to chill. Do not let it begin to freeze.

Cut the chilled meat into pieces small enough to fit in the throat of your grinder.

Using a Meat Grinder and Mixing with Your Hands

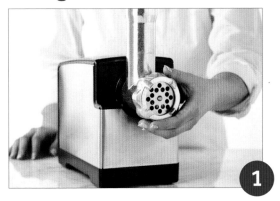

1

Attach the grinder plate specified in the recipe to the meat grinder.

2

Place a large bowl below the grinder head. Add meat to the grinder tray. Turn the grinder on (if using an electric grinder) or start turning the handle (if using a manual grinder) and use the stomper to push the meat into the feed chute.

3

Once all the meat is ground into the bowl, add all of the dry ingredients and seasonings specified in the recipe.

4

Using your hands, mix the seasonings into the meat until they are evenly distributed.

5

Add the liquid ingredients. Using your hands, mix until white strands appear and a handful of the mixture holds together. (*Note:* Mixtures that include vinegar will not hold together, but the white strands will still appear.)

6

Sauté a small amount of the sausage mixture until no longer pink or until juices run clear, as instructed in the recipe. Taste the sample. If desired, add additional seasonings to the meat mixture and mix until evenly distributed.

Grinding and Mixing with a Stand Mixer

Attach the mixer bowl and the food grinder attachment to your stand mixer, with the grinder plate specified in the recipe.

Add meat pieces to the grinder tray, without overfilling it. Set the mixer to the speed indicated in the manufacturer's user manual and use the food pusher to push the meat into the feed chute.

Once all the meat is ground into the stand mixer bowl, add all of the dry ingredients and seasonings specified in the recipe.

Remove the food grinder and attach the flat beater to the mixer. Set the mixer to Stir and mix until the seasonings are evenly distributed throughout the meat.

Add the liquid ingredients. Set the mixer to Stir and mix until white strands appear and a handful of the mixture holds together. (*Note:* Mixtures that include vinegar will not hold together, but the white strands will still appear.)

Sauté a small amount of the sausage mixture until no longer pink or until juices run clear, as instructed in the recipe. Taste the sample. If desired, add additional seasonings to the meat mixture and mix until evenly distributed.

Stuffing the Sausages and Twisting Links

1

If using a manual or electric meat grinder with stuffing capability or if using a stand-alone sausage stuffer, attach the appropriate-size extruding tube (see page 51) to the grinder or stuffer.

2

If using a stand mixer, remove the flat beater and reattach the food grinder, with the sausage stuffer tube in place of the grinder plate.

3

Pull one end of the casing out of the soaking bowl and open it. Scoop some water from the bowl into the casing so it will slide on and off the tube easily. Place the open end over the extruding tube. Slide the full length of the casing onto the tube, then tie a knot in the end.

4

Turn the grinder, stuffer or mixer on and, with one hand, slowly and steadily feed the meat mixture into the tray, pushing it down with the stomper or food pusher. With your other hand, hold the casing just beyond the end of the tube to help guide the sausage into the casing.

5

As the meat mixture begins to fill the casing, try to maintain a consistent thickness; the casing should be full, but not to the point of bursting.

6

Once all of the meat mixture is fed into the casing, cut off any excess casing and tie a knot in the open end. Gently twist the stuffed sausage into the desired number of links.

Bangers (page 66)

Sweet Italian Sausages (page 70)

Cajun Boudin Blanc (page 82)

Boudin Noir (page 84)

American Hot Dogs (page 92)

Pepperoni (page 103)

Spicy Fresh Kielbasa (page 125)

Cup o' Joe Morning Sausages (page 144)

Weisswurst (page 147)

Cabanossi (page 168)

Athenian Chicken Sausages (page 191)

Spicy Sicilian Chickpea Sausages (page 235)

Spiced and Peppered Sausages

When your taste buds demand a jolt, these sausages will fit the bill. The recipe includes three forms of pepper and a combination of ginger and coriander.

**MAKES
6 SAUSAGES**

Tip

Black peppercorns are picked when ripe and then dried, which turns the outer layer black. In contrast, the outer layer of white peppercorns is removed, leaving only the inner seed. White pepper is hotter, and is used in Chinese, Vietnamese and Swedish cuisines for this difference and because of its lack of color. Ground white pepper goes stale much more quickly than black pepper, so buy whole peppercorns if you use it infrequently.

2 lbs	trimmed boneless pork shoulder blade roast, chilled (see page 49)	1 kg
1 tbsp	hot pepper flakes	15 mL
2 tsp	garlic powder	10 mL
2 tsp	kosher salt	10 mL
1 tsp	ground ginger	5 mL
1 tsp	freshly cracked black pepper	5 mL
½ tsp	freshly ground white pepper	2 mL
⅛ tsp	ground coriander	0.5 mL
¼ cup	water	60 mL
4 to 5 feet	32/35 mm hog casing, soaked (see page 49)	120 to 150 cm

1. Cut pork into pieces small enough to fit in the throat of your grinder. Using the coarse grinder plate, grind pork into a large bowl or stand mixer bowl.

2. Add hot pepper flakes, garlic powder, salt, ginger, black pepper, white pepper and coriander to the ground pork. Using your hands or the stand mixer paddle attachment, mix until seasonings are evenly distributed. Add water and mix until white strands appear in the mixture and a handful of the mixture holds together.

3. In a small skillet, over medium-high heat, sauté a small amount of the sausage mixture until no longer pink. Taste the sample, then adjust seasonings as desired.

4. Stuff sausage mixture into prepared casing as described on page 51. Twist into 6 links, each about 6 inches (15 cm) in length.

Health Facts

Ginger's bountiful phytonutrients include limonene, gingerol, 6-dehydrogingerdione (DGE), shogaols and oxalic acid. Its biologic activities are numerous and include antioxidant and anti-inflammatory effects, which protect against heart disease and cancer. It is also widely used to counteract nausea.

Curry Sausages

The flavor of these unique sausages relies on two different types of curry powder, complex spice mixtures whose exact composition varies extensively by region. Malaysian curry powders typically contain turmeric, garlic, coconut, shallots, ginger, chile peppers and tamarind.

**MAKES
6 SAUSAGES**

Tips

Malaysian meat curry powder should be available at small grocers specializing in Indonesian, Thai and Filipino foods, and it's worth the hunt. However, if you can't find it, add an extra teaspoon (5 mL) of yellow curry powder and ½ teaspoon (2 mL) of coconut extract.

How long to make your sausage links is really up to you, although we suggest 6 inches (15 cm) for this recipe. Keep in mind that this is a rough guideline, and that you may have to adjust the length up or down so that you don't end up with one link smaller than the rest.

2 lbs	trimmed boneless pork shoulder blade roast, chilled (see page 49)	1 kg
1 tbsp	yellow curry powder	15 mL
2 tsp	garlic powder	10 mL
2 tsp	kosher salt	10 mL
1 tsp	freshly cracked black pepper	5 mL
1 tsp	Malaysian meat curry powder	5 mL
1 tsp	ground ginger	5 mL
1 tsp	ground cinnamon	5 mL
½ tsp	ground turmeric	2 mL
¼ cup	water	60 mL
4 to 5 feet	32/35 mm hog casing, soaked (see page 49)	120 to 150 cm

1. Cut pork into pieces small enough to fit in the throat of your grinder. Using the coarse grinder plate, grind pork into a large bowl or stand mixer bowl.

2. Add yellow curry powder, garlic powder, salt, pepper, Malaysian curry powder, ginger, cinnamon and turmeric to the ground pork. Using your hands or the stand mixer paddle attachment, mix until seasonings are evenly distributed. Add water and mix until white strands appear in the mixture and a handful of the mixture holds together.

3. In a small skillet, over medium-high heat, sauté a small amount of the sausage mixture until no longer pink. Taste the sample, then adjust seasonings as desired.

4. Stuff sausage mixture into prepared casing as described on page 51. Twist into 6 links, each about 6 inches (15 cm) in length.

Health Facts

This sausage is full of ingredients that provide phytonutrients, including ginger, cinnamon and turmeric. Turmeric, for example, contains curcumin, which has been studied for its anti-inflammatory, antioxidant and anticancer properties. Researchers have also reported that curcumin "reduces depressive symptoms in patients with major depression."

Ramen Sausages

Most college students are familiar with the small packages of ramen noodles in a variety of flavors. But the original ramen, created in Japan in the early 1900s, was actually a soup made with Chinese wheat noodles and a variety of spices. That flavor is captured in these sausages, which feature ginger, hot pepper flakes, chile sauce and garlic.

MAKES 6 SAUSAGES

Tip

Sriracha originated in Thailand, where it is used as a dipping sauce. This spicy sauce is quite versatile, so combine it with other condiments, such as mayonnaise or sour cream, to use both in recipes and as a dip.

Health Facts

Monosodium glutamate (MSG) has a bad but undeserved reputation. It consists of sodium and glutamic acid, an amino acid found naturally in the body and in protein foods. Connie Diekman, Director of Nutrition at Washington University in St. Louis, stated that "the USDA views MSG as a generally recognized as safe (GRAS) substance, since the scientific evidence does not exist to indicate that it has any negative health impacts."

2 lbs	trimmed boneless pork shoulder blade roast, chilled (see page 49)	1 kg
¼ cup	finely chopped green onions	60 mL
1 tsp	kosher salt	5 mL
1 tsp	freshly ground black pepper	5 mL
1 tsp	hot pepper flakes	5 mL
1 tsp	ground ginger	5 mL
1 tsp	garlic powder	5 mL
1 tsp	sweet paprika	5 mL
½ tsp	monosodium glutamate (MSG)	2 mL
2	beef bouillon cubes, smashed into powder (or 2 tsp/10 mL powdered beef bouillon)	2
¼ cup	water	60 mL
1 tbsp	sweet Thai chile sauce	15 mL
1 tsp	Asian hot pepper sauce (such as Sriracha)	5 mL
4 to 5 feet	32/35 mm hog casing, soaked (see page 49)	120 to 150 cm

1. Cut pork into pieces small enough to fit in the throat of your grinder. Using the coarse grinder plate, grind pork into a large bowl or stand mixer bowl.

2. Add green onions, salt, black pepper, hot pepper flakes, ginger, garlic powder, paprika, MSG and bouillon to the ground pork. Using your hands or the stand mixer paddle attachment, mix until seasonings are evenly distributed. Add water, chile sauce and hot pepper sauce; mix until white strands appear in the mixture and a handful of the mixture holds together.

3. In a small skillet, over medium-high heat, sauté a small amount of the sausage mixture until no longer pink. Taste the sample, then adjust seasonings as desired.

4. Stuff sausage mixture into prepared casing as described on page 51. Twist into 6 links, each about 6 inches (15 cm) in length.

Polynesian Sausages

Polynesia is a region of over 1000 islands in the central and southern Pacific Ocean. The sweet-and-sour flavor popular in Polynesian cuisine is achieved in these delicious sausages with the addition of pineapple, soy sauce, garlic and onion.

MAKES 7 SAUSAGES

Tips

Before chopping green onion shoots, run water through the stem. Soil containing bacteria can cling to the sticky coating that lines the shoots.

If you use your hands to mix the ground meat, have a bowl of water nearby in which to dip your fingers. This will help keep them from getting too sticky.

Health Facts

Pineapple contains numerous phytonutrients with antioxidant activity. Another of its phytochemicals, bromelain, has powerful anti-inflammatory and antitumor effects.

1 tsp	onion flakes	5 mL
1 tbsp	warm water	15 mL
2 lbs	trimmed boneless pork shoulder blade roast, chilled (see page 49)	1 kg
½ cup	drained canned pineapple tidbits, juice reserved	125 mL
3 tbsp	packed brown sugar	45 mL
2 tbsp	finely chopped green onion (green parts only)	30 mL
1½ tsp	grated lemon zest	7 mL
1 tsp	kosher salt	5 mL
1 tsp	freshly cracked black pepper	5 mL
1 tsp	garlic powder	5 mL
2 tbsp	soy sauce	30 mL
2 tbsp	pineapple juice (reserved from tidbits)	30 mL
4 to 5 feet	32/35 mm hog casing, soaked (see page 49)	120 to 150 cm

1. In a small bowl, combine onion flakes and warm water. Let stand for about 20 minutes or until softened.

2. Meanwhile, cut pork into pieces small enough to fit in the throat of your grinder. Using the coarse grinder plate, grind pork and pineapple into a large bowl or stand mixer bowl.

3. Add brown sugar, green onion, lemon zest, salt, pepper, garlic powder, onion flakes mixture and soy sauce to the ground pork mixture. Using your hands or the stand mixer paddle attachment, mix until seasonings are evenly distributed. Add pineapple juice and mix until white strands appear in the mixture and a handful of the mixture holds together.

4. In a small skillet, over medium-high heat, sauté a small amount of the sausage mixture until no longer pink. Taste the sample, then adjust seasonings as desired.

5. Stuff sausage mixture into prepared casing as described on page 51. Twist into 7 links, each about 6 inches (15 cm) in length.

Hawaiian Pizza Sausages

Hawaiian pizza burst onto the mainstream pizza scene in 1962, compliments of Canadian restaurateur Sam Panopoulos. These sausages evoke the flavor of that classic pizza and add a few more ingredient twists for an explosion of flavors to awaken the taste buds.

**MAKES
8 SAUSAGES**

Tips

Customize these sausages by adding your favorite pizza toppings, such as finely chopped green bell peppers, mushrooms or black olives. You can add up to ¼ cup (60 mL) of each without adversely affecting sausage texture.

How long to make your sausage links is really up to you, although we suggest 6 inches (15 cm) for this recipe. Keep in mind that this is a rough guideline, and that you may have to adjust the length up or down so that you don't end up with one link smaller than the rest.

2 lbs	trimmed boneless pork shoulder blade roast, chilled (see page 49)	1 kg
1 cup	shredded mozzarella cheese	250 mL
⅓ cup	diced Canadian bacon	75 mL
¼ cup	finely diced pineapple	60 mL
¼ cup	finely diced onion	60 mL
2 tbsp	tomato paste	30 mL
1 tbsp	roasted garlic paste (see page 47)	15 mL
2 tsp	freshly cracked fennel seeds (see tip, page 70)	10 mL
2 tsp	kosher salt	10 mL
1 tsp	freshly cracked black pepper	5 mL
1 tsp	dried oregano	5 mL
¼ cup	water	60 mL
4 to 5 feet	32/35 mm hog casing, soaked (see page 49)	120 to 150 cm

1. Cut pork into pieces small enough to fit in the throat of your grinder. Using the coarse grinder plate, grind pork into a large bowl or stand mixer bowl.

2. Add cheese, bacon, pineapple, onion, tomato paste, garlic paste, fennel seeds, salt, pepper and oregano to the ground pork. Using your hands or the stand mixer paddle attachment, mix until seasonings are evenly distributed. Add water and mix until white strands appear in the mixture and a handful of the mixture holds together.

3. In a small skillet, over medium-high heat, sauté a small amount of the sausage mixture until juices run clear. Taste the sample, then adjust seasonings as desired.

4. Stuff sausage mixture into prepared casing as described on page 51. Twist into 8 links, each about 6 inches (15 cm) in length.

Health Facts

In addition to several essential nutrients, pineapple contains many intriguing phytonutrients. One of these is gamma-aminobutyric acid (GABA), which is the main neurotransmitter in the central nervous system. It is sold as a supplement, with claims that it provides a calming effect.

American Brats

A German bratwurst can be any one of numerous regional specialties using different meats and spices. American brats became popular in the 1920s in Wisconsin, where a sizable German immigrant population resided, and came to mean sausages poached in beer and grilled. Here, the combination of spices and creamy porter or stout will take you back to that era, for a truly unique taste experience.

	MAKES 6 SAUSAGES

Tips

The dark beer adds significant character to these sausages, so don't be tempted to skip it. You can purchase a single bottle of either porter or stout and freeze the remainder for use in another recipe.

If you decide to use table salt in place of kosher salt, use 1½ tsp (7 mL), as table salt has a higher density.

2 lbs	trimmed boneless pork shoulder blade roast, chilled (see page 49)	1 kg
2 tsp	dried sage	10 mL
2 tsp	dry mustard	10 mL
2 tsp	kosher salt	10 mL
1½ tsp	granulated sugar	7 mL
1 tsp	freshly cracked black pepper	5 mL
½ tsp	ground coriander	2 mL
¼ tsp	sweet paprika	1 mL
¼ tsp	cayenne pepper	1 mL
⅛ tsp	ground nutmeg	0.5 mL
¼ cup	dark beer (porter or stout)	60 mL
4 to 5 feet	32/35 mm hog casing, soaked (see page 49)	120 to 150 cm

1. Cut pork into pieces small enough to fit in the throat of your grinder. Using the coarse grinder plate, grind pork into a large bowl or stand mixer bowl.

2. Add sage, mustard, salt, sugar, black pepper, coriander, paprika, cayenne and nutmeg to the ground pork. Using your hands or the stand mixer paddle attachment, mix until seasonings are evenly distributed. Add beer and mix until white strands appear in the mixture and a handful of the mixture holds together.

3. In a small skillet, over medium-high heat, sauté a small amount of the sausage mixture until no longer pink. Taste the sample, then adjust seasonings as desired.

4. Stuff sausage mixture into prepared casing as described on page 51. Twist into 6 links, each about 6 inches (15 cm) in length.

Health Facts

Coriander has traditionally been used in many countries to treat disorders of the digestive, respiratory and urinary systems, as a diuretic and as insomnia therapy. Its possible biologic effects include antimicrobial, antioxidant, analgesic, anti-inflammatory and anticancer activities.

Barbecue Sausages

For many of us, the word "barbecue" conjures up images of a fun-filled outdoor summer event featuring mouthwatering grilled foods. These sausages will bring your favorite barbecue memories flooding back, but they're just as perfect for dinner on a chilly winter day as they are for a summer picnic.

Tip

The combination of dry ingredients in this recipe is essentially a barbecue dry rub mix, which makes an excellent addition to your spice rack. Make a large batch to use in recipes such as chili, chip dip and vegetable dip.

2 lbs	trimmed boneless pork shoulder blade roast, chilled (see page 49)	1 kg
2 tbsp	packed brown sugar	30 mL
2 tsp	dry mustard	10 mL
2 tsp	sweet paprika	10 mL
2 tsp	garlic powder	10 mL
2 tsp	kosher salt	10 mL
1 tsp	freshly cracked black pepper	5 mL
1 tsp	cayenne pepper	5 mL
1 tsp	chili powder	5 mL
1 tsp	onion powder	5 mL
1 tsp	ground cumin	5 mL
2 tbsp	tomato paste	30 mL
1 tbsp	dark (cooking) molasses	15 mL
¼ cup	water	60 mL
4 to 5 feet	32/35 mm hog casing, soaked (see page 49)	120 to 150 cm

1. Cut pork into pieces small enough to fit in the throat of your grinder. Using the coarse grinder plate, grind pork into a large bowl or stand mixer bowl.

2. Add brown sugar, mustard, paprika, garlic powder, salt, black pepper, cayenne, chili powder, onion powder, cumin, tomato paste and molasses to the ground pork. Using your hands or the stand mixer paddle attachment, mix until seasonings are evenly distributed. Add water and mix until white strands appear in the mixture and a handful of the mixture holds together.

3. In a small skillet, over medium-high heat, sauté a small amount of the sausage mixture until juices run clear. Taste the sample, then adjust seasonings as desired.

4. Stuff sausage mixture into prepared casing as described on page 51. Twist into 6 links, each about 6 inches (15 cm) in length.

Health Facts

Molasses contains the essential minerals calcium, magnesium, manganese, potassium, copper, iron, phosphorus and chromium. It has a strong flavor, but it can replace some of the sugar in many recipes.

Pork Roast Sausages

These hearty sausages pack in all the flavors of a traditional pork roast dinner, including the side dishes of potatoes and carrots!

Tips

To always have rosemary on hand, wash it without removing it from the stem. Dry thoroughly, place it in a plastic freezer bag, press out excess air and freeze.

If you use your hands to mix the ground meat, have a bowl of water nearby in which to dip your fingers. This will help keep them from getting too sticky.

2 lbs	trimmed boneless pork shoulder blade roast, chilled (see page 49)	1 kg
5 oz	russet potatoes, peeled and cut lengthwise into quarters	150 g
½ cup	finely diced carrot	125 mL
2 tbsp	finely chopped caramelized onion (see tip, page 141)	30 mL
1 tbsp	minced fresh rosemary	15 mL
1 tbsp	garlic powder	15 mL
2 tsp	kosher salt	10 mL
1 tsp	freshly cracked black pepper	5 mL
1 tbsp	red wine	15 mL
1 tbsp	water	15 mL
4 to 5 feet	32/35 mm hog casing, soaked (see page 49)	120 to 150 cm

1. Cut pork into pieces small enough to fit in the throat of your grinder. Using the coarse grinder plate, grind pork and potatoes into a large bowl or stand mixer bowl.

2. Add carrot, onion, rosemary, garlic powder, salt and pepper to the ground pork. Using your hands or the stand mixer paddle attachment, mix until seasonings are evenly distributed. Add wine and water; mix until white strands appear in the mixture and a handful of the mixture holds together.

3. In a small skillet, over medium-high heat, sauté a small amount of the sausage mixture until no longer pink. Taste the sample, then adjust seasonings as desired.

4. Stuff sausage mixture into prepared casing as described on page 51. Twist into 7 links, each about 6 inches (15 cm) in length.

Health Facts

Rosemary is a superstar in the world of health-promoting herbs and spices. A 2015 study in rats reported that one of its phytonutrients, carnosic acid, improved memory and protected brain cells against free radical damage.

Hop Sausages

Hops are the flowers of a twining vine that is a member of the hemp family. They've been used for centuries in making beer, to which they confer a bitter flavor. In these sausages, a touch of Citra hops (a hybrid of several types of hops) provides a tropical fruit aroma.

MAKES 6 SAUSAGES

Tips

You can find hops at stores that sell home winemaking and beer-brewing supplies and online.

Don't skip the orange zest if you don't have a zester; it adds significant flavor. Instead, use a vegetable peeler to remove large strips of the peel, avoiding the white pith. Cut the peel into long, thin strips, then chop it to size.

2 lbs	trimmed boneless pork shoulder blade roast, chilled (see page 49)	1 kg
1 tbsp	grated orange zest	15 mL
2 tsp	kosher salt	10 mL
1 tsp	freshly cracked black pepper	5 mL
1 tsp	garlic powder	5 mL
1 tsp	onion powder	5 mL
1 tsp	ground coriander	5 mL
½ tsp	dried Citra hops, crumbled	2 mL
½ tsp	cayenne pepper	2 mL
2 tbsp	water	30 mL
4 to 5 feet	32/35 mm hog casing, soaked (see page 49)	120 to 150 cm

1. Cut pork into pieces small enough to fit in the throat of your grinder. Using the coarse grinder plate, grind pork into a large bowl or stand mixer bowl.

2. Add orange zest, salt, black pepper, garlic powder, onion powder, coriander, hops and cayenne to the ground pork. Using your hands or the stand mixer paddle attachment, mix until seasonings are evenly distributed. Add water and mix until white strands appear in the mixture and a handful of the mixture holds together.

3. In a small skillet, over medium-high heat, sauté a small amount of the sausage mixture until no longer pink. Taste the sample, then adjust seasonings as desired.

4. Stuff sausage mixture into prepared casing as described on page 51. Twist into 6 links, each about 6 inches (15 cm) in length.

Health Facts

A 2013 review of hop extract reported that it contains several compounds with estrogenic activity, pointing to studies on its effects on osteoporosis and menopause symptoms. The authors concluded that the extract holds promise, but that more clinical studies are needed on its safety and effectiveness.

Michigan Sausages

These sausages are a local favorite in the sausage makers' state of Michigan because of the prominence of two highly prized ingredients: morel mushrooms and asparagus. The traditional hunt for morels in early May finds Michiganders scouring the woods for this delicacy — and gathering up wild asparagus not much later. Both foods are nutritional powerhouses, but it's their flavor and texture that truly inspire this sausage's devotees.

**MAKES
7 SAUSAGES**

Tips

While morel mushrooms are available around the world, they may not be available when you're ready to make sausage. The best substitutes are highly textured mushroom varieties, such as portobello or oyster mushrooms. Alternatively, you can use 1 oz (30 g) dried morels and reconstitute them by soaking them in enough hot water to cover for 30 minutes. Drain and sauté in 1 tbsp (15 mL) olive oil for 3 minutes. Let cool completely.

To blanch asparagus, bring 2 cups (500 mL) water to a boil. Add trimmed asparagus and cook for 2 minutes or until bright green. Drain and plunge into a bowl of ice water. Drain again before chopping.

1½ tsp	olive oil	7 mL
1 cup	morel mushrooms (see tip, at left)	250 mL
2 lbs	trimmed boneless pork shoulder blade roast, chilled (see page 49)	1 kg
⅓ cup	chopped blanched asparagus (see tip, at left)	75 mL
2 tsp	finely minced fresh rosemary	10 mL
2 tsp	kosher salt	10 mL
1 tsp	freshly cracked black pepper	5 mL
1 tsp	dried thyme	5 mL
¼ cup	white wine	60 mL
4 to 5 feet	32/35 mm hog casing, soaked (see page 49)	120 to 150 cm

1. In a skillet, heat oil over medium-high heat. Add mushrooms and cook, stirring, for about 8 minutes or until browned and tender. Let cool completely.

2. Cut pork into pieces small enough to fit in the throat of your grinder. Using the coarse grinder plate, grind pork into a large bowl or stand mixer bowl.

3. Add mushrooms, asparagus, rosemary, salt, pepper and thyme to the ground pork. Using your hands or the stand mixer paddle attachment, mix until seasonings are evenly distributed. Add wine and mix until white strands appear in the mixture and a handful of the mixture holds together.

4. In a small skillet, over medium-high heat, sauté a small amount of the sausage mixture until no longer pink. Taste the sample, then adjust seasonings as desired.

5. Stuff sausage mixture into prepared casing as described on page 51. Twist into 7 links, each about 6 inches (15 cm) in length.

Health Facts

Asparagus contains a high level of vitamins A and C and several minerals, notably manganese and copper. It's also high in a type of soluble fiber known as fructooligosaccharides (FOS), which lower blood cholesterol and serve as a prebiotic, promoting the growth of healthy bacteria in the large intestine.

Pennsylvania Dutch Sausages

Chef Brent hails from Pennsylvania and still often visits his family's farm, where sausage making is a family tradition. This simple recipe melds the comfort-food cuisine of the early German settlers of the region with Brent's Irish family's recipe.

Tips

To help brown sugar maintain its moisture, seal it tightly in a heavy plastic food storage bag, or even double-wrap it. If it hardens on you, you can soften it: put a moist paper towel in a microwave-safe plastic bag with the brown sugar and microwave on High for 20 seconds.

How long to make your sausage links is really up to you, although we suggest 6 inches (15 cm) for this recipe. Keep in mind that this is a rough guideline, and that you may have to adjust the length up or down so that you don't end up with one link smaller than the rest.

2 lbs	trimmed boneless pork shoulder blade roast, chilled (see page 49)	1 kg
1 tbsp	packed dark brown sugar	15 mL
2 tsp	dried sage	10 mL
2 tsp	kosher salt	10 mL
1 tsp	freshly cracked black pepper	5 mL
1 tsp	dried thyme	5 mL
¼ cup	water	60 mL
4 to 5 feet	32/35 mm hog casing, soaked (see page 49)	120 to 150 cm

1. Cut pork into pieces small enough to fit in the throat of your grinder. Using the coarse grinder plate, grind pork into a large bowl or stand mixer bowl.

2. Add brown sugar, sage, salt, pepper and thyme to the ground pork. Using your hands or the stand mixer paddle attachment, mix until seasonings are evenly distributed. Add water and mix until white strands appear in the mixture and a handful of the mixture holds together.

3. In a small skillet, over medium-high heat, sauté a small amount of the sausage mixture until no longer pink. Taste the sample, then adjust seasonings as desired.

4. Stuff sausage mixture into prepared casing as described on page 51. Twist into 6 links, each about 6 inches (15 cm) in length.

Health Facts

Brown sugar consists of granulated (white) sugar mixed with molasses. Molasses contains many essential nutrients, and by extension, though to a lesser degree, so does brown sugar. But unless you're eating way too much brown sugar, it won't contribute much to your nutrient needs. Nevertheless, its touch of molasses makes it an enticing addition to many recipes in place of granulated sugar.

Super-Spicy Green Chorizo

Here's a spicier version of our Green Chorizo recipe (page 81), providing enough heat to satisfy even the most ardent heat-seeking sausage lover.

MAKES 8 SAUSAGES

Tips

The tomatillo is often called a "Mexican green tomato." While it's in the same plant family as the tomato, it has a tart flavor. Look for tomatillos at Latin American markets. If you can't find them, you can substitute an underripe tomato and add 1 tsp (5 mL) freshly squeezed lime juice.

To roast the tomatillo, preheat the broiler, with the rack set 2 inches (5 cm) from the heat source. Remove the papery covering from the tomatillo and rinse to remove the viscous coating. Place on broiler pan and broil for about 7 minutes or until slightly charred and soft. Let cool completely.

- Blender

1	tomatillo, roasted and cooled (see tips, at left)	1
2 oz	fresh cilantro leaves	60 g
1 oz	fresh parsley leaves	30 g
12	cloves garlic, roughly chopped	60 mL
¼ cup	canned diced hot green chile peppers, drained (see tip, page 141)	60 mL
1 tbsp	cayenne pepper	15 mL
2 tsp	dried oregano	10 mL
2 tsp	kosher salt	10 mL
1½ tsp	freshly cracked black pepper	7 mL
1 tsp	dried thyme	5 mL
	Cold water	
2 lbs	trimmed boneless pork shoulder blade roast, chilled (see page 49)	1 kg
3 tbsp	apple cider vinegar	45 mL
4 to 5 feet	32/35 mm hog casing, soaked (see page 49)	120 to 150 cm

1. In blender, combine tomatillo, cilantro, parsley, garlic, chiles, cayenne, oregano, salt, black pepper and thyme. With the motor running, through the feed tube, gradually add enough cold water to form a smooth purée.

2. Cut pork into pieces small enough to fit in the throat of your grinder. Using the coarse grinder plate, grind pork into a large bowl or stand mixer bowl.

3. Add purée to the ground pork. Using your hands or the stand mixer paddle attachment, mix until seasonings are evenly distributed. Add water and mix until white strands appear in the mixture.

4. In a small skillet, over medium-high heat, sauté a small amount of the sausage mixture until no longer pink. Taste the sample, then adjust seasonings as desired.

5. Stuff sausage mixture into prepared casing as described on page 51. Twist into 8 links, each about 6 inches (15 cm) in length.

Health Facts

Like other leafy greens, cilantro is high in essential nutrients and antioxidant phytonutrients.

Tamale Sausages

If you're on the hunt for south-of-the-border flavor, look no further. The tamale is a traditional Mesoamerican food made of masa (a corn-based dough), meat, chiles and spices, cooked in a leaf wrapper. The caramelized onion adds a sweet flavor to these zesty sausages.

**MAKES
7 SAUSAGES**

Tips

To always have caramelized onion on hand, use your slow cooker on the weekend to make enough for the week. Fill the slow cooker three-quarters full with thinly sliced peeled onions. Evenly distribute 1 tsp (5 mL) olive oil per 1 cup (250 mL) onions and toss to coat. Cover and cook for 10 hours on Low.

To drain canned chile peppers, pour them into a strainer and let drain for 5 minutes, then push down on them with a paper towel.

Health Facts

The compound that makes chile peppers hot is capsaicin, which may have anticancer benefits and has been shown to raise the metabolic rate. It's also widely used as a topical anesthetic ointment for nerve pain and arthritis.

2 lbs	trimmed boneless pork shoulder blade roast, chilled (see page 49)	1 kg
¼ cup	canned diced green chile peppers (hot or mild), drained (see tip, at left)	60 mL
3 tbsp	finely chopped fresh cilantro	45 mL
¼ cup	yellow cornmeal	60 mL
2 tbsp	finely minced caramelized onion (see tip, at left)	30 mL
2 tsp	kosher salt	10 mL
2 tsp	garlic powder	10 mL
1½ tsp	grated lime zest	7 mL
1½ tsp	sweet paprika	7 mL
1½ tsp	ground cumin	7 mL
1 tsp	freshly cracked black pepper	5 mL
½ tsp	chipotle chile powder	2 mL
1 tbsp	hot pepper sauce	15 mL
¼ cup	water	60 mL
4 to 5 feet	32/35 mm hog casing, soaked (see page 49)	120 to 150 cm

1. Cut pork into pieces small enough to fit in the throat of your grinder. Using the coarse grinder plate, grind pork into a large bowl or stand mixer bowl.

2. Add chiles, cilantro, cornmeal, onion, salt, garlic powder, lime zest, paprika, cumin, black pepper, chile powder and hot pepper sauce to the ground pork. Using your hands or the stand mixer paddle attachment, mix until seasonings are evenly distributed. Add water and mix until white strands appear in the mixture and a handful of the mixture holds together.

3. In a small skillet, over medium-high heat, sauté a small amount of the sausage mixture until no longer pink. Taste the sample, then adjust seasonings as desired.

4. Stuff sausage mixture into prepared casing as described on page 51. Twist into 7 links, each about 6 inches (15 cm) in length.

Jamaican Jerk Sausages

Historians believe Jamaica's jerk cuisine to be West African in origin, although the word "jerk" most likely has its roots in Spanish. Jerk seasoning is a spice blend that is most often used as a rub for meats, traditionally pork and chicken. These days, jerk seasoning is also used to add a lively flavor to vegetables and even tofu, and it certainly gives a flavor boost to these delectable sausages!

MAKES 6 SAUSAGES

Tip

You can purchase jerk seasoning, or you can make your own. Here's a typical recipe that you can tweak to your preferences: ¼ cup (60 mL) packed light brown sugar, 1 tbsp (15 mL) ground allspice, 2 tsp (10 mL) salt, 1 tsp (5 mL) freshly ground black pepper, 1 tsp (5 mL) hot pepper flakes, ¼ tsp (1 mL) ground cinnamon, ¼ tsp (1 mL) ground cloves and ¼ tsp (1 mL) ground cumin. Store in a tightly sealed jar at room temperature for up to 1 year.

2 lbs	trimmed boneless pork shoulder blade roast, chilled (see page 49)	1 kg
2 tbsp	jerk seasoning spice blend (with salt)	30 mL
1 tbsp	garlic powder	15 mL
1½ tsp	grated orange zest	7 mL
1½ tsp	packed light brown sugar	7 mL
1 tsp	kosher salt	5 mL
1 tsp	freshly cracked black pepper	5 mL
¼ cup	water	60 mL
4 to 5 feet	32/35 mm hog casing, soaked (see page 49)	120 to 150 cm

1. Cut pork into pieces small enough to fit in the throat of your grinder. Using the coarse grinder plate, grind pork into a large bowl or stand mixer bowl.

2. Add jerk seasoning, garlic powder, orange zest, brown sugar, salt and pepper to the ground pork. Using your hands or the stand mixer paddle attachment, mix until seasonings are evenly distributed. Add water and mix until white strands appear in the mixture and a handful of the mixture holds together.

3. In a small skillet, over medium-high heat, sauté a small amount of the sausage mixture until no longer pink. Taste the sample, then adjust seasonings as desired.

4. Stuff sausage mixture into prepared casing as described on page 51. Twist into 6 links, each about 6 inches (15 cm) in length.

Health Facts

Orange zest contains potassium and riboflavin, as well as vitamin A in the form of the potent antioxidant beta-carotene. Some of its phytonutrients might alleviate indigestion, according to the University of Michigan Health System, which suggests simmering 1 to 2 grams of dried peel in 3 cups (750 mL) of water to make tea.

Beef Sausages

Beef has been one of the most popular meats for centuries, and is second only to pork as the favored meat for sausages. It is also often combined with pork for certain sausages, as with the Bockwurst, Weisswurst, Golabki Bras, Cabanossi and Meatloaf Sausages in this chapter.

With the exception of the Cabanossi (a dried smoked sausage) and the All-Beef Hot Dogs (which are smoked), all of the sausages in this chapter taste best if they are refrigerated for at least 1 day before they are cooked.

Cup o' Joe Morning Sausages

Nothing says "good morning" like a cup of joe — and a breakfast sausage, for that matter. This recipe combines two morning favorites for an unexpected and robust flavor that blends well with the aromatic seasonings, including rosemary and smoked paprika.

MAKES
MAKES 6 SAUSAGES

Tips

Sauerkraut is enjoying a resurgence in popularity thanks to the fermentation process used to make it — a process that creates probiotics. Buy it in bulk and freeze it in smaller quantities to preserve the probiotics and keep other spoiling microbes at bay.

How long to make your sausage links is really up to you, although we suggest 6 inches (15 cm) for this recipe. Keep in mind that this is a rough guideline, and that you may have to adjust the length up or down so that you don't end up with one link smaller than the rest.

2 lbs	85/15 beef brisket, chilled (see page 49)	1 kg
2 tsp	minced garlic	10 mL
1½ tsp	kosher salt	7 mL
1 tsp	finely minced fresh rosemary	5 mL
1 tsp	ground coffee	5 mL
1 tsp	ground cumin	5 mL
1 tsp	onion powder	5 mL
1 tsp	smoked paprika	5 mL
1 tsp	freshly cracked black pepper	5 mL
½ tsp	freshly cracked white pepper	2 mL
½ tsp	dry mustard	2 mL
½ cup	roughly chopped drained sauerkraut	125 mL
4 to 5 feet	32/35 mm hog casing, soaked (see page 49)	120 to 150 cm

1. Cut beef into pieces small enough to fit in the throat of your grinder. Using the coarse grinder plate, grind beef into a large bowl or stand mixer bowl.

2. Add garlic, salt, rosemary, coffee, cumin, onion powder, paprika, black pepper, white pepper and mustard to the ground beef. Using your hands or the stand mixer paddle attachment, mix until seasonings are evenly distributed. Add sauerkraut and mix until white strands appear in the mixture and a handful of the mixture holds together.

3. In a small skillet, over medium-high heat, sauté a small amount of the sausage mixture until no longer pink. Taste the sample, then adjust seasonings as desired.

4. Stuff sausage mixture into prepared casing as directed on page 51. Twist into 6 links, each about 6 inches (15 cm) in length.

Health Facts

Although relegated to the "avoid" food list for many years, coffee is taking its place among the superstars of the nutrition world. Numerous studies have pointed to its various health benefits. In 2015, researchers reported that regular coffee drinking was associated with a lower risk for developing diabetes. They theorized that the mechanism was coffee's content of anti-inflammatory compounds.

Corned Beef Bratwurst

Although it's a favorite on St. Patrick's Day in North America, the combination of corned beef and cabbage is probably not originally Irish. Food historians believe that colcannon is the true traditional Irish meal upon which corned beef and cabbage is based. This recipe combines colcannon's traditional elements — corned beef, potato, onion and cabbage — for delicious and unique sausages.

Tips

Cabbage freezes well. You can add the minced onion to chopped or shredded cabbage, then freeze in freezer bags for up to 3 months. Drain liquid before using.

If you use your hands to mix the ground meat, have a bowl of water nearby in which to dip your fingers. This will help keep them from getting too sticky.

Health Facts

Cabbage is one of the most widely consumed cruciferous vegetables. In addition to a high content of vitamins C and K, it contains an important phytochemical known as sulforaphane. Some studies have shown that sulforaphane may help prevent prostate and other types of cancer.

1	medium russet potato, peeled and diced	1
1 tsp	butter	5 mL
½ cup	finely chopped green cabbage	125 mL
2 tbsp	finely minced onion	30 mL
1½ lbs	corned beef	750 g
8 oz	85/15 boneless beef shoulder	250 g
1 tsp	kosher salt	5 mL
1 tsp	freshly cracked black pepper	5 mL
1 tsp	mustard seeds	5 mL
1 tsp	dried dillweed	5 mL
½ tsp	hot pepper flakes	2 mL
2 tbsp	water	30 mL
4 to 5 feet	32/35 mm hog casing, soaked (see page 49)	120 to 150 cm

1. Place potato in a small saucepan and cover with 1 inch (2.5 cm) of cold water. Bring to a boil over high heat. Reduce heat and simmer for about 10 minutes or until fork-tender. Drain and let cool completely.

2. Meanwhile, in a small skillet, melt butter over medium heat. Add cabbage and onion; cook, stirring, for about 10 minutes or until tender. Let cool completely.

3. Meanwhile, chill corned beef and beef shoulder as directed on page 50.

4. Cut corned beef and beef shoulder into pieces small enough to fit in the throat of your grinder. Using the coarse grinder plate, grind beef into a large bowl or stand mixer bowl.

5. Add potato, cabbage mixture, salt, black pepper, mustard seeds, dill and hot pepper flakes to the ground beef. Using your hands or the stand mixer paddle attachment, mix until seasonings are evenly distributed. Add water and mix until white strands appear in the mixture and a handful of the mixture holds together.

6. In a small skillet, over medium-high heat, sauté a small amount of the sausage mixture until no longer pink. Taste the sample, then adjust seasonings as desired.

7. Stuff sausage mixture into prepared casing as directed on page 51. Twist into 7 links, each about 6 inches (15 cm) in length.

Bockwurst

Bockwurst is traditionally made with a combination of meats, in contrast to its cousin, bratwurst. Although the German word *bock* means "goat," that's not the meat typically used. The most common combination is veal and pork, although a bockwurst in northern Germany uses fish. These sausages stick with tradition (at least within the same animal group) and add a nice blend of herbs and spices for intense flavor.

**MAKES
6 SAUSAGES**

Tips

Many cooks substitute green onions for chives, but they are completely different. Chives are considered an herb, and while they add an oniony flavor, they also add a hint of garlic. Dried chives don't have the same depth of flavor. If you freeze fresh chives, they will impart more flavor than dried.

If you decide to use table salt in place of kosher salt, use 1¼ tsp (6 mL), as table salt has a higher density.

1 lb	85/15 boneless beef shoulder, chilled (see page 49)	500 g
1 lb	trimmed boneless pork shoulder blade roast, chilled	500 g
2 tbsp	finely minced fresh parsley	30 mL
2 tbsp	finely minced fresh chives	30 mL
1½ tsp	kosher salt	7 mL
1 tsp	freshly ground white pepper	5 mL
1 tsp	sweet paprika	5 mL
¼ cup	water	60 mL
4 to 5 feet	32/35 mm hog casing, soaked (see page 49)	120 to 150 cm

1. Cut beef and pork into pieces small enough to fit in the throat of your grinder. Using the coarse grinder plate, grind meat into a large bowl or stand mixer bowl.

2. Add parsley, chives, salt, pepper and paprika to the ground meat. Using your hands or the stand mixer paddle attachment, mix until seasonings are evenly distributed. Add water and mix until white strands appear in the mixture and a handful of the mixture holds together.

3. In a small skillet, over medium-high heat, sauté a small amount of the sausage mixture until no longer pink. Taste the sample, then adjust seasonings as desired.

4. Stuff sausage mixture into prepared casing as directed on page 51. Twist into 6 links, each about 6 inches (15 cm) in length.

Health Facts

Chives are a member of the allium family, which also includes garlic, green onions, onions and leeks, all of which contain the same phytonutrients with health benefits such as helping to prevent cancers of the prostate, colon and stomach. They also contain the nutrient choline, which helps with sleep, muscle movement, learning and memory.

Weisswurst

Weisswurst is German for "white sausage." It comes by its characteristic color thanks to its content of cream, which also adds a smooth flavor. Weisswurst was traditionally a breakfast sausage, but you can enjoy it at any meal. Its flavors combine well with many side dishes and vegetables.

**MAKES
6 SAUSAGES**

Tip

A container of powdered egg white solids is useful to have on hand, as they make an excellent binding agent to hold other ingredients together. Unopened egg white solids can be stored at room temperature indefinitely, but refrigerate in an airtight container after opening.

1 lb	85/15 boneless beef shoulder, chilled (see page 49)	500 g
1 lb	trimmed boneless pork shoulder blade roast, chilled	500 g
¼ cup	finely minced onion	60 mL
1 tbsp	grated lemon zest	15 mL
2 tsp	powdered egg white solids	10 mL
1½ tsp	kosher salt	7 mL
1 tsp	freshly cracked black pepper	5 mL
¼ tsp	ground mace	1 mL
¼ tsp	ground ginger	1 mL
¼ cup	heavy or whipping (35%) cream	60 mL
2 tbsp	water	30 mL
4 to 5 feet	32/35 mm hog casing, soaked (see page 49)	120 to 150 cm

1. Cut beef and pork into pieces small enough to fit in the throat of your grinder. Using the coarse grinder plate, grind meat into a large bowl or stand mixer bowl.

2. Add onion, lemon zest, egg white solids, salt, pepper, mace and ginger to the ground meat. Using your hands or the stand mixer paddle attachment, mix until seasonings are evenly distributed. Add cream and water; mix until white strands appear in the mixture and a handful of the mixture holds together.

3. In a small skillet, over medium-high heat, sauté a small amount of the sausage mixture until no longer pink. Taste the sample, then adjust seasonings as desired.

4. Stuff sausage mixture into prepared casing as directed on page 51. Twist into 6 links, each about 6 inches (15 cm) in length.

Health Facts

Mace is the outer seed covering of the nutmeg fruit, from which nutmeg also comes. Mace has a more intense aroma than nutmeg and has been used in traditional medicines for centuries. Its phytonutrients aid in digestion and have antifungal and antidepressant activities. Two of mace's compounds, myristicin and elemicin, may have both soothing and stimulant effects on the brain.

Italian Corned Beef Sausages

The flavor of corned beef takes on an Italian flair with this recipe that combines many favorite spices and herbs from the sunny peninsula. An authentic version of Italian corned beef is known as *carne salada*, which translates as "meat salad." It is a specialty of the northern region of the country, where it's enjoyed raw, smoked or cooked drizzled with herbs and white wine.

MAKES 6 SAUSAGES

Tips

The best way to crush whole peppercorns to the exact texture you want is to use a mortar and pestle. You can achieve any texture, from finely ground to coarsely crushed to cracked, much more easily than with a peppermill, and it's easier to adjust as needed.

Rosemary is easy to grow indoors — it's very forgiving when you forget to water, and it doesn't mind the reduced sunlight in winter. Purchase a plant in the fall and transplant it to a large pot, as it can become large quite quickly. Place it in a spot with southeastern exposure and enjoy fresh rosemary throughout the year.

1½ lbs	corned beef	750 g
8 oz	85/15 boneless beef shoulder, chilled (see page 49)	250 g
2 tsp	coarsely crushed black peppercorns	10 mL
1 tsp	kosher salt	5 mL
1 tsp	finely minced fresh rosemary	5 mL
1 tsp	finely minced fresh sage	5 mL
1 tsp	finely minced fresh parsley	5 mL
⅛ tsp	ground bay leaf	0.5 mL
2 tsp	roasted garlic paste (see page 47)	10 mL
1 tbsp	white wine	15 mL
4 to 5 feet	32/35 mm hog casing, soaked (see page 49)	120 to 150 cm

1. Cut corned beef and beef shoulder into pieces small enough to fit in the throat of your grinder. Using the coarse grinder plate, grind beef into a large bowl or stand mixer bowl.

2. Add peppercorns, salt, rosemary, sage, parsley, bay leaf and garlic paste to the ground beef. Using your hands or the stand mixer paddle attachment, mix until seasonings are evenly distributed. Add wine and mix until white strands appear in the mixture and a handful of the mixture holds together.

3. In a small skillet, over medium-high heat, sauté a small amount of the sausage mixture until no longer pink. Taste the sample, then adjust seasonings as desired.

4. Stuff sausage mixture into prepared casing as directed on page 51. Twist into 6 links, each about 6 inches (15 cm) in length.

Health Facts

Everyone has heard about the health benefits of red wine, but white wine is also good for your heart. A 2009 study in the *Journal of Agricultural and Food Chemistry* compared the antioxidants in red wine and those in white wine. The results indicated that white wine's antioxidants were just as powerful at improving heart function and preventing artery blockage.

Steak Siciliano Sausages

Although there are many variations, steak Siciliano generally combines beef (usually steak) with tomatoes, garlic, grated cheese and traditional Italian herbs. These flavorful sausages bring the same elements together for a great centerpiece to a plate of pasta and marinara sauce. They will enliven any meal and please both the sophisticated diner and the picky eater.

**MAKES
7 SAUSAGES**

Tip

Although you can substitute Parmesan cheese, if you've never tried Parmigiano-Reggiano, it's worth splurging a bit. In Europe, the term "Parmigiano-Reggiano" can only be used on the label if the cheese is from specific Italian provinces. In North America, the term can be used if a cheese is deemed similar to Parmigiano-Reggiano. Cheese experts point to a unique flavor that cannot be duplicated.

2 lbs	85/15 boneless beef shoulder, chilled (see page 49)	1 kg
1 cup	diced seeded peeled plum (Roma) tomatoes	250 mL
¼ cup	finely chopped fresh basil	60 mL
¼ cup	freshly grated Parmigiano-Reggiano cheese	60 mL
1½ tsp	kosher salt	7 mL
1 tsp	freshly cracked black pepper	5 mL
1 tsp	onion powder	5 mL
1 tsp	dried oregano	5 mL
2 tsp	roasted garlic paste (see page 47)	10 mL
¼ cup	water	60 mL
2 tsp	olive oil	10 mL
4 to 5 feet	32/35 mm hog casing, soaked (see page 49)	120 to 150 cm

1. Cut beef into pieces small enough to fit in the throat of your grinder. Using the coarse grinder plate, grind beef into a large bowl or stand mixer bowl.

2. Add tomatoes, basil, cheese, salt, pepper, onion powder, oregano and garlic paste to the ground beef. Using your hands or the stand mixer paddle attachment, mix until seasonings are evenly distributed. Add water and oil; mix until white strands appear in the mixture and a handful of the mixture holds together.

3. In a small skillet, over medium-high heat, sauté a small amount of the sausage mixture until no longer pink. Taste the sample, then adjust seasonings as desired.

4. Stuff sausage mixture into prepared casing as directed on page 51. Twist into 7 links, each about 6 inches (15 cm) in length.

Health Facts

The high content of lycopene in tomatoes has been a topic of research for its potential role in preventing prostate cancer. A 2015 study also points to its ability to protect the heart and blood vessels, thanks to its antioxidant activity.

Minestrone Sausages

These fun and tasty sausages bring together the flavors of an Italian staple, minestrone.

Tips

Pesto is a handy substitute for fresh basil if a recipe also includes either Parmesan or Pecorino Romano cheese. It keeps in the refrigerator for up to 6 weeks, but you can freeze it in small portions. In this recipe, use 2 tsp (10 mL) pesto and add it with the tomato paste in step 4.

If you use your hands to mix the ground meat, have a bowl of water nearby in which to dip your fingers. This will help keep them from getting too sticky.

1 tbsp	olive oil	15 mL
¼ cup	finely minced onion	60 mL
¼ cup	finely diced celery	60 mL
2 tbsp	finely minced fresh basil	30 mL
2 lbs	85/15 boneless beef shoulder	1 kg
¼ cup	diced drained canned green beans	60 mL
¼ cup	roughly chopped rinsed drained canned cannellini (white kidney) beans	60 mL
¼ cup	freshly grated Parmesan cheese	60 mL
2 tsp	garlic powder	10 mL
1½ tsp	kosher salt	7 mL
1 tsp	freshly cracked black pepper	5 mL
1 tbsp	tomato paste	15 mL
¼ cup	ready-to-use beef broth	60 mL
4 to 5 feet	32/35 mm hog casing, soaked (see page 49)	120 to 150 cm

1. In a small skillet, heat oil over medium heat. Add onion, celery and basil; cook, stirring, for 10 minutes or until softened. Let cool completely.

2. Meanwhile, chill beef as directed on page 50.

3. Cut beef into pieces small enough to fit in the throat of your grinder. Using the coarse grinder plate, grind beef into a large bowl or stand mixer bowl.

4. Add onion mixture, green beans, cannellini beans, cheese, garlic powder, salt, pepper and tomato paste to the ground beef. Using your hands or the stand mixer paddle attachment, mix until seasonings are evenly distributed. Add broth and mix until white strands appear in the mixture and a handful of the mixture holds together.

5. In a small skillet, over medium-high heat, sauté a small amount of the sausage mixture until no longer pink. Taste the sample, then adjust seasonings as desired.

6. Stuff sausage mixture into prepared casing as directed on page 51. Twist into 7 links, each about 6 inches (15 cm) in length.

Health Facts

Cannellini beans, like other legumes, are high in several nutrients, especially soluble fiber. The fiber is most likely the beneficial component that helps lower blood cholesterol and glucose levels. Cannellini beans are also high in inositol hexaphosphate, which researchers say may reduce tumor development.

Polenta Sausages

The word "polenta" is derived from the Latin pollenta, for peeled barley. In rural regions, polenta is traditionally made by cooking cornmeal into a thick, spreadable mixture, spreading it on a large wooden board and topping it with tomato sauce, cheese, ground meat or sausage and sometimes mushrooms. The family would gather around the board and enjoy polenta as a communal dish. These sausages bring all these elements together, except for the wooden board.

MAKES 6 SAUSAGES

Tip

Mushrooms, especially portobellos, have a texture and umami taste that simulates meat. You can use chopped mushrooms to extend recipes containing ground beef and save significant calories while adding several phytonutrients.

Health Facts

In a 2009 Australian study, two foods, mushrooms and green tea, were associated with a lower risk for breast cancer. Unexpectedly, women who consumed both had an even lower risk, showing a possible synergism of benefit. Women who consumed mushrooms and green tea every day had one-fifth of the breast cancer risk compared to women who consumed neither.

1 tsp	olive oil	5 mL
½ cup	finely chopped portobello mushrooms	125 mL
2 lbs	85/15 boneless beef shoulder	1 kg
¼ cup	yellow cornmeal	60 mL
2 tbsp	finely minced fresh basil	30 mL
2 tbsp	freshly grated Parmesan cheese	30 mL
1 tbsp	finely minced sun-dried tomato (see tip, page 128)	15 mL
1½ tsp	kosher salt	7 mL
1 tsp	freshly cracked black pepper	5 mL
2 tbsp	tomato paste	30 mL
1 tbsp	roasted garlic paste (see page 47)	15 mL
¼ cup	water	60 mL
4 to 5 feet	32/35 mm hog casing, soaked (see page 49)	120 to 150 cm

1. In a skillet, heat oil over medium-high heat. Add mushrooms and cook, stirring, for about 8 minutes or until browned and tender. Let cool completely.

2. Meanwhile, chill beef as directed on page 50.

3. Cut beef into pieces small enough to fit in the throat of your grinder. Using the coarse grinder plate, grind beef into a large bowl or stand mixer bowl.

4. Add mushrooms, cornmeal, basil, cheese, sun-dried tomato, salt, pepper, tomato paste and garlic paste to the ground beef. Using your hands or the stand mixer paddle attachment, mix until seasonings are evenly distributed. Add water and mix until white strands appear in the mixture and a handful of the mixture holds together.

5. In a small skillet, over medium-high heat, sauté a small amount of the sausage mixture until no longer pink. Taste the sample, then adjust seasonings as desired.

6. Stuff sausage mixture into prepared casing as directed on page 51. Twist into 6 links, each about 6 inches (15 cm) in length.

Golabki Brats

Golabki is the traditional Polish rolled cabbage that many North Americans refer to as "pigs in a blanket." In these sausages, you'll find all the tasty ingredients of golabki: rice, cabbage, tomatoes and meat. Each sausage is a meal all by itself.

Tips

Many recipes call for canned tomatoes in a quantity that is smaller than the entire can. To store the leftover tomatoes for another recipe, pour them into an ice cube tray and freeze. Once frozen, transfer the cubes to a freezer bag. Determine the volume measurement of each cube and write that amount, along with the date, on the bag.

How long to make your sausage links is really up to you, although we suggest 6 inches (15 cm) for this recipe. Keep in mind that this is a rough guideline, and that you may have to adjust the length up or down so that you don't end up with one link smaller than the rest.

Health Facts

A 2015 analysis reported that people who ate garlic and onions, both members of the allium family, had a lower risk for head and neck cancers.

1 tbsp	butter	15 mL
2 cups	chopped green cabbage	500 mL
¼ cup	minced onion	60 mL
1½ lbs	85/15 boneless beef shoulder	750 g
8 oz	trimmed boneless pork shoulder blade roast	250 g
½ cup	drained canned tomatoes, with 2 tbsp (30 mL) juice reserved	125 mL
¼ cup	cooked white rice, cooled	60 mL
2 tsp	minced garlic	10 mL
1½ tsp	kosher salt	7 mL
1 tsp	freshly cracked black pepper	5 mL
1 tsp	finely minced fresh thyme	5 mL
1 tsp	finely minced fresh rosemary	5 mL
1 tsp	tomato paste	5 mL
2 tbsp	water	30 mL
4 to 5 feet	32/35 mm hog casing, soaked (see page 49)	120 to 150 cm

1. In a small skillet, melt butter over medium heat. Add cabbage and onion; cook, stirring, for about 10 minutes or until tender. Let cool completely.

2. Meanwhile, chill beef and pork as directed on page 50.

3. Cut beef and pork into pieces small enough to fit in the throat of your grinder. Using the coarse grinder plate, grind meat into a large bowl or stand mixer bowl.

4. Add cabbage mixture, tomatoes, rice, garlic, salt, pepper, thyme, rosemary and tomato paste to the ground meat. Using your hands or the stand mixer paddle attachment, mix until seasonings are evenly distributed. Add water and the reserved tomato juice; mix until white strands appear in the mixture and a handful of the mixture holds together.

5. In a small skillet, over medium-high heat, sauté a small amount of the sausage mixture until no longer pink. Taste the sample, then adjust seasonings as desired.

6. Stuff sausage mixture into prepared casing as directed on page 51. Twist into 8 links, each about 6 inches (15 cm) in length.

North African Sausages

North African cuisine shares common elements with countries across the Mediterranean Sea, but has also developed unique ingredients. One of these is harissa, a chile pepper paste usually containing roasted red peppers, serrano peppers, garlic, coriander, caraway and olive oil. The unique flavor and heat of the harissa in these sausages will add an exotic flair to any meal.

MAKES 6 SAUSAGES

Tips

If you decide to use table salt in place of kosher salt, use 1¼ tsp (6 mL), as table salt has a higher density.

You can buy harissa in many forms, but one of the most convenient is in a tube. With this product, you can easily squeeze out the amount you need directly into your measuring spoon or the mixing bowl.

2 lbs	85/15 boneless beef shoulder, chilled (see page 49)	1 kg
2 tbsp	finely minced garlic	30 mL
1½ tsp	kosher salt	7 mL
1 tsp	freshly cracked black pepper	5 mL
½ tsp	ground coriander	2 mL
½ tsp	ground caraway seeds	2 mL
½ tsp	curry powder	2 mL
½ tsp	ground allspice	2 mL
½ tsp	ground cumin	2 mL
1 tbsp	harissa	15 mL
¼ cup	water	60 mL
2 tbsp	olive oil	30 mL
4 to 5 feet	32/35 mm hog casing, soaked (see page 49)	120 to 150 cm

1. Cut beef into pieces small enough to fit in the throat of your grinder. Using the coarse grinder plate, grind beef into a large bowl or stand mixer bowl.

2. Add garlic, salt, pepper, coriander, caraway seeds, curry powder, allspice, cumin and harissa to the ground beef. Using your hands or the stand mixer paddle attachment, mix until seasonings are evenly distributed. Add water and oil; mix until white strands appear in the mixture and a handful of the mixture holds together.

3. In a small skillet, over medium-high heat, sauté a small amount of the sausage mixture until no longer pink. Taste the sample, then adjust seasonings as desired.

4. Stuff sausage mixture into prepared casing as directed on page 51. Twist into 6 links, each about 6 inches (15 cm) in length.

Health Facts

A 2015 study published in *PLoS One* reported on the possible antioxidant and antimicrobial effects of combining various herbs and spices. One of the most effective combinations was cumin and coriander. The authors stated that this combination showed potential as a "safe and effective natural antimicrobial and antioxidant."

Persian Beef Sausages

Persian cuisine is known for its reliance on heady aromatic spices and herbs. Another common thread is the use of dried fruits and nuts. This delicious sausage features many of the ingredients used in traditional Persian cooking, including dried apricots, a classic favorite throughout the Mediterranean.

**MAKES
6 SAUSAGES**

Tips

If you prefer a slightly sweeter taste to your sausage, substitute 3 tbsp (45 mL) pomegranate syrup (pomegranate molasses) for the juice and add 1 tbsp (15 mL) water.

If you use your hands to mix the ground meat, have a bowl of water nearby in which to dip your fingers. This will help keep them from getting too sticky.

How long to make your sausage links is really up to you, although we suggest 6 inches (15 cm) for this recipe. Keep in mind that this is a rough guideline, and that you may have to adjust the length up or down so that you don't end up with one link smaller than the rest.

1 tsp	olive oil	5 mL
¼ cup	finely minced onion	60 mL
2 tbsp	finely minced garlic	30 mL
½ tsp	ground turmeric	2 mL
½ tsp	ground cumin	2 mL
2 lbs	85/15 boneless beef shoulder	1 kg
¼ cup	finely chopped dried apricots	60 mL
1 tbsp	finely minced fresh mint	15 mL
1½ tsp	kosher salt	7 mL
1 tsp	freshly cracked black pepper	5 mL
¼ cup	unsweetened pomegranate juice	60 mL
4 to 5 feet	32/35 mm hog casing, soaked (see page 49)	120 to 150 cm

1. In a small skillet, heat oil over medium heat. Add onion and garlic; cook, stirring, for about 6 minutes or until softened. Stir in turmeric and cumin; cook, stirring, for 3 minutes. Let cool completely.

2. Meanwhile, chill beef as directed on page 50.

3. Cut beef into pieces small enough to fit in the throat of your grinder. Using the coarse grinder plate, grind beef into a large bowl or stand mixer bowl.

4. Add onion mixture, apricots, mint, salt and pepper to the ground beef. Using your hands or the stand mixer paddle attachment, mix until seasonings are evenly distributed. Add pomegranate juice and mix until white strands appear in the mixture and a handful of the mixture holds together.

5. In a small skillet, over medium-high heat, sauté a small amount of the sausage mixture until no longer pink. Taste the sample, then adjust seasonings as desired.

6. Stuff sausage mixture into prepared casing as directed on page 51. Twist into 6 links, each about 6 inches (15 cm) in length.

Health Facts

There are around 20 different varieties of mint, including the familiar peppermint and spearmint. Mint is widely used in numerous products, from tea to toothpaste, and studies show that has one of the highest levels of antioxidants of any plant.

Polo Kadu Sausages

Iran's cuisine has been influenced by its neighbors and its historical conquests throughout the Middle East and Asia. These sausages bring together many flavors of Persian cuisine. The Farsi words for rice and squash — *polo* and *kadu*, respectively — give them their name.

**MAKES
8 SAUSAGES**

Tip

Another way to cook squash is in the microwave. Scrub the squash, remove the stem, cut the squash in half and scoop out the seeds. Place the two halves, cut side down, in a shallow glass dish with 1 tbsp (15 mL) water. Cover and microwave on High for about 18 minutes (depending on squash size and microwave wattage) or until tender. Let cool completely, then peel and dice for the recipe. Skip step 1 and add the diced squash as directed in step 2.

Health Facts

Cardamom has been used throughout history to treat digestive problems, respiratory infections and sore throat. A 2015 study showed that it helped prevent stomach cancer induced in mice.

1 cup	diced butternut squash	250 mL
2 tbsp	olive oil	30 mL
½ cup	finely minced onion	125 mL
2 lbs	85/15 boneless beef shoulder	1 kg
½ cup	cooked basmati rice, cooled	125 mL
1½ tsp	kosher salt	7 mL
1 tsp	freshly cracked black pepper	5 mL
1 tsp	ground cardamom	5 mL
1 tsp	ground turmeric	5 mL
1 tsp	ground cumin	5 mL
2 tsp	liquid honey	10 mL
2 tbsp	water	30 mL
4 to 5 feet	32/35 mm hog casing, soaked (see page 49)	120 to 150 cm

1. In a small saucepan of boiling water, boil squash for about 20 minutes or until just tender.

2. In a large skillet, heat oil over medium heat. Add onion and cook, stirring, for 6 minutes. Stir in parboiled squash and cook, stirring, for 2 minutes or until onion and squash are tender. Let cool completely.

3. Meanwhile, chill beef as directed on page 50.

4. Cut beef into pieces small enough to fit in the throat of your grinder. Using the coarse grinder plate, grind beef into a large bowl or stand mixer bowl.

5. Add squash mixture, rice, salt, pepper, cardamom, turmeric, cumin and honey to the ground beef. Using your hands or the stand mixer paddle attachment, mix until seasonings are evenly distributed. Add water and mix until white strands appear in the mixture and a handful of the mixture holds together.

6. In a small skillet, over medium-high heat, sauté a small amount of the sausage mixture until no longer pink. Taste the sample, then adjust seasonings as desired.

7. Stuff sausage mixture into prepared casing as directed on page 51. Twist into 8 links, each about 6 inches (15 cm) in length.

Cambodian Sausages

Some culinary enthusiasts describe Cambodian cuisine as a palette of contrasts: sweet and bitter, salty and sour, raw and cooked. It shares many staple foods, spices and seasonings with its Southeast Asian neighbors. There is also a French influence from its history as a French colony. These sausages incorporate many of these elements, for a traditional Cambodian flavor.

**MAKES
6 SAUSAGES**

Tip

Galangal (also called galanga) is a root similar to ginger, but hard and woody. Its flavor is different from that of ginger, with a strong citrus and pine flavor. You can purchase it fresh at Asian markets or online. You can mince, sliver or grind it. Minced and slivered galangal will add a more intense flavor to recipes. To mince it for this recipe, first cut it into splinters, then finely mince it.

2 lbs	85/15 boneless beef shoulder, chilled (see page 49)	1 kg
½ cup	cooked long-grain white rice, cooled	125 mL
2 tbsp	finely minced garlic	30 mL
1 tbsp	finely minced galangal	15 mL
1 tbsp	granulated sugar	15 mL
1½ tsp	kosher salt	7 mL
1 tsp	freshly cracked black pepper	5 mL
¼ cup	red wine	60 mL
4 to 5 feet	32/35 mm hog casing, soaked (see page 49)	120 to 150 cm

1. Cut beef into pieces small enough to fit in the throat of your grinder. Using the coarse grinder plate, grind beef into a large bowl or stand mixer bowl.

2. Add rice, garlic, galangal, sugar, salt and pepper to the ground beef. Using your hands or the stand mixer paddle attachment, mix until seasonings are evenly distributed. Add wine and mix until white strands appear in the mixture and a handful of the mixture holds together.

3. In a small skillet, over medium-high heat, sauté a small amount of the sausage mixture until no longer pink. Taste the sample, then adjust seasonings as desired.

4. Stuff sausage mixture into prepared casing as directed on page 51. Twist into 6 links, each about 6 inches (15 cm) in length

Health Facts

Galangal is used in several traditional Asian systems of medicine, most often for digestive ailments. Researchers have found that it contains key phytonutrients that function as antioxidants and anti-inflammatory agents, including eugenol and gingerol.

Coney Dogs

While most people think of New York as the birthplace of the Coney dog, its origins actually lie in Detroit, Michigan. A Greek immigrant named Gust Keros opened American Coney Island in 1917 in Detroit, and the Coney dog was born. The New York version is the Coney Island hot dog, which did indeed originate on Coney Island in that state. These fresh sausages bring the flavors of that tradition to the table.

MAKES 6 SAUSAGES

Tip

Any type of prepared mustard will work in this recipe. Use your favorite or try experimenting with specialty varieties to make subtle changes in the flavor of this tasty sausage. One that works especially well is a honey chipotle mustard (although most of our taste panel preferred a spicy brown, or deli, mustard).

2 lbs	85/15 boneless beef shoulder, chilled (see page 49)	1 kg
¼ cup	finely minced onion	60 mL
1½ tsp	kosher salt	7 mL
1 tsp	freshly cracked black pepper	5 mL
1 tsp	chili powder	5 mL
½ tsp	sweet paprika	2 mL
1 tbsp	prepared mustard	15 mL
¼ cup	water	60 mL
4 to 5 feet	32/35 mm hog casing, soaked (see page 49)	120 to 150 cm

1. Cut beef into pieces small enough to fit in the throat of your grinder. Using the coarse grinder plate, grind beef into a large bowl or stand mixer bowl.

2. Add onion, salt, pepper, chili powder, paprika and mustard to the ground beef. Using your hands or the stand mixer paddle attachment, mix until seasonings are evenly distributed. Add water and mix until white strands appear in the mixture and a handful of the mixture holds together.

3. In a small skillet, over medium-high heat, sauté a small amount of the sausage mixture until no longer pink. Taste the sample, then adjust seasonings as desired.

4. Stuff sausage mixture into prepared casing as directed on page 51. Twist into 6 links, each about 6 inches (15 cm) in length.

Health Facts

In addition to providing essential nutrients, vitamins C and B_6, potassium and manganese, onions contain the flavonoid compound quercetin. Quercetin is an antioxidant that helps prevent several chronic diseases, and a 2015 study in rats reported that the compound was effective as an antidepressant.

All-Beef Hot Dogs

While many North Americans think of the hot dog as one of their own traditional foods, its roots are traced to the year 1487 in Frankfurt, Germany, which feted this sausage in 1987, on its 500th birthday. German immigrants to the United States in the 1800s brought their traditional frankfurter with them, and the North American hot dog is a direct descendant. There have been a few tweaks to the recipe, one of which is an all-beef version.

**MAKES
8 SAUSAGES**

Tips

For even better flavor, buy whole nutmeg and grate it yourself. Whole nutmeg maintains its flavor for up to 9 years, while ground nutmeg remains aromatic and flavorful for only a year.

To press minced garlic into paste, press a chef's knife down with both hands and pull it toward you across the garlic. Repeat the motion until you achieve a paste-like consistency.

- Large bowl, chilled in the refrigerator for 30 minutes
- Food processor, bowl chilled in the refrigerator for 30 minutes
- Meat thermometer
- Smoker

2 lbs	85/15 boneless beef shoulder, chilled (see page 49)	1 kg
1½ tsp	kosher salt	7 mL
1 tsp	freshly cracked black pepper	5 mL
1 tsp	sweet paprika	5 mL
1 tsp	dry mustard	5 mL
¼ tsp	ground mace	1 mL
¼ tsp	ground nutmeg	1 mL
¼ tsp	ground marjoram	1 mL
1	large egg white	1
2	cloves garlic, minced and pressed into paste (see tip, at left)	2
2 tbsp	cold water	30 mL
2 tbsp	crushed ice	30 mL
4 to 5 feet	24/26 mm sheep casing, soaked (see page 49)	120 to 150 cm

1. Cut beef into pieces small enough to fit in the throat of your grinder. Using the fine grinder plate, grind beef into chilled large bowl.

2. Transfer ground beef to chilled food processor bowl and add salt, pepper, paprika, mustard, mace, nutmeg, marjoram and egg white. With the motor running, through the feed tube, gradually add puréed garlic, cold water and ice. Continue processing the mixture, carefully monitoring the temperature. As the mixture gets warmer, it will begin to appear pasty, indicating that it is emulsified. When it reaches 57°F (14°C), the mixture should be a uniform consistency and you should stop processing. The mixture must not exceed 57°F (14°C) or the emulsion will break down.

You'll get the best results with 24/26 mm sheep casing in this recipe, but if you cannot find it, 32/35 mm hog casing will work just fine, though your hot dogs will be more sausage-shaped and you'll end up with 6 links instead of 8.

3. In a small skillet, over medium-high heat, sauté a small amount of the sausage mixture until juices run clear. Taste the sample, then adjust seasonings as desired.

4. Stuff sausage mixture into prepared casing as directed on page 51. Twist into 8 links, each about 6 inches (15 cm) in length. Let dry at room temperature for 20 to 30 minutes or until casings have a slightly tacky feel.

5. Meanwhile, prepare a fire in your smoker. Smoke sausages at 170°F to 180°F (77°C to 82°C) for 2 to 3 hours or until a meat thermometer inserted in the center of a sausage link registers 160°F (71°C). Let cool completely, then refrigerate.

Health Facts

Nutmeg is used in traditional Chinese and Indian medicines to treat ailments of the nervous and digestive systems. It contains the phytonutrient eugenol, which was shown, in a 2014 study in mice, to help prevent fatty liver.

Loaded Dogs

Imagine this: as you bite into a hot dog loaded with all your favorite toppings, savoring the wonderful meld of flavors, gobs of mustard squirt out the end and down your shirt. It's a common experience. By combining the toppings into one flavorful fresh sausage, this recipe has all of the taste you'd enjoy at a summer baseball game, but none of the mess.

**MAKES
6 SAUSAGES**

Tip

Everyone's idea of the perfect hot dog toppings is different. You can easily adjust the ingredients to match your preference. For example, you can increase the amount of dry mustard and/ or relish (up to double the amount of each). You can even add up to ¼ cup (60 mL) of any other favorite toppings.

2 lbs	85/15 boneless beef shoulder, chilled (see page 49)	1 kg
¼ cup	finely minced onion	60 mL
2 tsp	garlic powder	10 mL
1½ tsp	kosher salt	7 mL
1 tsp	freshly cracked black pepper	5 mL
1 tsp	sweet smoked paprika	5 mL
1 tsp	dry mustard	5 mL
2 tbsp	pickle relish	30 mL
2 tbsp	ketchup	30 mL
¼ cup	water	60 mL
4 to 5 feet	32/35 mm hog casing, soaked (see page 49)	120 to 150 cm

1. Cut beef into pieces small enough to fit in the throat of your grinder. Using the coarse grinder plate, grind beef into a large bowl or stand mixer bowl.

2. Add onion, garlic powder, salt, pepper, paprika, mustard, relish and ketchup to the ground beef. Using your hands or the stand mixer paddle attachment, mix until seasonings are evenly distributed. Add water and mix until white strands appear in the mixture and a handful of the mixture holds together.

3. In a small skillet, over medium-high heat, sauté a small amount of the sausage mixture until no longer pink. Taste the sample, then adjust seasonings as desired.

4. Stuff sausage mixture into prepared casing as directed on page 51. Twist into 6 links, each about 6 inches (15 cm) in length.

Health Facts

Dry mustard is made by grinding mustard seeds and therefore contains the same phytonutrients found in the whole seeds, most notably the sulfur-based glucosinolates, which are linked to cancer prevention.

Philly Steak and Cheese Sausages

The history of the Philly cheesesteak sandwich is full of interesting conjecture. One theory holds that Pat Olivieri, of Pat's King of Steaks Restaurant in the Italian immigrant section of South Philadelphia, created it in 1930 and added the cheese years later. The controversial history was even the subject of a National Public Radio broadcast in 2000. Whatever its origins, it remains a favorite in all its different recipe incarnations, including these flavorful sausages.

MAKES 7 SAUSAGES

Tip

Just as you can make caramelized onions in a large batch to store for use in several recipes, you can also make a large batch of a caramelized onion and pepper combination. Use 2 tbsp (30 mL) oil, 2 cups (500 mL) each onion and green pepper, and 1 cup (250 mL) red pepper and follow the instructions in step 1, using a large skillet and working in batches as necessary. If you don't use the combination as often as the onion alone, you can freeze it for up to 4 months. Use about ⅓ cup (75 mL) of the caramelized vegetable mixture in this recipe.

1 tsp	vegetable oil	5 mL
¼ cup	finely minced fresh onion	60 mL
¼ cup	finely minced green bell pepper	60 mL
2 tbsp	finely minced red bell pepper	30 mL
2 lbs	85/15 beef brisket	1 kg
½ cup	shredded Cheddar cheese	125 mL
1 tbsp	garlic powder	15 mL
1½ tsp	kosher salt	7 mL
1 tsp	freshly cracked black pepper	5 mL
¼ cup	water	60 mL
4 to 5 feet	32/35 mm hog casing, soaked (see page 49)	120 to 150 cm

1. In a small skillet, heat oil over medium heat. Add onion, green pepper and red pepper; cook, stirring, for about 8 minutes or until lightly caramelized. Let cool completely.

2. Meanwhile, chill beef as directed on page 50.

3. Cut beef into pieces small enough to fit in the throat of your grinder. Using the coarse grinder plate, grind beef into a large bowl or stand mixer bowl.

4. Add onion mixture, cheese, garlic powder, salt and pepper to the ground beef. Using your hands or the stand mixer paddle attachment, mix until seasonings are evenly distributed. Add water and mix until white strands appear in the mixture and a handful of the mixture holds together.

5. In a small skillet, over medium-high heat, sauté a small amount of the sausage mixture until no longer pink. Taste the sample, then adjust seasonings as desired.

6. Stuff sausage mixture into prepared casing as directed on page 51. Twist into 7 links, each about 6 inches (15 cm) in length.

Health Facts

Bell peppers are loaded with essential nutrients and phytonutrients. All varieties are good sources of vitamins C and A, although red pepper is significantly higher in both. In addition to beta-carotene, which the body converts to vitamin A, red peppers also contain lycopene, another carotenoid that is one of the most potent antioxidants.

Salisbury Steak Sausages

The Salisbury steak is attributed to a 19th-century American, Dr. James H. Salisbury, who promoted a high-protein diet. It lost its connection to a "health prescription" in the 20th century and became known as a "glorified hamburger steak," which continues to be a popular dinner entrée. These tasty sausages bring together all the traditional ingredients of a true American favorite.

MAKES 7 SAUSAGES

Tips

You can swap in your usual dry bread crumbs for the panko, though panko is more coarsely ground.

If you use your hands to mix the ground meat, have a bowl of water nearby in which to dip your fingers. This will help keep them from getting too sticky.

Health Facts

People tend to think of mushrooms as a vegetable, but they are actually fungi. They're high in the nutrients folate, niacin and zinc. They also contain lectins, which several studies have shown may help prevent cancer.

1 tsp	olive oil	5 mL
½ cup	finely chopped mushrooms	125 mL
2 lbs	85/15 boneless beef shoulder	1 kg
½ cup	panko (Japanese bread crumbs)	125 mL
2 tbsp	finely minced onion	30 mL
1 tbsp	finely chopped fresh parsley	15 mL
1 tsp	finely chopped fresh rosemary	5 mL
2 tsp	onion powder	10 mL
2 tsp	freshly cracked black pepper	10 mL
1½ tsp	kosher salt	7 mL
1 tsp	sweet paprika	5 mL
1 tsp	dry mustard	5 mL
2	large eggs, beaten	2
2 tbsp	ketchup	30 mL
1 tsp	Worcestershire sauce	5 mL
2 tbsp	water	30 mL
4 to 5 feet	32/35 mm hog casing, soaked (see page 49)	120 to 150 cm

1. In a small skillet, heat oil over medium-high heat. Add mushrooms and cook, stirring, for about 8 minutes or until browned and tender. Let cool completely.

2. Meanwhile, chill beef as directed on page 50.

3. Cut beef into pieces small enough to fit in the throat of your grinder. Using the coarse grinder plate, grind beef into a large bowl or stand mixer bowl.

4. Add panko, mushrooms, onion, parsley, rosemary, onion powder, pepper, salt, paprika, mustard, eggs, ketchup and Worcestershire sauce to the ground beef. Using your hands or the stand mixer paddle attachment, mix until seasonings are evenly distributed. Add water and mix until white strands appear in the mixture and a handful of the mixture holds together.

5. In a small skillet, over medium-high heat, sauté a small amount of the sausage mixture until no longer pink. Taste the sample, then adjust seasonings as desired.

6 Stuff sausage mixture into prepared casing as directed on page 51. Twist into 7 links, each about 6 inches (15 cm) in length.

Cheeseburger Sausages

The cheeseburger, virtually a staple food item for some people, is often credited to Lionel Sternberger. A story in the *Los Angeles Times* claimed that Lionel was a short-order cook in his father's Pasadena restaurant in the 1920s and, on a whim, added a slice of cheese to a burger, giving birth to an American classic. With all of the traditional ingredients of the classic cheeseburger, these sausages are sure to become a new favorite.

Tip

To complete the cheeseburger experience, top this sausage with shredded lettuce or slaw on your favorite bun. It's a complete meal, including all the condiments.

Health Facts

Like other preserved tomato products, ketchup is an excellent source of the carotenoid lycopene, a powerful antioxidant. Studies of lycopene show a protective effect against prostate cancer. Ketchup is a particularly good source of lycopene because of the concentration of the tomatoes and because the high processing temperature makes the lycopene more absorbable in the intestinal tract.

1 tsp	onion flakes	5 mL
1 tbsp	warm water	15 mL
2 lbs	85/15 boneless beef shoulder, chilled (see page 49)	1 kg
½ cup	shredded Cheddar cheese	125 mL
¼ cup	finely diced seeded tomato	60 mL
2 tbsp	finely minced onion	30 mL
1½ tsp	kosher salt	7 mL
1 tsp	freshly cracked black pepper	5 mL
2 tbsp	ketchup	30 mL
1 tbsp	prepared mustard	15 mL
2 tsp	Worcestershire sauce	10 mL
4 to 5 feet	32/35 mm hog casing, soaked (see page 49)	120 to 150 cm

1. In a small bowl, combine onion flakes and warm water. Let stand for about 20 minutes or until softened.

2. Meanwhile, cut beef into pieces small enough to fit in the throat of your grinder. Using the coarse grinder plate, grind beef into a large bowl or stand mixer bowl.

3. Add cheese, tomato, minced onion, salt, pepper, ketchup, mustard, Worcestershire sauce and onion flakes mixture to the ground beef. Using your hands or the stand mixer paddle attachment, mix until seasonings are evenly distributed, white strands appear in the mixture and a handful of the mixture holds together.

4. In a small skillet, over medium-high heat, sauté a small amount of the sausage mixture until no longer pink. Taste the sample, then adjust seasonings as desired.

5. Stuff sausage mixture into prepared casing as directed on page 51. Twist into 7 links, each about 6 inches (15 cm) in length.

Meatloaf Sausages

The combination of ground meat with bread and flavorings is a time-honored way to make meat "go further." The modern meatloaf got its start in the 1800s, when the Industrial Revolution made ground meat an available and economical product. These delicious sausages, which bring together all of the classic meatloaf ingredients, will make you forget every bad meatloaf joke you've ever heard.

**MAKES
7 SAUSAGES**

Tip

The sautéed onion, celery and carrot combination makes a great recipe ingredient. Make a large batch starting with 3 tbsp (45 mL) butter, 4 cups (1 L) onion and ½ cup (125 mL) each carrot and celery. Freeze the mixture in commonly used portion sizes for up to 4 months. Use 3 tbsp (45 mL) of the mixture in this recipe.

1 tsp	butter	5 mL
¼ cup	finely minced onion	60 mL
2 tsp	finely diced celery	10 mL
2 tsp	finely diced carrot	10 mL
1 lb	85/15 boneless beef shoulder	500 g
1 lb	trimmed boneless pork shoulder blade roast	500 g
½ cup	dry bread crumbs	125 mL
1½ tsp	kosher salt	7 mL
1 tsp	freshly cracked black pepper	5 mL
1 tsp	finely minced fresh rosemary	5 mL
1 tsp	finely minced fresh thyme	5 mL
1 tsp	garlic powder	5 mL
2	large eggs, beaten	2
2 tsp	Worcestershire sauce	10 mL
2 tsp	chili sauce	10 mL
1 tsp	spicy brown (deli) mustard	5 mL
¼ cup	water	60 mL
4 to 5 feet	32/35 mm hog casing, soaked (see page 49)	120 to 150 cm

1. In a small skillet, melt butter over medium heat. Add onion, celery and carrot; cook, stirring, for about 6 minutes or until tender. Let cool completely.

2. Meanwhile, chill beef and pork as directed on page 50.

3. Cut beef and pork into pieces small enough to fit in the throat of your grinder. Using the coarse grinder plate, grind meat into a large bowl or stand mixer bowl.

4. Add onion mixture, bread crumbs, salt, pepper, rosemary, thyme, garlic powder, eggs, Worcestershire sauce, chili sauce and mustard to the ground meat. Using your hands or the stand mixer paddle attachment, mix until seasonings are evenly distributed. Add water and mix until white strands appear in the mixture and a handful of the mixture holds together.

How long to make your sausage links is really up to you, although we suggest 6 inches (15 cm) for this recipe. Keep in mind that this is a rough guideline, and that you may have to adjust the length up or down so that you don't end up with one link smaller than the rest.

5. In a small skillet, over medium-high heat, sauté a small amount of the sausage mixture until no longer pink. Taste the sample, then adjust seasonings as desired.

6. Stuff sausage mixture into prepared casing as directed on page 51. Twist into 7 links, each about 6 inches (15 cm) in length.

Health Facts

A 2015 study of a compound in onions — allium cepa agglutinin (ACA) — reported that it stimulated a specific type of immune response important for fighting infection. The authors noted that, although ACA is present in low amounts, it contributes to the immune-boosting power of onions "since considerable amounts are consumed on a daily basis universally."

Sweet 'n' Neat Joe Sausages

The inspiration for these sausages is the sloppy joe, an American classic. The first print citation for the sloppy joe is from 1935, and food experts believe "Joe" is a stand-in for the average guy on the street, rather than a historical figure. The "sloppy" moniker comes from the tendency for the sauce to drip off the bun. Since everything is contained in a tidy casing here, though, it becomes a "neat joe."

MAKES 7 SAUSAGES

Tip

Crystallization is a natural occurrence in liquid honey and doesn't affect the quality. To reliquefy, place the jar in a saucepan filled with cold water to reach the level of honey in the jar. Heat over medium-high heat until the water reaches 95°F to 104°F (35°C to 40°C). Turn off heat, remove jar lid and let stand for 30 minutes, stirring occasionally.

Health Facts

Honey has long been known to be an effective antibacterial, but a recent study suggests it may also help fight cancer. When researchers combined honey with ginger and used the mix against a line of colon cancer cells, they observed a reduction in cancer cell growth.

2 lbs	85/15 boneless beef shoulder, chilled (see page 49)	1 kg
½ cup	finely chopped green bell pepper	125 mL
¼ cup	finely chopped red bell pepper	60 mL
¼ cup	drained canned diced tomatoes, with 1 tsp (5 mL) juice reserved	60 mL
2 tsp	packed brown sugar	10 mL
2 tsp	sweet paprika	10 mL
2 tsp	freshly cracked black pepper	10 mL
1½ tsp	kosher salt	7 mL
1 tsp	onion powder	5 mL
1 tsp	chili powder	5 mL
½ tsp	ground cumin	2 mL
1 tbsp	liquid honey	15 mL
1 tsp	water	5 mL
4 to 5 feet	32/35 mm hog casing, soaked (see page 49)	120 to 150 cm

1. Cut beef into pieces small enough to fit in the throat of your grinder. Using the coarse grinder plate, grind beef into a large bowl or stand mixer bowl.

2. Add green pepper, red pepper, tomatoes, brown sugar, paprika, pepper, salt, onion powder, chili powder and cumin to the ground beef. Using your hands or the stand mixer paddle attachment, mix until seasonings are evenly distributed. Add honey, water and the reserved tomato juice; mix until white strands appear in the mixture and a handful of the mixture holds together.

3. In a small skillet, over medium-high heat, sauté a small amount of the sausage mixture until no longer pink. Taste the sample, then adjust seasonings as desired.

4. Stuff sausage mixture into prepared casing as directed on page 51. Twist into 7 links, each about 6 inches (15 cm) in length.

Tex-Mex Sausages

Tex-Mex cuisine appears to date back hundreds of years, to when Spanish and Mexican cuisines first combined with British cuisine. The first use of the term "Tex-Mex" in print was in the 1940s, and Tex-Mex restaurants soon appeared throughout the southwestern United States. These flavorful sausages include many ingredients common to Tex-Mex recipes, with a few new twists.

MAKES 7 SAUSAGES

Tips

Crumbled queso blanco can be used in place of the queso fresco in this recipe; however, there is a difference: queso fresco is made with an enzyme that curdles the milk, whereas queso blanco is made from milk curdled with an acid, such as lemon juice. Both can be frozen without affecting texture.

If you use your hands to mix the ground meat, have a bowl of water nearby in which to dip your fingers. This will help keep them from getting too sticky.

Health Facts

A 2015 review of capsaicin, an active ingredient in hot peppers, reported several health benefits, including anticancer, antioxidant and anti-inflammatory activities. It was also shown to help lower blood cholesterol and stimulate digestion to help prevent and heal stomach ulcers.

2 lbs	85/15 beef brisket, chilled (see page 49)	1 kg
1 cup	crumbled queso fresco	250 mL
2 tsp	minced canned chipotle peppers	10 mL
1 tsp	finely minced drained pickled jalapeño pepper	5 mL
2 tsp	ground cumin	10 mL
2 tsp	chili powder	10 mL
2 tsp	kosher salt	10 mL
1 tsp	freshly cracked black pepper	5 mL
1 tsp	garlic powder	5 mL
½ tsp	onion powder	2 mL
½ tsp	dried thyme	2 mL
½ tsp	ground coriander	2 mL
2 tbsp	water	30 mL
4 to 5 feet	32/35 mm hog casing, soaked (see page 49)	120 to 150 cm

1. Cut beef into pieces small enough to fit in the throat of your grinder. Using the coarse grinder plate, grind beef into a large bowl or stand mixer bowl.

2. Add queso fresco, chipotles, jalapeño, cumin, chili powder, salt, pepper, garlic powder, onion powder, thyme and coriander to the ground beef. Using your hands or the stand mixer paddle attachment, mix until seasonings are evenly distributed. Add water and mix until white strands appear in the mixture and a handful of the mixture holds together.

3. In a small skillet, over medium-high heat, sauté a small amount of the sausage mixture until no longer pink. Taste the sample, then adjust seasonings as desired.

4. Stuff sausage mixture into prepared casing as directed on page 51. Twist into 7 links, each about 6 inches (15 cm) in length.

Cabanossi

Cabanossi is a dry-fermented smoked sausage that contains beef and pork, though it's sometimes made with poultry, such as duck. It's often described as mild salami.

Tips

The traditional Polish version of this sausage, *kabanosy*, uses pork alone. If you enjoy this sausage, try making it that way, too.

Although the narrow diameter of the sheep casing is more traditional, this recipe will also work with 32/35 mm hog casing.

Health Facts

Many European cuisines use caraway seeds, and use of caraway as a medicine dates far back in history. Of its many phytonutrients, two compounds, thujone and carvone, have significant antibacterial properties. Carvone has also demonstrated anticancer activity.

- Smoker
- Meat thermometer
- Drying chamber

1 lb	85/15 boneless beef shoulder, chilled (see page 49)	500 g
1 lb	trimmed boneless pork shoulder blade roast, chilled	500 g
1½ tsp	kosher salt	7 mL
1 tsp	freshly cracked black pepper	5 mL
½ tsp	ground caraway seeds	2 mL
½ tsp	ground nutmeg	2 mL
½ tsp	ground coriander	2 mL
¼ tsp	cure #1 curing salts	1 mL
¼ tsp	granulated sugar	1 mL
¼ cup	water	60 mL
4 to 5 feet	22/22 mm sheep casing, soaked (see page 49)	120 to 150 cm

1. Cut beef and pork into pieces small enough to fit in the throat of your grinder. Using the coarse grinder plate, grind meat into a large bowl or stand mixer bowl.

2. Add salt, pepper, caraway seeds, nutmeg, coriander, curing salts and sugar to the ground meat. Using your hands or the stand mixer paddle attachment, mix until seasonings are evenly distributed. Add water and mix until white strands appear and a handful of the mixture holds together.

3. In a small skillet, over medium-high heat, sauté a small amount of the sausage mixture until juices run clear. Taste the sample, then adjust seasonings as desired.

4. Stuff sausage mixture into prepared casing as described on page 51, starting a new strand every 18 inches (45 cm). Twist each strand into three 6-inch (15 cm) links. Lay sausage strands flat and prick generously to remove air bubbles. Let dry at room temperature for 20 to 30 minutes or until casings have a slightly tacky feel.

5. Meanwhile, prepare a fire in your smoker. Smoke sausages at 170°F to 180°F (77°C to 82°C) for about 3 hours or until a meat thermometer inserted in the center of a sausage link registers 160°F (71°C).

6. Weigh a sausage strand and document its weight. Hang sausage strands in your drying chamber until the strand you weighed has lost 30% of its original weight.

Lamb Sausages

Sheep were among the first animals to be domesticated, likely in Turkey and Iran, and their meat provides high-quality protein. The meat is considered lamb when the sheep is under a year old; after that, it's mutton. Although lamb is considered more desirable by many cultures, some have a preference for mutton. From a culinary standpoint, there are two types of lamb: lamb that is still fed its mother's milk and lamb between 4 and 12 months old. In addition to a tougher texture, which is not significant for sausage making, mutton is higher in fat and has a stronger flavor.

All of the sausages in this chapter taste best if they are refrigerated for at least 1 day before they are cooked.

Traditional Lamb Sausages

This mild sausage is a traditional recipe for those who love lamb and don't want too many spices and herbs to dilute the flavor of the meat.

MAKES 6 SAUSAGES

Tips

Many countries produce lamb, with Australia and New Zealand being major exporters. Debates rage over which is better, but both are primarily grass-fed, providing a nutritional advantage. As to taste, try both and see which you prefer.

If you use your hands to mix the ground meat, have a bowl of water nearby in which to dip your fingers. This will help keep them from getting too sticky.

2 lbs	trimmed leg of lamb, chilled (see page 49)	1 kg
1 tbsp	finely minced garlic	15 mL
2 tsp	kosher salt	10 mL
1 tsp	freshly cracked black pepper	5 mL
¼ cup	water	60 mL
4 to 5 feet	32/35 mm hog casing, soaked (see page 49)	120 to 150 cm

1. Cut lamb into pieces small enough to fit in the throat of your grinder. Using the coarse grinder plate, grind lamb into a large bowl or stand mixer bowl.

2. Add garlic, salt and pepper to the ground lamb. Using your hands or the stand mixer paddle attachment, mix until seasonings are evenly distributed. Add water and mix until white strands appear in the mixture and a handful of the mixture holds together.

3. In a small skillet, over medium-high heat, sauté a small amount of the sausage mixture until no longer pink. Taste the sample, then adjust seasonings as desired.

4. Stuff sausage mixture into prepared casing as directed on page 51. Twist into 6 links, each about 6 inches (15 cm) in length.

Health Facts

Omega-3 fatty acids are healthy fats that may protect against heart disease and fight inflammation. Lamb can be a good source of these fats, depending on the diet of both the young sheep and its mother. One way to assure the highest amount of these healthy compounds is to select lamb that is labeled "100% grass fed," as it contains 25% more omega-3s than grain-fed lamb. Grass-fed lamb also contains 49% more alpha-linolenic acid, a precursor for omega-3s, than grain-fed.

Irish Stew Sausages

The traditional Irish stew — created, no doubt, of necessity because of the scarcity of meat — has become an iconic food. Chefs often quibble about what the exact ingredients should be, but most would agree on the ones included in these sausages.

MAKES 9 SAUSAGES

Tips

You can peel and dice the potatoes up to a day ahead and place them in a bowl of cold water in the refrigerator. Make sure the potatoes are entirely covered with water. Drain well and pat dry before using.

If you decide to use table salt in place of kosher salt, use 1½ tsp (7 mL), as table salt has a higher density.

2 lbs	trimmed leg of lamb, chilled (see page 49)	1 kg
8 oz	russet potatoes, peeled and diced	250 g
¼ cup	diced carrots	60 mL
¼ cup	diced celery	60 mL
¼ cup	minced onion	60 mL
2 tbsp	finely minced garlic	30 mL
1 tbsp	minced fresh rosemary	15 mL
2 tsp	minced fresh parsley	10 mL
1½ tsp	minced fresh thyme	7 mL
2 tsp	kosher salt	10 mL
1 tsp	freshly cracked black pepper	5 mL
⅛ tsp	ground bay leaves	0.5 mL
¼ cup	water	60 mL
4 to 5 feet	32/35 mm hog casing, soaked (see page 49)	120 to 150 cm

1. Cut lamb into pieces small enough to fit in the throat of your grinder. Using the coarse grinder plate, grind lamb into a large bowl or stand mixer bowl.

2. Add potatoes, carrots, celery, onion, garlic, rosemary, parsley, thyme, salt, pepper and bay leaves to the ground lamb. Using your hands or the stand mixer paddle attachment, mix until seasonings are evenly distributed. Add water and mix until white strands appear in the mixture and a handful of the mixture holds together.

3. In a small skillet, over medium-high heat, sauté a small amount of the sausage mixture until no longer pink. Taste the sample, then adjust seasonings as desired.

4. Stuff sausage mixture into prepared casing as directed on page 51. Twist into 9 links, each about 6 inches (15 cm) in length.

Health Facts

A 2015 review reported that two compounds contained in bay leaves, costunolide and dehydrocostus lactone, exhibit anti-inflammatory, anticancer, antiviral, antimicrobial, antifungal, antioxidant, antidiabetic and antiulcer activities.

Contadina Sausages

These sausages get their name from the Italian word for "peasant" or "farmer." The combination of lamb, pork and other robust and rustic ingredients brings to mind the sunny Italian countryside. The sausages make a hearty accompaniment to vegetable soup or pasta.

MAKES 6 SAUSAGES

Tip

Most cooks have faced the dilemma of needing only 1 or 2 tbsp (15 or 30 mL) of tomato paste for a recipe, so they tuck the small can somewhere in the refrigerator, only to find it weeks later sporting a beard of mold. You can freeze the paste in small portions, but another alternative is to buy it in a tube. Once opened, the tube can be safely refrigerated for up to 45 days.

1 lb	trimmed leg of lamb, chilled (see page 49)	500 g
1 lb	trimmed boneless pork shoulder blade roast, chilled	500 g
2 tbsp	tomato paste (see tip, at left)	30 mL
1 tbsp	pesto	15 mL
2 tsp	kosher salt	10 mL
1 tsp	freshly cracked black pepper	5 mL
¼ cup	dry red wine	60 mL
4 to 5 feet	32/35 mm hog casing, soaked (see page 49)	120 to 150 cm

1. Cut lamb and pork into pieces small enough to fit in the throat of your grinder. Using the coarse grinder plate, grind lamb and pork into a large bowl or stand mixer bowl.

2. Add tomato paste, pesto, salt and pepper to the ground meat. Using your hands or the stand mixer paddle attachment, mix until seasonings are evenly distributed. Add wine and mix until white strands appear in the mixture and a handful of the mixture holds together.

3. In a small skillet, over medium-high heat, sauté a small amount of the sausage mixture until juices run clear. Taste the sample, then adjust seasonings as desired.

4. Stuff sausage mixture into prepared casing as directed on page 51. Twist into 6 links, each about 6 inches (15 cm) in length.

Health Facts

Pesto's base is olive oil, used throughout the Mediterranean for centuries. Olive oil is a good source of vitamins E and K, and it contains antioxidant polyphenols and phytosterols, both of which may protect against heart disease.

Milanese Sausages

The cuisine of Milan, Italy, includes elements from Italy's northern neighbors as well as familiar Italian cuisine. It favors rice over pasta, butter rather than olive oil, and the frequent use of spinach. These sausages make an elegant meal served with risotto, another Milan favorite.

MAKES 8 SAUSAGES

Tips

Another great ingredient combination is the mix of sautéed spinach and onions. You can make up a big batch and freeze portions to add these savory flavors to rice, pasta and meat dishes.

If you use your hands to mix the ground meat, have a bowl of water nearby in which to dip your fingers. This will help keep them from getting too sticky.

1 tsp	butter	5 mL
¼ cup	minced onion	60 mL
2 oz	trimmed spinach leaves (2 cups/ 500 mL packed), coarsely chopped	60 g
2 lbs	trimmed leg of lamb, chilled (see page 49)	1 kg
1 cup	freshly grated Parmesan cheese	250 mL
2 tbsp	roasted garlic paste (see page 47)	30 mL
2 tsp	kosher salt	10 mL
1 tsp	freshly cracked black pepper	5 mL
¼ cup	water	60 mL
4 to 5 feet	32/35 mm hog casing, soaked (see page 49)	120 to 150 cm

1. In a large skillet, melt butter over medium heat. Add onion and cook, stirring, for 4 minutes or until softened. Add spinach, reduce heat to medium-low, cover and cook for 4 minutes or until wilted. Let cool completely, then drain off any excess liquid.

2. Cut lamb into pieces small enough to fit in the throat of your grinder. Using the coarse grinder plate, grind lamb into a large bowl or stand mixer bowl.

3. Add spinach mixture, cheese, garlic paste, salt and pepper to the ground lamb. Using your hands or the stand mixer paddle attachment, mix until seasonings are evenly distributed. Add water and mix until white strands appear in the mixture and a handful of the mixture holds together.

4. In a small skillet, over medium-high heat, sauté a small amount of the sausage mixture until no longer pink. Taste the sample, then adjust seasonings as desired.

5. Stuff sausage mixture into prepared casing as directed on page 51. Twist into 8 links, each about 6 inches (15 cm) in length.

Health Facts

Spinach is one of the most nutrient-dense vegetables, with levels of vitamins A, C and folate (to name just a few) exceeding the daily value. In a study on how intake of spinach, kale and broccoli affects the risk of prostate cancer, only spinach demonstrated protection against the development of aggressive prostate cancer.

Loukaniko

The name of these sausages (also spelled lukániko) comes from the Greek for a sausage made of pork. However, it has come to represent a Greek-style sausage recipe that usually includes orange zest, leeks and a variety of spices. This recipe, though made with lamb, maintains those elements, including several Greek spices.

**MAKES
6 SAUSAGES**

Tips

The easiest way to crack fennel seeds is to place them on a piece of parchment paper on the kitchen counter and roll over them with a heavy rolling pin.

Citrus zest livens up just about any recipe. Instead of discarding your citrus rinds, take a few extra minutes before peeling the fruit to grate the zest, then freeze it for up to 4 months. It will maintain all its flavor and healthy compounds and be ready whenever culinary inspiration strikes.

2 lbs	trimmed leg of lamb, chilled (see page 49)	1 kg
2 tbsp	minced leek	30 mL
1 tsp	finely minced garlic	5 mL
1 tbsp	grated orange zest	15 mL
1 tbsp	freshly cracked fennel seeds (see tip, at left)	15 mL
2 tsp	kosher salt	10 mL
1 tsp	freshly cracked black pepper	5 mL
1 tsp	dried thyme	5 mL
1 tsp	dried oregano	5 mL
¼ cup	water	60 mL
4 to 5 feet	32/35 mm hog casing, soaked (see page 49)	120 to 150 cm

1. Cut lamb into pieces small enough to fit in the throat of your grinder. Using the coarse grinder plate, grind lamb into a large bowl or stand mixer bowl.

2. Add leek, garlic, orange zest, fennel seeds, salt, pepper, thyme and oregano to the ground lamb. Using your hands or the stand mixer paddle attachment, mix until seasonings are evenly distributed. Add water and mix until white strands appear in the mixture and a handful of the mixture holds together.

3. In a small skillet, over medium-high heat, sauté a small amount of the sausage mixture until no longer pink. Taste the sample, then adjust seasonings as desired.

4. Stuff sausage mixture into prepared casing as directed on page 51. Twist into 6 links, each about 6 inches (15 cm) in length.

Health Facts

A 2015 study reported that orange peel extract (along with other citrus peel extracts) inhibited various activities in colon cancer cells. The authors concluded that this "suggests the potential use of citrus peels as functional food in the management and/or prevention of colon cancer."

Moussaka Sausages

If you've never tasted the layered eggplant and ground lamb casserole that inspired these sausages, you've missed something special, but now's your chance to savor the same combination of ingredients.

Tip

To make roasted eggplant purée, peel a medium eggplant and cut into ¼-inch (0.5 cm) dice. Toss with 1 tbsp (15 mL) olive oil and 1 tsp (5 mL) each salt and freshly ground black pepper. Spread in a single layer on a baking sheet lined with parchment paper. Bake in a 400°F (200°C) oven for 5 to 8 minutes or until starting to brown. Let cool, then purée until smooth in a food processor. You can freeze leftover purée in an airtight container for up to 3 months. It's a great addition to soups and sauces.

Health Facts

Eggplant contains several intriguing phytonutrients that demonstrate beneficial effects on blood vessels and may help lower blood cholesterol levels and reduce the risk of heart disease.

2 lbs	trimmed leg of lamb, chilled (see page 49)	1 kg
4 oz	goat cheese (chèvre)	125 g
½ cup	roasted eggplant purée (see tip, at left)	125 mL
¼ cup	minced onion	60 mL
¼ cup	minced drained roasted red bell peppers, patted dry	60 mL
¼ cup	panko (Japanese bread crumbs)	60 mL
2 tbsp	roasted garlic paste (see page 47)	30 mL
2 tbsp	finely chopped fresh basil	30 mL
1 tbsp	minced fresh oregano	15 mL
1 tbsp	finely grated lemon zest	15 mL
2 tsp	kosher salt	10 mL
1 tsp	freshly cracked black pepper	5 mL
½ tsp	ground cinnamon	2 mL
¼ tsp	ground allspice	1 mL
¼ cup	heavy or whipping (35%) cream	60 mL
2 tbsp	water	30 mL
4 to 5 feet	32/35 mm hog casing, soaked (see page 49)	120 to 150 cm

1. Cut lamb into pieces small enough to fit in the throat of your grinder. Using the coarse grinder plate, grind lamb into a large bowl or stand mixer bowl.

2. Add goat cheese, eggplant purée, onion, roasted peppers, panko, garlic paste, basil, oregano, lemon zest, salt, pepper, cinnamon and allspice to the ground lamb. Using your hands or the stand mixer paddle attachment, mix until seasonings are evenly distributed. Add cream and water; mix until white strands appear in the mixture and a handful of the mixture holds together.

3. In a small skillet, over medium-high heat, sauté a small amount of the sausage mixture until no longer pink. Taste the sample, then adjust seasonings as desired.

4. Stuff sausage mixture into prepared casing as directed on page 51. Twist into 9 links, each about 6 inches (15 cm) in length.

Tabbouleh Sausages

You'll find as many variations in the recipe for tabbouleh as there are different spellings (tabouli and tabbuleh, among others). The Mediterranean salad is made of bulgur, parsley and an assortment of spices. These ingredients find a new home in these sausages made with lamb, another Mediterranean staple.

**MAKES
8 SAUSAGES**

Tip

Many chefs prefer to use a large chef's knife to mince parsley, but a food processor works well for those who are less adept at wielding a knife. Use a series of short pulses, and be careful not to overprocess. For the best taste and texture, the stems are best omitted. Use a pair of kitchen scissors to cut them off as closely to the leaves as possible while still in a bunch.

2 lbs	trimmed leg of lamb, chilled (see page 49)	1 kg
1 cup	cooked coarse bulgur, cooled	250 mL
1 cup	minced fresh parsley	250 mL
½ cup	minced onion	125 mL
2 tsp	finely grated lemon zest	10 mL
2 tsp	sesame seeds	10 mL
2 tsp	ground cumin	10 mL
2 tsp	kosher salt	10 mL
1 tsp	freshly cracked black pepper	5 mL
1 tsp	ground turmeric	5 mL
¼ cup	water	60 mL
4 to 5 feet	32/35 mm hog casing, soaked (see page 49)	120 to 150 cm

1. Cut lamb into pieces small enough to fit in the throat of your grinder. Using the coarse grinder plate, grind lamb into a large bowl or stand mixer bowl.

2. Add bulgur, parsley, onion, lemon zest, sesame seeds, cumin, salt, pepper and turmeric to the ground lamb. Using your hands or the stand mixer paddle attachment, mix until seasonings are evenly distributed. Add water and mix until white strands appear in the mixture and a handful of the mixture holds together.

3. In a small skillet, over medium-high heat, sauté a small amount of the sausage mixture until no longer pink. Taste the sample, then adjust seasonings as desired.

4. Stuff sausage mixture into prepared casing as directed on page 51. Twist into 8 links, each about 6 inches (15 cm) in length.

Health Facts

In addition to a high concentration of vitamins and minerals, parsley contains the phytonutrient apigenin. A large epidemiologic study reported that diets high in this flavonoid, which is a powerful antioxidant and anti-inflammatory, were associated with a lower risk for both heart disease and cancer.

Makanek

Makanek is a Lebanese sausage made with lamb, beef or a combination, and is full of aromatic spices. The links are traditionally cut short, to about 3 inches (7.5 cm), although you can make them any length you prefer. A traditional way to eat these delicious sausages is to sauté them with onion, then drizzle them with pomegranate syrup (sometimes called pomegranate molasses).

**MAKES
12 SAUSAGES**

Tips

To toast pine nuts, spread them evenly on a baking sheet and bake in a 375°F (190°C) oven for 5 to 8 minutes, stirring occasionally, until lightly browned and fragrant. For a small amount, as in this recipe, you can also use a toaster oven set at 325°F (160°C) for about 4 minutes. Let cool completely, then roughly chop.

If you find your shelf bereft of cognac, a fortified wine, such as port, will also work well in this recipe.

Health Facts

A 2014 study of the effects of fenugreek seeds on a small group of people with type 2 diabetes showed that it provided several benefits, including improved blood glucose and cholesterol levels. The authors concluded that fenugreek seeds "may be useful in the control of diabetes risk factors in type 2 diabetes."

2 lbs	trimmed leg of lamb, chilled (see page 49)	1 kg
¼ cup	roughly chopped toasted pine nuts (see tip, at left)	60 mL
2 tbsp	finely minced garlic	30 mL
1 tbsp	ground cumin	15 mL
2 tsp	kosher salt	10 mL
1½ tsp	curry powder	7 mL
1 tsp	freshly cracked black pepper	5 mL
½ tsp	ground coriander	2 mL
½ tsp	ground fenugreek seeds	2 mL
¼ tsp	ground nutmeg	1 mL
⅛ tsp	ground cloves	0.5 mL
¼ cup	white wine	60 mL
1 tbsp	cognac	15 mL
½ tsp	white vinegar	2 mL
4 to 5 feet	32/35 mm hog casing, soaked (see page 49)	120 to 150 cm

1. Cut lamb into pieces small enough to fit in the throat of your grinder. Using the coarse grinder plate, grind lamb into a large bowl or stand mixer bowl.

2. Add pine nuts, garlic, cumin, salt, curry powder, pepper, coriander, fenugreek, nutmeg and cloves to the ground lamb. Using your hands or the stand mixer paddle attachment, mix until seasonings are evenly distributed. Add wine, cognac and vinegar; mix until white strands appear in the mixture and a handful of the mixture holds together.

3. In a small skillet, over medium-high heat, sauté a small amount of the sausage mixture until no longer pink. Taste the sample, then adjust seasonings as desired.

4. Stuff sausage mixture into prepared casing as directed on page 51. Twist into 12 links, each about 3 inches (7.5 cm) in length.

Gyro Sausages

All of the ingredients of the gyro sandwich have a long history in the Middle East, as does the use of a vertical rotisserie. The name is a more recent creation — food historians say it originated in New York City in the 1970s. Meaning "turn" in Greek, it is a nod to the rotating meat. The many flavors of the Mediterranean in this recipe make for delectable sausages that would be perfect snuggled inside warm grilled pitas.

**MAKES
7 SAUSAGES**

Tip

Serve these sausages with tzatziki. In a food processor, combine 1 roughly chopped peeled cucumber, 1 chopped garlic clove, 1½ tsp (7 mL) roughly chopped fresh dill, salt and freshly ground black pepper to taste, 1 cup (250 mL) plain yogurt, 1 tbsp (15 mL) olive oil and the juice of ¼ lemon; purée until smooth.

Health Facts

Cucumbers contain a high level of phytonutrients in the lignans group, which studies show may reduce the risk for heart disease and cancer.

½ cup	finely diced seeded peeled cucumber	125 mL
	Kosher salt	
2 lbs	trimmed leg of lamb, chilled (see page 49)	2 kg
½ cup	minced onion	125 mL
½ cup	finely diced seeded peeled tomatoes	125 mL
2 tbsp	roasted garlic paste (see page 47)	30 mL
1 tbsp	coarsely chopped fresh dill	15 mL
1 tbsp	coarsely chopped fresh oregano	15 mL
½ tsp	minced fresh rosemary	2 mL
½ tsp	minced fresh marjoram	2 mL
1 tsp	freshly cracked black pepper	5 mL
2 tbsp	water	30 mL
4 to 5 feet	32/35 mm hog casing, soaked (see page 49)	120 to 150 cm

1. Place cucumber in a strainer placed over a bowl and sprinkle with a pinch of salt to extract liquid. Reserve 2 tbsp (30 mL) liquid, adding water to make up the difference, if needed. Set cucumber aside.

2. Cut lamb into pieces small enough to fit in the throat of your grinder. Using the coarse grinder plate, grind lamb into a large bowl or stand mixer bowl.

3. Add cucumber, onion, tomatoes, garlic paste, dill, oregano, rosemary, marjoram, 2 tsp (10 mL) salt and pepper to the ground lamb. Using your hands or the stand mixer paddle attachment, mix until seasonings are evenly distributed. Add water and reserved cucumber liquid; mix until white strands appear in the mixture and a handful of the mixture holds together.

4. In a small skillet, over medium-high heat, sauté a small amount of the sausage mixture until no longer pink. Taste the sample, then adjust seasonings as desired.

5. Stuff sausage mixture into prepared casing as directed on page 51. Twist into 7 links, each about 6 inches (15 cm) in length.

Kafta Sausages

The word "kafta" is used to refer to many meat items from various Middle Eastern countries, including seasoned lamb or beef meatloaves, meatballs or kebabs. And, as here, it can also mean a fresh Lebanese sausage with a hint of allspice. The sausages are sometimes skewered and grilled, or may be baked with tomatoes and potatoes.

MAKES 6 SAUSAGES

Tips

Choose garlic bulbs that are plump and intact, without cuts. Make sure they are firm when squeezed and not moist, which might be a sign of mold. Store garlic in a loosely covered container in a cool, dry spot, and it should stay fresh for a month.

If you use your hands to mix the ground meat, have a bowl of water nearby in which to dip your fingers. This will help keep them from getting too sticky.

2 tsp	onion flakes	10 mL
2 tbsp	warm water	30 mL
2 lbs	trimmed leg of lamb, chilled (see page 49)	1 kg
3 tbsp	minced drained oil-packed sun-dried tomatoes	45 mL
1 tbsp	minced fresh mint	15 mL
1 tsp	finely minced garlic	5 mL
2 tsp	ground cumin	10 mL
2 tsp	kosher salt	10 mL
1 tsp	freshly cracked black pepper	5 mL
½ tsp	ground cinnamon	2 mL
¼ tsp	ground allspice	1 mL
¼ cup	water	60 mL
4 to 5 feet	32/35 mm hog casing, soaked (see page 49)	120 to 150 cm

1. In a small bowl, combine onion flakes and warm water. Let stand for about 20 minutes or until softened.

2. Meanwhile, cut lamb into pieces small enough to fit in the throat of your grinder. Using the coarse grinder plate, grind lamb into a large bowl or stand mixer bowl.

3. Add sun-dried tomatoes, mint, garlic, cumin, salt, pepper, cinnamon, allspice and onion flakes mixture to the ground lamb. Using your hands or the stand mixer paddle attachment, mix until seasonings are evenly distributed. Add ¼ cup (60 mL) water and mix until white strands appear in the mixture and a handful of the mixture holds together.

4. In a small skillet, over medium-high heat, sauté a small amount of the sausage mixture until no longer pink. Taste the sample, then adjust seasonings as desired.

5. Stuff sausage mixture into prepared casing as directed on page 51. Twist into 6 links, each about 6 inches (15 cm) in length.

Health Facts

Some of allspice's purported health benefits include improving digestive problems, relieving pain and improving circulation.

Kibbeh Sausages

Kibbeh is a Middle Eastern dish of lamb and bulgur that originated with the Levantines, who also made it with beef, goat or camel. The combination of herbs and spices in these sausages gives them a flavor characteristic of that region of the world.

Tips

You can use cracked wheat in place of bulgur in this recipe. People often think they are the same, but there is a slight difference: bulgur is parboiled and dried with some of the bran removed, while cracked wheat is crushed but not parboiled.

Choose mint leaves that are a rich green with no dark or yellow spots. Consider growing your own mint: it's easy to grow outside or in a planter in the house.

2 tsp	onion flakes	10 mL
2 tbsp	warm water	30 mL
2 lbs	trimmed leg of lamb, chilled (see page 49)	1 kg
½ cup	cooked coarse bulgur, cooled	125 mL
2 tsp	minced fresh mint	10 mL
1 tsp	finely minced garlic	5 mL
2 tsp	ground cumin	10 mL
2 tsp	kosher salt	10 mL
1 tsp	freshly cracked black pepper	5 mL
⅛ tsp	ground allspice	0.5 mL
¼ cup	water	60 mL
4 to 5 feet	32/35 mm hog casing, soaked (see page 49)	120 to 150 cm

1. In a small bowl, combine onion flakes and warm water. Let stand for about 20 minutes or until softened.

2. Meanwhile, cut lamb into pieces small enough to fit in the throat of your grinder. Using the coarse grinder plate, grind lamb into a large bowl or stand mixer bowl.

3. Add bulgur, mint, garlic, cumin, salt, pepper, allspice and onion flakes mixture to the ground lamb. Using your hands or the stand mixer paddle attachment, mix until seasonings are evenly distributed. Add ¼ cup (60 mL) water and mix until white strands appear in the mixture and a handful of the mixture holds together.

4. In a small skillet, over medium-high heat, sauté a small amount of the sausage mixture until no longer pink. Taste the sample, then adjust seasonings as desired.

5. Stuff sausage mixture into prepared casing as directed on page 51. Twist into 6 links, each about 6 inches (15 cm) in length.

Health Facts

Mint has long been linked to a soothing effect on the digestive system, with many cultures steeping it in hot water as a medicinal beverage.

Persian Lamb Sausages

These sausages contains two essentials in Persian cuisine: pistachios and advieh (a spice blend). Lamb is a popular meat in Iran, in part because of Islam's ban on eating pork.

Tips

If you like both eating pistachios as a snack and using them in cooking, consider buying them unsalted. Salted pistachios are definitely tastier than unsalted, but for cooking, the salt is too high. If you buy them unsalted, you can whip up a salted batch by placing the nuts on a baking sheet, sprinkling them with salt, and roasting them in a 300°F (150°C) oven for 8 minutes, stirring occasionally.

A typical advieh mix consists of ground cinnamon, nutmeg, rose petals, cardamom and cumin. Since most people don't have rose petals lying around, you probably won't be able to make your own, and you may not find it even in well-stocked grocery stores, but it's readily available online.

2 lbs	trimmed leg of lamb, chilled (see page 49)	1 kg
2 tbsp	finely chopped unsalted roasted pistachios	30 mL
2 tbsp	minced dried cranberries	30 mL
2 tsp	advieh (see tip, at left)	10 mL
2 tsp	kosher salt	10 mL
1 tsp	freshly cracked black pepper	5 mL
1/2 tsp	ground turmeric	2 mL
1/2 tsp	ground cumin	2 mL
1/4 cup	water	60 mL
4 to 5 feet	32/35 mm hog casing, soaked (see page 49)	120 to 150 cm

1. Cut lamb into pieces small enough to fit in the throat of your grinder. Using the coarse grinder plate, grind lamb into a large bowl or stand mixer bowl.

2. Add pistachios, cranberries, advieh, salt, pepper, turmeric and cumin to the ground lamb. Using your hands or the stand mixer paddle attachment, mix until seasonings are evenly distributed. Add water and mix until white strands appear in the mixture and a handful of the mixture holds together.

3. In a small skillet, over medium-high heat, sauté a small amount of the sausage mixture until no longer pink. Taste the sample, then adjust seasonings as desired.

4. Stuff sausage mixture into prepared casing as directed on page 51. Twist into 6 links, each about 6 inches (15 cm) in length.

Health Facts

In addition to being delicious, pistachios pack several health benefits. One 2014 study reported on the nut's positive effects on blood cholesterol levels, while another study in the same year noted its ability to reduce abdominal fat in people with type 2 diabetes.

Persian Stuffed Pepper Sausages

Every culture seems to have a stuffed pepper recipe, and the use of lamb, sweet basmati rice, nuts and traditional herbs and spices transforms these colorful sausages into a Persian delicacy.

**MAKES
7 SAUSAGES**

Tip

Since these sausages are full of aromatic spices and herbs, they work well as an addition to many different soups and stews. Cut them into chunks and sauté them, let cool, then freeze in small portions to add to various dishes.

1 tsp	onion flakes	5 mL
1 tbsp	warm water	15 mL
2 lbs	trimmed leg of lamb, chilled (see page 49)	1 kg
½ cup	cooked white basmati rice, cooled	125 mL
2 tbsp	minced orange bell pepper	30 mL
2 tbsp	finely chopped walnuts	30 mL
1 tbsp	minced fresh dill	15 mL
1 tsp	minced fresh mint	5 mL
2 tsp	kosher salt	10 mL
1 tsp	freshly cracked black pepper	5 mL
½ tsp	ground turmeric	2 mL
1 tbsp	tomato paste	15 mL
¼ cup	ready-to-use beef broth	60 mL
4 to 5 feet	32/35 mm hog casing, soaked (see page 49)	120 to 150 cm

1. In a small bowl, combine onion flakes and warm water. Let stand for about 20 minutes or until softened.

2. Meanwhile, cut lamb into pieces small enough to fit in the throat of your grinder. Using the coarse grinder plate, grind lamb into a large bowl or stand mixer bowl.

3. Add rice, orange pepper, walnuts, dill, mint, salt, pepper, turmeric, tomato paste and onion flakes mixture to the ground lamb. Using your hands or the stand mixer paddle attachment, mix until seasonings are evenly distributed. Add broth and mix until white strands appear in the mixture and a handful of the mixture holds together.

4. In a small skillet, over medium-high heat, sauté a small amount of the sausage mixture until juices run clear. Taste the sample, then adjust seasonings as desired.

5. Stuff sausage mixture into prepared casing as directed on page 51. Twist into 7 links, each about 6 inches (15 cm) in length.

Health Facts

Dill contains the phytonutrients eugenol and limonene, which may help to reduce blood glucose levels in people with diabetes, although more studies are needed.

Easter Lamb Sausages

These highly seasoned sausages make a great addition to a spring holiday table. The combination of lamb, herbs and spices invoke a Middle Eastern flavor palette.

Tips

Try making a double batch of the dried herbs and spices from this recipe and saving the other half so you can add this flavor palette to other dishes.

If you decide to use table salt in place of kosher salt, use 1½ tsp (7 mL), as table salt has a higher density.

How long to make your sausage links is really up to you, although we suggest 6 inches (15 cm) for this recipe. Keep in mind that this is a rough guideline, and that you may have to adjust the length up or down so that you don't end up with one link smaller than the rest.

1 tsp	onion flakes	5 mL
1 tbsp	warm water	15 mL
2 lbs	trimmed leg of lamb, chilled (see page 49)	1 kg
1 tsp	finely minced garlic	5 mL
1 tsp	minced fresh mint	5 mL
2 tsp	kosher salt	10 mL
1 tsp	freshly cracked black pepper	5 mL
½ tsp	dried thyme	2 mL
½ tsp	dried rosemary	2 mL
⅛ tsp	ground coriander	0.5 mL
¼ cup	water	60 mL
4 to 5 feet	32/35 mm hog casing, soaked (see page 49)	120 to 150 cm

1. In a small bowl, combine onion flakes and warm water. Let stand for about 20 minutes or until softened.

2. Meanwhile, cut lamb into pieces small enough to fit in the throat of your grinder. Using the coarse grinder plate, grind lamb into a large bowl or stand mixer bowl.

3. Add garlic, mint, salt, pepper, thyme, rosemary, coriander and onion flakes mixture to the ground lamb. Using your hands or the stand mixer paddle attachment, mix until seasonings are evenly distributed. Add ¼ cup (60 mL) water and mix until white strands appear in the mixture and a handful of the mixture holds together.

4. In a small skillet, over medium-high heat, sauté a small amount of the sausage mixture until no longer pink. Taste the sample, then adjust seasonings as desired.

5. Stuff sausage mixture into prepared casing as directed on page 51. Twist into 6 links, each about 6 inches (15 cm) in length.

Health Facts

Even just smelling rosemary has been shown to provide health benefits, but, of course, eating it is the best way to take advantage of its numerous phytonutrients, whose beneficial effects include stimulating the immune system, improving digestion and reducing the severity of asthma.

Australian Kransky Sausages

These Australian sausages get their name from the Slovenian *kranjska klobasa* (Carniolan sausages). They were introduced to Australia by Slovenian immigrants and quickly became very popular. They are made with a mix of lamb and pork, both plentiful in Australia, and with cheese, another favorite sausage ingredient in that country.

**MAKES
7 SAUSAGES**

Tips

We chose white Cheddar cheese for this recipe mainly for its lack of color. Cheddar cheese is naturally white, but the plant extract annatto is added to it to produce the familiar orange color. You can use orange Cheddar cheese here, if you prefer.

If you use your hands to mix the ground meat, have a bowl of water nearby in which to dip your fingers. This will help keep them from getting too sticky.

1 lb	trimmed leg of lamb, chilled (see page 49)	500 g
1 lb	trimmed boneless pork shoulder blade roast, chilled	500 g
1 cup	shredded white Cheddar cheese	250 mL
3 tbsp	instant nonfat dry milk (skim milk powder)	45 mL
2 tsp	finely minced garlic	10 mL
2 tsp	kosher salt	10 mL
1 tsp	freshly cracked black pepper	5 mL
¼ cup	white wine	60 mL
4 to 5 feet	32/35 mm hog casing, soaked (see page 49)	120 to 150 cm

1. Cut lamb and pork into pieces small enough to fit in the throat of your grinder. Using the coarse grinder plate, grind lamb and pork into a large bowl or stand mixer bowl.

2. Add cheese, dry milk, garlic, salt and pepper to the ground meat. Using your hands or the stand mixer paddle attachment, mix until seasonings are evenly distributed. Add wine and mix until white strands appear in the mixture and a handful of the mixture holds together.

3. In a small skillet, over medium-high heat, sauté a small amount of the sausage mixture until no longer pink. Taste the sample, then adjust seasonings as desired.

4. Stuff sausage mixture into prepared casing as directed on page 51. Twist into 7 links, each about 6 inches (15 cm) in length.

Health Facts

Ajoene, a compound found in crushed garlic, appears to target a protein in cancer cells, causing them to destroy themselves, a process known as apoptosis.

Chicken and Turkey Sausages

Poultry has long been used in sausage making, although traditional recipes tended to use game birds rather than chicken or turkey. Today, however, chicken and turkey sausages are among the most popular choices, and for good reason: they tend to be lower in total fat and saturated fat. In an attempt to compensate for perceived flavor deficiencies due to the lower fat content, chicken and turkey sausages also tend to include more interesting ingredients.

All of the sausages in this chapter taste best if they are refrigerated for at least 1 day before they are cooked.

Cherry Chicken Sausages

These super-lean sausages combine sage and marjoram with the rich flavors of tart cherries and walnuts — all healthy ingredients that provide phytonutrients for a disease-fighting punch.

**MAKES
7 SAUSAGES**

Tips

Dried tart cherries are readily available in the produce section of most large grocery stores. You can also use an equal amount of frozen tart cherries, but make sure to thaw them thoroughly, press out excess liquid and pat dry.

How long to make your sausage links is really up to you, although we suggest 6 inches (15 cm) for this recipe. Keep in mind that this is a rough guideline, and that you may have to adjust the length up or down so that you don't end up with one link smaller than the rest.

1 lb	trimmed boneless skinless chicken breasts, chilled (see page 49)	500 g
1 lb	untrimmed boneless skinless chicken thighs, chilled	500 g
¼ cup	chopped walnuts	60 mL
¼ cup	chopped dried tart cherries	60 mL
2½ tsp	kosher salt	12 mL
1 tsp	freshly cracked black pepper	5 mL
¼ tsp	ground rubbed sage	1 mL
¼ tsp	ground marjoram	1 mL
1 tbsp	pure maple syrup	15 mL
½ cup	water	125 mL
4 to 5 feet	32/35 mm hog casing, soaked (see page 49)	120 to 150 cm

1. Cut chicken breasts and thighs into pieces small enough to fit in the throat of your grinder, keeping them separate. Using the coarse grinder plate, grind chicken breasts into a large bowl or stand mixer bowl. Using the fine grinder plate, grind chicken thighs into the same bowl.

2. Add walnuts, cherries, salt, pepper, sage, marjoram and maple syrup to the ground chicken. Using your hands or the stand mixer paddle attachment, mix until seasonings are evenly distributed. Add water and mix until a handful of the mixture holds together.

3. In a small skillet, over medium-high heat, sauté a small amount of the sausage mixture until no longer pink. Taste the sample, then adjust seasonings as desired.

4. Stuff sausage mixture into prepared casing as directed on page 51. Twist into 7 links, each about 6 inches (15 cm) in length.

Health Facts

Cherries, and in particular tart cherries, contain many phenol compounds that fight both inflammation and free radicals. One group of phytonutrients, anthocyanins, appear to be powerful mediators of blood levels of insulin, glucose and cholesterol, as well as blood pressure.

Bolognese Chicken Sausages

The city of Bologna, Italy, has its own unique culinary flavors. As in many Italian regions, tomatoes feature prominently, but Bolognese cooking also often incorporates heavy cream, which is not typical of other areas of the country.

**MAKES
7 SAUSAGES**

Tips

To roast garlic, remove the outer skin from a head of garlic, keeping the head intact, and cut off the tops of the cloves. Place the garlic head on a sheet of foil, drizzle cloves with 1 tbsp (15 mL) olive oil and gather foil at the top to enclose the head. Roast in a 400°F (200°C) oven for 45 minutes or until cloves are fork-tender. Let cool completely.

Even with the heavy cream, these are lean sausages. For even lower-fat sausages, substitute whole milk for the cream.

1 lb	trimmed boneless skinless chicken breasts, chilled (see page 49)	500 g
1 lb	untrimmed boneless skinless chicken thighs, chilled	500 g
¼ cup	drained canned diced tomatoes, with 3 tbsp (45 mL) juice reserved	60 mL
1 tbsp	mashed roasted garlic (see tip, at left)	15 mL
2½ tsp	kosher salt	12 mL
1 tsp	freshly cracked black pepper	5 mL
1 tsp	granulated sugar	5 mL
½ tsp	dried Italian seasoning	2 mL
¼ cup	heavy or whipping (35%) cream	60 mL
4 to 5 feet	32/35 mm hog casing, soaked (see page 49)	120 to 150 cm

1. Cut chicken breasts and thighs into pieces small enough to fit in the throat of your grinder, keeping them separate. Using the coarse grinder plate, grind chicken breasts into a large bowl or stand mixer bowl. Using the fine grinder plate, grind chicken thighs into the same bowl.

2. Add tomatoes, roasted garlic, salt, pepper, sugar and Italian seasoning to the ground chicken. Using your hands or the stand mixer paddle attachment, mix until seasonings are evenly distributed. Add cream and reserved tomato juice; mix until a handful of the mixture holds together.

3. In a small skillet, over medium-high heat, sauté a small amount of the sausage mixture until no longer pink. Taste the sample, then adjust seasonings as desired.

4. Stuff sausage mixture into prepared casing as directed on page 51. Twist into 7 links, each about 6 inches (15 cm) in length.

Health Facts

Tomatoes and garlic, two staples of Italian cuisine, contain many healthy nutrients. Tomatoes contain the carotenoid lycopene, a powerful antioxidant that may help prevent prostate cancer. Garlic has made headlines for its role in helping to prevent cardiovascular disease by reducing inflammation and discouraging blood clotting cells from sticking together.

Gorgonzola Chicken Sausages

Gorgonzola, a type of blue cheese, has been produced in an Italian town of the same name since the late ninth century. It can be made with either cow's milk or goat's milk, although cow's milk is more common. In these sausages, the intensity and creaminess of the Gorgonzola melds with the tart-sweet cranberries and spinach for a burst of flavor in every bite.

MAKES 7 SAUSAGES

Tip

Molds can grow on blue cheese, adversely affecting flavor and safety. Plan to keep it (even if unopened) in the refrigerator for only up to 4 weeks. You can freeze it for up to 6 months, but freezing will affect its texture, making it more suitable for cooked dishes.

1 lb	trimmed boneless skinless chicken breasts, chilled (see page 49)	500 g
1 lb	untrimmed boneless skinless chicken thighs, chilled	500 g
⅓ cup	crumbled Gorgonzola cheese	75 mL
¼ cup	minced dried cranberries	60 mL
¼ cup	minced baby spinach	60 mL
2½ tsp	kosher salt	12 mL
1 tsp	freshly cracked black pepper	5 mL
1 tsp	garlic powder	5 mL
½ cup	water	125 mL
4 to 5 feet	32/35 mm hog casing, soaked (see page 49)	120 to 150 cm

1. Cut chicken breasts and thighs into pieces small enough to fit in the throat of your grinder, keeping them separate. Using the coarse grinder plate, grind chicken breasts into a large bowl or stand mixer bowl. Using the fine grinder plate, grind chicken thighs into the same bowl.

2. Add cheese, cranberries, spinach, salt, pepper and garlic powder to the ground chicken. Using your hands or the stand mixer paddle attachment, mix until seasonings are evenly distributed. Add water and mix until a handful of the mixture holds together.

3. In a small skillet, over medium-high heat, sauté a small amount of the sausage mixture until no longer pink. Taste the sample, then adjust seasonings as desired.

4. Stuff sausage mixture into prepared casing as directed on page 51. Twist into 7 links, each about 6 inches (15 cm) in length.

Health Facts

A 2010 study reported that, of various highly ripened cheeses, blue cheeses caused the strongest suppression of cell growth. The authors concluded that the results "suggest a potential role of highly ripened cheeses in the prevention of leukemic cell proliferation."

Piedmont Chicken Sausages

The Piedmont region of northwestern Italy is in many ways the heart of traditional Italian cuisine. One specialty is salami made with poultry or trout. This fresh sausage recipe mimics the Piedmont style.

Tips

Pecorino Romano is made from sheep's milk and has a more robust flavor than Parmesan cheese. Although it's not as widely available as Parmesan — you may need to go to an Italian specialty store or a well-stocked cheese shop to find it — it's worthwhile to try to find it.

If you use your hands to mix the ground meat, have a bowl of water nearby in which to dip your fingers. This will help keep them from getting too sticky.

1 lb	trimmed boneless skinless chicken breasts, chilled (see page 49)	500 g
1 lb	untrimmed boneless skinless chicken thighs, chilled	500 g
½ cup	grated Pecorino Romano cheese	125 mL
1 tbsp	dried parsley	15 mL
2½ tsp	kosher salt	12 mL
2 tsp	garlic powder	10 mL
1 tsp	freshly cracked black pepper	5 mL
½ tsp	dried basil	2 mL
½ cup	water	125 mL
4 to 5 feet	32/35 mm hog casing, soaked (see page 49)	120 to 150 cm

1. Cut chicken breasts and thighs into pieces small enough to fit in the throat of your grinder, keeping them separate. Using the coarse grinder plate, grind chicken breasts into a large bowl or stand mixer bowl. Using the fine grinder plate, grind chicken thighs into the same bowl.

2. Add cheese, parsley, salt, garlic powder, pepper and basil to the ground chicken. Using your hands or the stand mixer paddle attachment, mix until seasonings are evenly distributed. Add water and mix until a handful of the mixture holds together.

3. In a small skillet, over medium-high heat, sauté a small amount of the sausage mixture until no longer pink. Taste the sample, then adjust seasonings as desired.

4. Stuff sausage mixture into prepared casing as directed on page 51. Twist into 7 links, each about 6 inches (15 cm) in length.

Health Facts

Basil is used in Ayurveda, a traditional Indian system of medicine, to treat stomach, liver, respiratory and inflammatory disorders.

Pesto Chicken Sausages

Basil and other pesto ingredients provide these sausages with an intense Mediterranean flavor that is only enhanced by the roasted garlic and sun-dried tomatoes.

**MAKES
7 SAUSAGES**

Tips

Fresh basil can be kept in the freezer for up to 6 months and retains its fragrant aroma. Wash and dry the leaves thoroughly, then place them in an airtight freezer bag. When needed, simply crumble the frozen leaves into the recipe.

You can use either oil-packed or dry-packed sun-dried tomatoes. If you use oil-packed, drain well before mincing and measuring. An opened container of oil-packed tomatoes will remain fresh in the refrigerator for up to 6 months. The oil will turn into a white solid, but it will liquefy in 30 minutes at room temperature. To store dry-packed tomatoes, squeeze any air out of the bag before sealing it; this will keep them fresh for about a year in the refrigerator.

1 lb	trimmed boneless skinless chicken breasts, chilled (see page 49)	500 g
1 lb	untrimmed boneless skinless chicken thighs, chilled	500 g
¼ cup	finely chopped fresh basil	60 mL
2 tbsp	finely chopped fresh parsley	30 mL
3 tbsp	coarsely chopped toasted pine nuts (see tip, page 177)	45 mL
3 tbsp	roasted garlic paste (see page 47)	45 mL
2 tbsp	finely minced sun-dried tomatoes (see tip, at left)	30 mL
2½ tsp	kosher salt	12 mL
1 tsp	freshly cracked black pepper	5 mL
½ cup	water	125 mL
4 to 5 feet	32/35 mm hog casing, soaked (see page 49)	120 to 150 cm

1. Cut chicken breasts and thighs into pieces small enough to fit in the throat of your grinder, keeping them separate. Using the coarse grinder plate, grind chicken breasts into a large bowl or stand mixer bowl. Using the fine grinder plate, grind chicken thighs into the same bowl.

2. Add basil, parsley, pine nuts, garlic paste, sun-dried tomatoes, salt and pepper to the ground chicken. Using your hands or the stand mixer paddle attachment, mix until seasonings are evenly distributed. Add water and mix until a handful of the mixture holds together.

3. In a small skillet, over medium-high heat, sauté a small amount of the sausage mixture until no longer pink. Taste the sample, then adjust seasonings as desired.

4. Stuff sausage mixture into prepared casing as directed on page 51. Twist into 7 links, each about 6 inches (15 cm) in length.

Health Facts

The essential oils in basil have been shown to lower blood glucose, triglyceride and cholesterol levels, all of which may help in fighting both diabetes and heart disease.

Athenian Chicken Sausages

These sausages contain many ingredients associated with Greek cuisine, including kalamata olives. These distinctive olives contain many healthy phytonutrients with antioxidant activity.

**MAKES
8 SAUSAGES**

Tip

Look for jars of grape leaves packed in brine in the international aisle of well-stocked grocery stores. Make sure to remove the woody veins and use only the tender leaf portion. Refrigerate the jar after opening and make sure to keep the leaves covered with brine. They should be used within 2 weeks after opening.

Health Facts

Oregano contains the phytonutrients carvacrol, ursolic acid and caffeic acid, all of which have antioxidant and anti-inflammatory activity. In addition, carvacrol is an antimicrobial and ursolic acid may help fight cancer.

2 oz	coarsely chopped trimmed spinach leaves	60 g
1 lb	trimmed boneless skinless chicken breasts, chilled (see page 49)	500 g
1 lb	untrimmed boneless skinless chicken thighs, chilled	500 g
1	brine-packed grape leaf, drained and finely minced	1
½ cup	crumbled feta cheese	125 mL
¼ cup	finely chopped pitted kalamata olives	60 mL
¼ cup	minced drained roasted red bell peppers	60 mL
2 tbsp	finely grated lemon zest	30 mL
1 tbsp	dried oregano	15 mL
1½ tsp	kosher salt	7 mL
1 tsp	freshly cracked black pepper	5 mL
½ cup	water	125 mL
4 to 5 feet	32/35 mm hog casing, soaked (see page 49)	120 to 150 cm

1. Place spinach in a skillet over medium heat. Toss with tongs so that all of the spinach comes into contact with the bottom of the pan. Cook, tossing, for about 4 minutes or until all of the spinach is wilted. Transfer spinach to a colander and plunge into a bowl of ice water. Carefully squeeze out all of the liquid and pat dry.

2. Cut chicken breasts and thighs into pieces small enough to fit in the throat of your grinder, keeping them separate. Using the coarse grinder plate, grind chicken breasts into a large bowl or stand mixer bowl. Using the fine grinder plate, grind chicken thighs into the same bowl.

3. Add spinach, grape leaf, cheese, olives, roasted peppers, lemon zest, oregano, salt and pepper to the ground chicken. Using your hands or the stand mixer paddle attachment, mix until seasonings are evenly distributed. Add water and mix until a handful of the mixture holds together.

4. In a small skillet, over medium-high heat, sauté a small amount of the sausage mixture until no longer pink. Taste the sample, then adjust seasonings as desired.

5. Stuff sausage mixture into prepared casing as directed on page 51. Twist into 8 links, each about 6 inches (15 cm) in length.

Shawarma Chicken Sausages

Shawarma is a Levantine method of preparing meat. The meat is placed on a spit and grilled throughout the day; some is shaved off for a meal or a sandwich while the remaining meat continues to cook. The traditional Middle Eastern spices used here lend the distinctive shawarma flavor to these sausages. Try serving them in pitas!

**MAKES
8 SAUSAGES**

Tip

Za'atar is a Middle Eastern spice blend. If you can't find it in stores, you can make your own, though you will still need to source sumac berries at a Middle Eastern market or online. In a food processor, combine ¼ cup (60 mL) sumac berries, 2 tbsp (30 mL) dried thyme, 2 tbsp (30 mL) dried marjoram, 2 tbsp (30 mL) dried oregano, 1 tbsp (15 mL) roasted sesame seeds and 1 tsp (5 mL) salt; process to a medium-coarse grind.

Health Facts

Sumac (a key ingredient in za'atar) has been used as a medicinal plant in the Middle East throughout history. Several medical studies have shown it to be a potent antioxidant.

1 tsp	onion flakes	5 mL
1 tbsp	warm water	15 mL
1 lb	trimmed boneless skinless chicken breasts, chilled (see page 49)	500 g
1 lb	untrimmed boneless skinless chicken thighs, chilled	500 g
1	medium tomato, seeded and finely chopped	1
¼ cup	drained pickled radishes, finely minced	60 mL
1 tbsp	minced garlic	15 mL
1 tbsp	finely chopped fresh parsley	15 mL
1 tbsp	grated lemon zest	15 mL
2 tsp	kosher salt	10 mL
1½ tsp	za'atar (see tip, at left)	7 mL
1 tsp	freshly cracked black pepper	5 mL
½ cup	water	125 mL
4 to 5 feet	32/35 mm hog casing, soaked (see page 49)	120 to 150 cm

1. In a small bowl, combine onion flakes and warm water. Let stand for about 20 minutes or until softened.

2. Meanwhile, cut chicken breasts and thighs into pieces small enough to fit in the throat of your grinder, keeping them separate. Using the coarse grinder plate, grind chicken breasts into a large bowl or stand mixer bowl. Using the fine grinder plate, grind chicken thighs into the same bowl.

3. Add tomato, radishes, garlic, parsley, lemon zest, salt, za'atar, pepper and onion flakes mixture to the ground chicken. Using your hands or the stand mixer paddle attachment, mix until seasonings are evenly distributed. Add ½ cup (125 mL) water and mix until a handful of the mixture holds together.

4. In a small skillet, over medium-high heat, sauté a small amount of the sausage mixture until no longer pink. Taste the sample, then adjust seasonings as desired.

5. Stuff sausage mixture into prepared casing as directed on page 51. Twist into 8 links, each about 6 inches (15 cm) in length.

Persian Chicken Sausages

These sausages incorporate several ingredients associated with Persian (Iranian) cuisine. Advieh is a Persian spice mixture that comes in two main varieties: advieh-e polo, used with rice dishes, and advieh-e khoresh, used as a meat rub and in stews. Persia is also the birthplace of the pomegranate, which has always been a staple in Persian cuisine.

MAKES 6 SAUSAGES

Tip

Pomegranate syrup (also known as pomegranate molasses) is available at Middle Eastern markets or online. You can also make your own. In a saucepan, combine ¼ cup (60 mL) granulated sugar, 2 cups (500 mL) unsweetened pomegranate juice and 2 tbsp (30 mL) freshly squeezed lemon juice. Bring to a simmer over medium-high heat. Reduce heat and simmer for 1 hour or until reduced to a syrup-like consistency. Let cool, then pour into an airtight container and refrigerate for up to 6 months.

1 lb	trimmed boneless skinless chicken breasts, chilled (see page 49)	500 g
1 lb	untrimmed boneless skinless chicken thighs, chilled	500 g
2 tbsp	coarsely chopped unsalted pistachios	30 mL
2 tbsp	finely chopped fresh parsley	30 mL
2 tbsp	minced onion	30 mL
1 tbsp	finely minced garlic	15 mL
2½ tsp	kosher salt	12 mL
2 tsp	advieh (see tip, page 181)	10 mL
1 tsp	freshly cracked black pepper	5 mL
1 tsp	Middle Eastern curry powder	5 mL
¼ cup	pomegranate syrup (pomegranate molasses)	60 mL
2 tbsp	water	30 mL
4 to 5 feet	32/35 mm hog casing, soaked (see page 49)	120 to 150 cm

1. Cut chicken breasts and thighs into pieces small enough to fit in the throat of your grinder, keeping them separate. Using the coarse grinder plate, grind chicken breasts into a large bowl or stand mixer bowl. Using the fine grinder plate, grind chicken thighs into the same bowl.

2. Add pistachios, parsley, onion, garlic, salt, advieh, pepper and curry powder to the ground chicken. Using your hands or the stand mixer paddle attachment, mix until seasonings are evenly distributed. Add pomegranate syrup and water; mix until a handful of the mixture holds together.

3. In a small skillet, over medium-high heat, sauté a small amount of the sausage mixture until no longer pink. Taste the sample, then adjust seasonings as desired.

4. Stuff sausage mixture into prepared casing as directed on page 51. Twist into 6 links, each about 6 inches (15 cm) in length.

Health Facts

Pomegranates contain many health-promoting phytonutrients. One study reported that pomegranate extract reduced a marker for prostate cancer, suggesting that it may slow progression of the disease.

Curry Chicken Sausages

The wonderfully exotic flavors of curry and turmeric not only enhance the flavor of these chicken sausages, but also add the health benefits of many phytonutrients.

**MAKES
6 SAUSAGES**

Tips

Curry powder is a combination of ground spices that may include coriander, fenugreek, cumin, turmeric, black pepper, bay leaves, celery seeds, nutmeg, cloves, onion, red pepper and ginger. To emphasize one particular spice, add more of just that spice, as is done with turmeric in this recipe.

If you use your hands to mix the ground meat, have a bowl of water nearby in which to dip your fingers. This will help keep them from getting too sticky.

1 lb	trimmed boneless skinless chicken breasts, chilled (see page 49)	500 g
1 lb	untrimmed boneless skinless chicken thighs, chilled	500 g
2½ tsp	kosher salt	12 mL
2 tsp	curry powder	10 mL
2 tsp	garlic powder	10 mL
1 tsp	freshly cracked black pepper	5 mL
½ tsp	freshly ground white pepper	2 mL
½ tsp	ground turmeric	2 mL
½ tsp	hot paprika	2 mL
½ tsp	dried basil	2 mL
½ cup	water	125 mL
4 to 5 feet	32/35 mm hog casing, soaked (see page 49)	120 to 150 cm

1. Cut chicken breasts and thighs into pieces small enough to fit in the throat of your grinder, keeping them separate. Using the coarse grinder plate, grind chicken breasts into a large bowl or stand mixer bowl. Using the fine grinder plate, grind chicken thighs into the same bowl.

2. Add salt, curry powder, garlic powder, black pepper, white pepper, turmeric, paprika and basil to the ground chicken. Using your hands or the stand mixer paddle attachment, mix until seasonings are evenly distributed. Add water and mix until a handful of the mixture holds together.

3. In a small skillet, over medium-high heat, sauté a small amount of the sausage mixture until no longer pink. Taste the sample, then adjust seasonings as desired.

4. Stuff sausage mixture into prepared casing as directed on page 51. Twist into 6 links, each about 6 inches (15 cm) in length.

Health Facts

Turmeric is one of the most studied spices in the field of disease prevention. Its most active compound is curcumin, which has anti-inflammatory and antioxidant effects that may help prevent cancer and other chronic diseases.

Thai Chicken Sausages

Thai cuisine has become ubiquitous throughout the world, and while many people associate it with extremely spicy food, it can also be relatively mild. These sausages exemplify the harmony of traditional Thai ingredients, but are definitely not mild.

**MAKES
6 SAUSAGES**

Tips

Thai basil is quite different from the more widely available sweet basil. It is characterized by a spicy anise flavor, and can withstand longer cooking times. Freeze leftover Thai basil to use in Thai-inspired stir-fries.

How long to make your sausage links is really up to you, although we suggest 6 inches (15 cm) for this recipe. Keep in mind that this is a rough guideline, and that you may have to adjust the length up or down so that you don't end up with one link smaller than the rest.

1 lb	trimmed boneless skinless chicken breasts, chilled (see page 49)	500 g
1 lb	untrimmed boneless skinless chicken thighs, chilled	500 g
¼ cup	finely chopped unsalted peanuts	60 mL
1 tbsp	minced fresh Thai basil	15 mL
1½ tsp	grated lime zest	7 mL
1 tbsp	hot pepper flakes	15 mL
2 tsp	garlic powder	10 mL
2 tsp	kosher salt	10 mL
1 tsp	freshly cracked black pepper	5 mL
¼ cup	coconut milk	60 mL
4 to 5 feet	32/35 mm hog casing, soaked (see page 49)	120 to 150 cm

1. Cut chicken breasts and thighs into pieces small enough to fit in the throat of your grinder, keeping them separate. Using the coarse grinder plate, grind chicken breasts into a large bowl or stand mixer bowl. Using the fine grinder plate, grind chicken thighs into the same bowl.

2. Add peanuts, basil, lime zest, hot pepper flakes, garlic powder, salt and black pepper to the ground chicken. Using your hands or the stand mixer paddle attachment, mix until seasonings are evenly distributed. Add coconut milk and mix until a handful of the mixture holds together.

3. In a small skillet, over medium-high heat, sauté a small amount of the sausage mixture until no longer pink. Taste the sample, then adjust seasonings as desired.

4. Stuff sausage mixture into prepared casing as directed on page 51. Twist into 6 links, each about 6 inches (15 cm) in length.

Health Facts

Limes are loaded with nutrients and phytonutrients, including a group of flavonoids known as flavonol glycosides, which have been shown to stop cell division in some types of cancer cells and to have an antibiotic effect. In West Africa, adding lime juice to the diet has been protective against outbreaks of cholera.

Aloha Chicken Sausages

Nothing says "aloha" like pineapple and macadamia nuts. But you may be surprised to learn that these healthy foods came to Hawaii from Australia. In fact, macadamia nuts didn't hit the shores of the Big Island until the late 1800s, and pineapple only arrived in the early 1800s.

MAKES 8 SAUSAGES		

Tip

Red bell peppers are full of healthy nutrients and add a wonderfully sweet flavor to recipes. To have some always on hand, freeze quartered peppers in a sealable plastic bag.

1 tsp	onion flakes	5 mL
1 tbsp	warm water	15 mL
1	can (14 to 15 oz/400 to 425 mL) pineapple tidbits	1
1 lb	trimmed boneless skinless chicken breasts, chilled (see page 49)	500 g
1 lb	untrimmed boneless skinless chicken thighs, chilled	500 g
½ cup	finely chopped unsalted macadamia nuts	125 mL
¼ cup	minced red bell pepper	60 mL
2½ tsp	kosher salt	12 mL
1 tsp	dried marjoram	5 mL
½ tsp	freshly ground white pepper	2 mL
½ tsp	ground ginger	2 mL
½ tsp	garlic powder	2 mL
½ tsp	sweet paprika	2 mL
4 to 5 feet	32/35 mm hog casing, soaked (see page 49)	120 to 150 cm

1. In a small bowl, combine onion flakes and warm water. Let stand for about 20 minutes or until softened.

2. Meanwhile, drain juice from pineapple, reserving ½ cup (125 mL) juice. Finely chop pineapple tidbits and measure out ½ cup (125 mL). (Store any remaining juice and pineapple in an airtight container in the refrigerator for another use.)

3. Cut chicken breasts and thighs into pieces small enough to fit in the throat of your grinder, keeping them separate. Using the coarse grinder plate, grind chicken breasts into a large bowl or stand mixer bowl. Using the fine grinder plate, grind chicken thighs into the same bowl.

4. Add pineapple, macadamia nuts, red pepper, salt, marjoram, white pepper, ginger, garlic powder, paprika and onion flakes mixture to the ground chicken. Using your hands or the stand mixer paddle attachment, mix until seasonings are evenly distributed. Add the reserved pineapple juice and mix until a handful of the mixture holds together.

Tip

How long to make your sausage links is really up to you, although we suggest 6 inches (15 cm) for this recipe. Keep in mind that this is a rough guideline, and that you may have to adjust the length up or down so that you don't end up with one link smaller than the rest.

5. In a small skillet, over medium-high heat, sauté a small amount of the sausage mixture until no longer pink. Taste the sample, then adjust seasonings as desired.

6. Stuff sausage mixture into prepared casing as directed on page 51. Twist into 8 links, each about 6 inches (15 cm) in length.

Health Facts

Like all nuts, macadamia nuts are high in healthy fatty acids. A study published in 2014 reported that macadamia oil supplementation in obese mice reduced inflammation, which is common in obese mice and people. A 2008 study showed that just 1½ ounces (45 g) of these nuts added to the diet each day lowered cholesterol in men and women who had high levels.

Buffalo Chicken Sausages

The Buffalo wing experience began in 1964, at a family bar in Buffalo, New York. At the Anchor Bar, Teressa Bellissimo deep-fried chicken wings, covered them in a special sauce she created and served them with a side order of blue cheese dressing and celery. These savory chicken sausages incorporate many of the traditional elements, including our homemade Buffalo Sauce.

Tip

If you use your hands to mix the ground meat, have a bowl of water nearby in which to dip your fingers. This will help keep them from getting too sticky.

1 lb	trimmed boneless skinless chicken breasts, chilled (see page 49)	500 g
1 lb	untrimmed boneless skinless chicken thighs, chilled	500 g
½ cup	crumbled blue cheese	125 mL
1 tbsp	dried parsley	15 mL
2 tsp	garlic powder	10 mL
1½ tsp	kosher salt	7 mL
1 tsp	freshly cracked black pepper	5 mL
1 tsp	celery seeds	5 mL
¼ cup	water	60 mL
¼ cup	Buffalo Sauce (see recipe, opposite)	60 mL
4 to 5 feet	32/35 mm hog casing, soaked (see page 49)	120 to 150 cm

1. Cut chicken breasts and thighs into pieces small enough to fit in the throat of your grinder, keeping them separate. Using the coarse grinder plate, grind chicken breasts into a large bowl or stand mixer bowl. Using the fine grinder plate, grind chicken thighs into the same bowl.

2. Add cheese, parsley, garlic powder, salt, pepper and celery seeds to the ground chicken. Using your hands or the stand mixer paddle attachment, mix until seasonings are evenly distributed. Add water and Buffalo Sauce; mix until a handful of the mixture holds together.

3. In a small skillet, over medium-high heat, sauté a small amount of the sausage mixture until no longer pink. Taste the sample, then adjust seasonings as desired.

4. Stuff sausage mixture into prepared casing as directed on page 51. Twist into 7 links, each about 6 inches (15 cm) in length.

Health Facts

Celery seeds are one of the most concentrated sources of luteolin, a phytonutrient with many biologic activities. The large Nurses' Health Study reported that women consuming the highest amounts of several phytonutrients, including luteolin, had a 25% reduced risk of developing ovarian cancer when compared with women consuming the least.

Buffalo Sauce

This spicy sauce will do double duty as an ingredient in recipes, such as our Buffalo Chicken Sausages (opposite), and as a dipping sauce.

(opposite)

Tip

A host of recipes will be enhanced by this sauce, whether you add it right to the recipe or use it as a condiment or dip. Any sauce you don't use right away can be frozen in individual portion amounts in airtight containers for up to 3 months. Try adding it to meatloaves, casseroles and hearty stews.

¼ tsp	cayenne pepper	1 mL
½ tsp	celery salt	2 mL
½ tsp	garlic powder	2 mL
¼ tsp	freshly ground white pepper	1 mL
⅔ cup	hot pepper sauce (such as Frank's RedHot)	150 mL
½ cup	unsalted butter	125 mL
1½ tbsp	white vinegar	22 mL
¼ tsp	Worcestershire sauce	1 mL

1. In a small saucepan, combine cayenne, celery salt, garlic powder, white pepper, hot pepper sauce, butter, vinegar and Worcestershire sauce. Bring to a simmer over medium heat, whisking constantly. When sauce begins to bubble, remove from heat and whisk for 1 minute.

BBQ Chicken Pizza Sausages

What could be better than sausages that combine two North American favorites, barbecue and pizza? This recipe includes Kansas City–style sauce and some popular pizza toppings. Wrapped in a pita or hoagie bun, the sausages are great for tailgating.

Tip

Onions are great for adding flavor and nutrients to foods, but no one likes the tears. Here are some tricks to avoid them when cutting onions: keep your tongue at the roof of your mouth while cutting; wear swim goggles; run a fan, blowing away from the cutting board; chew gum slowly.

1 lb	trimmed boneless skinless chicken breasts, chilled (see page 49)	500 g
1 lb	untrimmed boneless skinless chicken thighs, chilled	500 g
¼ cup	minced onion	60 mL
¼ cup	shredded smoked provolone cheese	60 mL
¼ cup	shredded mozzarella cheese	60 mL
¼ cup	shredded Muenster cheese	60 mL
1 tbsp	real bacon bits (or crumbled cooked bacon)	15 mL
1½ tsp	kosher salt	7 mL
1 tsp	freshly cracked black pepper	5 mL
⅓ cup	water	75 mL
¼ cup	Kansas City–Style BBQ Sauce (see recipe, opposite)	60 mL
4 to 5 feet	32/35 mm hog casing, soaked (see page 49)	120 to 150 cm

1. Cut chicken breasts and thighs into pieces small enough to fit in the throat of your grinder, keeping them separate. Using the coarse grinder plate, grind chicken breasts into a large bowl or stand mixer bowl. Using the fine grinder plate, grind chicken thighs into the same bowl.

2. Add onion, provolone, mozzarella, Muenster, bacon bits, salt and pepper to the ground chicken. Using your hands or the stand mixer paddle attachment, mix until seasonings are evenly distributed. Add water and barbecue sauce; mix until a handful of the mixture holds together.

3. In a small skillet, over medium-high heat, sauté a small amount of the sausage mixture until no longer pink. Taste the sample, then adjust seasonings as desired.

4. Stuff sausage mixture into prepared casing as directed on page 51. Twist into 8 links, each about 6 inches (15 cm) in length.

Health Facts

Although onions aren't colorful (which is the usual sign of healthy plant pigments), they have a higher polyphenol content than garlic, tomatoes, carrots or red bell peppers. Polyphenols are one of the largest groups of phytonutrients in foods, and many possess numerous biologic activities, including antioxidant and anti-inflammatory effects.

Tips

To mash garlic, use a large chef's knife and a cutting board. Trim off the ends of the cloves and cut in half lengthwise. Turn the cloves flat side down and lay the side of the blade on each clove, smashing down with the heel of your palm. Repeat until the garlic has a paste-like consistency.

The cooled sauce can be stored in individual portion amounts in airtight containers in the refrigerator for up to 2 weeks or the freezer for up to 3 months.

Kansas City–Style BBQ Sauce

Of the numerous types of barbecue sauce, Kansas City–style is among the most famous. KC BBQ, as it's known to its legions of devotees, is characterized by vinegary, hot and sweet flavors.

2 tbsp	vegetable oil	30 mL
5	cloves garlic, mashed (see tip, at left)	5
1½ tbsp	sweet smoked paprika	22 mL
1 tbsp	chili powder	15 mL
1 tbsp	dry mustard	15 mL
1 tbsp	kosher salt	15 mL
2 tsp	hot pepper flakes	10 mL
1 tsp	freshly cracked black pepper	5 mL
¼ tsp	ground allspice	1 mL
2½ tbsp	tomato paste	37 mL
¼ cup	packed dark brown sugar	60 mL
2 cups	ketchup	500 mL
2 cups	water	500 mL
½ cup	apple cider vinegar	125 mL
3 tbsp	blackstrap molasses	45 mL
1 tbsp	tamari	15 mL
1 tbsp	Worcestershire sauce	15 mL

1. In a large saucepan, heat oil over medium heat. Add garlic, paprika, chili powder, mustard, salt, hot pepper flakes, black pepper, allspice and tomato paste; cook, stirring, for 4 minutes.

2. Stir in brown sugar, ketchup, water, vinegar, molasses, tamari and Worcestershire sauce; bring to a simmer. Reduce heat and simmer for 40 minutes to blend the flavors.

Philly Chicken Sausages

The traditional Philly cheesesteak sandwich is made with thinly sliced steak served in a hoagie bun and topped with melted cheese. These ingredients serve as the inspiration for our Philly Chicken Sausages, with chicken subbing in for the steak. Hoagie buns are de rigueur for serving them, of course.

Tips

For a more authentic Philly experience, serve these sausages in hoagie rolls, topped with melted American cheese.

How long to make your sausage links is really up to you, although we suggest 6 inches (15 cm) for this recipe. Keep in mind that this is a rough guideline, and that you may have to adjust the length up or down so that you don't end up with one link smaller than the rest.

1 lb	trimmed boneless skinless chicken breasts, chilled (see page 49)	500 g
1 lb	untrimmed boneless skinless chicken thighs, chilled	500 g
½ cup	diced provolone cheese	125 mL
3 tbsp	minced green bell pepper	45 mL
3 tbsp	minced onion	45 mL
1 tbsp	garlic powder	15 mL
2½ tsp	kosher salt	12 mL
1 tsp	freshly cracked black pepper	5 mL
½ cup	water	125 mL
4 to 5 feet	32/35 mm hog casing, soaked (see page 49)	120 to 150 cm

1. Cut chicken breasts and thighs into pieces small enough to fit in the throat of your grinder, keeping them separate. Using the coarse grinder plate, grind chicken breasts into a large bowl or stand mixer bowl. Using the fine grinder plate, grind chicken thighs into the same bowl.

2. Add cheese, green pepper, onion, garlic powder, salt and pepper to the ground chicken. Using your hands or the stand mixer paddle attachment, mix until seasonings are evenly distributed. Add water and mix until a handful of the mixture holds together.

3. In a small skillet, over medium-high heat, sauté a small amount of the sausage mixture until no longer pink. Taste the sample, then adjust seasonings as desired.

4. Stuff sausage mixture into prepared casing as directed on page 51. Twist into 8 links, each about 6 inches (15 cm) in length.

Health Facts

Even with the provolone cheese, this sausage is low in fat and high in protein. This profile qualifies it as a lean meat according to the guidelines of the American Diabetes Association.

Parmesan Chicken Sausages

Don't let the Italian name fool you: chicken Parmesan is a modern North American creation — much like these sausages that replicate its flavor!

**MAKES
8 SAUSAGES**

Tip

Grated cheese kept in the refrigerator can become moldy. To save money and prevent mold, buy a large chunk of Parmigiano-Reggiano at an Italian specialty store and ask for it to be grated. Freeze the grated cheese in a large freezer bag. Every few weeks, scoop out the amount you'll use in that time and store it in an airtight container in the refrigerator.

1 lb	trimmed boneless skinless chicken breasts, chilled (see page 49)	500 g
1 lb	untrimmed boneless skinless chicken thighs, chilled	500 g
½ cup	grated Parmigiano-Reggiano cheese	125 mL
2 tbsp	finely minced sun-dried tomatoes (see tip, page 190)	30 mL
1 tbsp	finely minced fresh basil	15 mL
1 tbsp	roasted garlic paste (see page 47)	15 mL
1½ tsp	kosher salt	7 mL
1 tsp	freshly cracked black pepper	5 mL
½ cup	water	125 mL
4 to 5 feet	32/35 mm hog casing, soaked (see page 49)	120 to 150 cm

1. Cut chicken breasts and thighs into pieces small enough to fit in the throat of your grinder, keeping them separate. Using the coarse grinder plate, grind chicken breasts into a large bowl or stand mixer bowl. Using the fine grinder plate, grind chicken thighs into the same bowl.

2. Add cheese, sun-dried tomatoes, basil, garlic paste, salt and pepper to the ground chicken. Using your hands or the stand mixer paddle attachment, mix until seasonings are evenly distributed. Add water and mix until a handful of the mixture holds together.

3. In a small skillet, over medium-high heat, sauté a small amount of the sausage mixture until no longer pink. Taste the sample, then adjust seasonings as desired.

4. Stuff sausage mixture into prepared casing as directed on page 51. Twist into 8 links, each about 6 inches (15 cm) in length.

Health Facts

One of the lesser-known phytonutrients in tomatoes is campesterol, a plant sterol. In addition to its antioxidant function, campesterol may help lower cholesterol. A 2015 study reported that plant sterols further lowered blood cholesterol levels in patients already taking cholesterol-lowering medications.

Turkey de Provence Sausages

Provence is a region in southeast France, but its cuisine borrows from Italian, Greek and Spanish influences. These sausages are filled with aromatic herbs that call to mind the rustic French countryside.

MAKES 6 SAUSAGES

Tip

A Provence-inspired herb mix makes a handy seasoning for your cabinet. Combine equal amounts of dried rosemary, thyme, oregano, marjoram and sage. You can use 2 tbsp (30 mL) of this herb mix in this recipe in place of the fresh rosemary and dried herbs.

Health Facts

One of the phytonutrients in marjoram is terpinolene, which acts as an antioxidant and an antifungal. A 2015 study reported that terpinolene was one of the most effective plant compounds tested in inhibiting the growth of many types of bacteria.

1 tsp	onion flakes	5 mL
1 tbsp	warm water	15 mL
1 lb	trimmed boneless skinless turkey breast, chilled (see page 49)	500 g
1 lb	untrimmed boneless skinless turkey thighs, chilled	500 g
1 tbsp	finely minced fresh rosemary	15 mL
2½ tsp	kosher salt	12 mL
2 tsp	dried thyme	10 mL
1 tsp	dried oregano	5 mL
1 tsp	dried marjoram	5 mL
1 tsp	ground rubbed sage	5 mL
1 tsp	freshly cracked black pepper	5 mL
¼ cup	heavy or whipping (35%) cream	60 mL
¼ cup	water	60 mL
4 to 5 feet	32/35 mm hog casing, soaked (see page 49)	120 to 150 cm

1. In a small bowl, combine onion flakes and warm water. Let stand for about 20 minutes or until softened.

2. Meanwhile, cut turkey breast and thighs into pieces small enough to fit in the throat of your grinder, keeping them separate. Using the coarse grinder plate, grind turkey breast into a large bowl or stand mixer bowl. Using the fine grinder plate, grind turkey thighs into the same bowl.

3. Add rosemary, salt, thyme, oregano, marjoram, sage, pepper and onion flakes mixture to the ground turkey. Using your hands or the stand mixer paddle attachment, mix until seasonings are evenly distributed. Add cream and ¼ cup (60 mL) water; mix until a handful of the mixture holds together.

4. In a small skillet, over medium-high heat, sauté a small amount of the sausage mixture until no longer pink. Taste the sample, then adjust seasonings as desired.

5. Stuff sausage mixture into prepared casing as directed on page 51. Twist into 6 links, each about 6 inches (15 cm) in length.

Sweet-and-Sour Turkey Sausages

Although beloved by many patrons of Chinese restaurants outside China, sweet-and-sour chicken and pork dishes are not, in fact, part of traditional Chinese cuisine. These sausages carry on the trend of adapting Chinese foods to North American tastes, incorporating all of the flavorful ingredients that blend so well in a sweet-and-sour dish.

MAKES 9 SAUSAGES

Tips

To get all the health benefits, buy raw honey, which has not been heated or pasteurized. You can purchase it locally or online.

If you use your hands to mix the ground meat, have a bowl of water nearby in which to dip your fingers. This will help keep them from getting too sticky.

Health Facts

Unlike processed honey, raw honey has not been heated or filtered. Both provide essential micronutrients and phytonutrients, but raw honey also contains propolis, a resin that bees use to seal the hive and protect it against bacteria. Propolis provides additional phytonutrients that appear to protect against cancer.

1	can (8 oz/227 mL) pineapple tidbits	1
1 lb	trimmed boneless skinless turkey breast, chilled (see page 49)	500 g
1 lb	untrimmed boneless skinless turkey thighs, chilled	500 g
¼ cup	minced red bell pepper	60 mL
¼ cup	minced green bell pepper	60 mL
¼ cup	minced green onions	60 mL
2½ tsp	kosher salt	12 mL
1 tsp	freshly cracked black pepper	5 mL
1 tsp	garlic powder	5 mL
½ tsp	ground ginger	2 mL
1 tbsp	liquid honey	15 mL
1 tbsp	soy sauce	15 mL
4 to 5 feet	32/35 mm hog casing, soaked (see page 49)	120 to 150 cm

1. Drain juice from pineapple, reserving ¼ cup (60 mL) juice. Finely chop pineapple tidbits and measure out ¼ cup (60 mL). (Store any remaining juice and pineapple in an airtight container in the refrigerator for another use.)

2. Cut turkey breast and thighs into pieces small enough to fit in the throat of your grinder, keeping them separate. Using the coarse grinder plate, grind turkey breast into a large bowl or stand mixer bowl. Using the fine grinder plate, grind turkey thighs into the same bowl.

3. Add pineapple, red pepper, green pepper, green onions, salt, pepper, garlic powder, ginger, honey and soy sauce to the ground turkey. Using your hands or the stand mixer paddle attachment, mix until seasonings are evenly distributed. Add the reserved pineapple juice and mix until a handful of the mixture holds together.

4. In a small skillet, over medium-high heat, sauté a small amount of the sausage mixture until no longer pink. Taste the sample, then adjust seasonings as desired.

5. Stuff sausage mixture into prepared casing as directed on page 51. Twist into 9 links, each about 6 inches (15 cm) in length.

Szechuan Turkey Sausages

These sausages combine typical ingredients from Szechuan cuisine. Based on your heat tolerance, you may want to dial up or down on the chili paste.

**MAKES
7 SAUSAGES**

Tips

You can buy chili paste, which is a staple in many Asian cuisines, but it's easy to make your own, following our recipe, and you'll know exactly what went into it.

How long to make your sausage links is really up to you, although we suggest 6 inches (15 cm) for this recipe. Keep in mind that this is a rough guideline, and that you may have to adjust the length up or down so that you don't end up with one link smaller than the rest.

1 lb	trimmed boneless skinless turkey breast, chilled (see page 49)	500 g
1 lb	untrimmed boneless skinless turkey thighs, chilled	500 g
¼ cup	finely chopped green onions	60 mL
1 tbsp	finely minced ginger	15 mL
1 tbsp	finely minced garlic	15 mL
2 tsp	kosher salt	10 mL
1 tsp	freshly cracked black pepper	5 mL
1 tbsp	Chili Paste (see recipe, opposite)	15 mL
1 tbsp	soy sauce	15 mL
¼ cup	water	60 mL
4 to 5 feet	32/35 mm hog casing, soaked (see page 49)	120 to 150 cm

1. Cut turkey breast and thighs into pieces small enough to fit in the throat of your grinder, keeping them separate. Using the coarse grinder plate, grind turkey breast into a large bowl or stand mixer bowl. Using the fine grinder plate, grind turkey thighs into the same bowl.

2. Add green onions, ginger, garlic, salt, pepper, chili paste and soy sauce to the ground turkey. Using your hands or the stand mixer paddle attachment, mix until seasonings are evenly distributed. Add water and mix until a handful of the mixture holds together.

3. In a small skillet, over medium-high heat, sauté a small amount of the sausage mixture until no longer pink. Taste the sample, then adjust seasonings as desired.

4. Stuff sausage mixture into prepared casing as directed on page 51. Twist into 7 links, each about 6 inches (15 cm) in length.

Health Facts

Of the many phytonutrients in ginger, one of the most intriguing is 6-dehydrogingerdione (DGE), which has numerous biologic effects, especially as a powerful antioxidant. A 2014 study reported that DGE destroyed free radicals in the nerve cells of rats in which oxidative stress had been induced, thereby protecting the cells.

Chili Paste

This chili paste is a great addition to any recipe you want to spice up. It has many ingredients (and they're all important), but it's still an easy recipe to make.

MAKES ABOUT 4 CUPS (1 L)

Tip

To store the paste, pour it into glass jars with secure lids. Some people don't refrigerate chili paste, but refrigeration is recommended for both food safety and to prevent spoilage. It can be safely stored in the refrigerator for up to 4 months.

- Food processor

6	shallots, peeled	6
5	cloves garlic, peeled	5
3	Thai bird chile peppers	3
2	serrano chile peppers	2
2	stalks lemongrass (tender white part only), chopped	2
2 tbsp	minced gingerroot	30 mL
1 tbsp	granulated sugar	15 mL
1 tbsp	kosher salt	15 mL
1 tbsp	coarsely ground black pepper	15 mL
1 tbsp	Worcestershire sauce	15 mL
	Juice of 2 limes (¼ cup/60 mL)	
2 tbsp	peanut oil (approx.)	30 mL

1. In food processor, combine shallots, garlic, Thai bird and serrano chile peppers, lemongrass, ginger, sugar, salt, pepper, Worcestershire sauce and lime juice; process for 3 minutes or until finely chopped.

2. With the motor running, through the feed tube, add just enough oil to achieve a paste-like consistency, making sure not to thin the paste. Adjust seasonings to taste.

Autumn Harvest Turkey Sausages

In many parts of North America, autumn air carries memories of biting into a crisp apple, with thoughts of turkey dinners not far behind. These delightful sausages blend the sweetness of autumn apples and maple syrup with the tang of fresh cranberries. They're a natural fit with roasted acorn squash for an autumnal dinner.

**MAKES
8 SAUSAGES**

Tips

It's hard to match the flavor of a Honeycrisp apple, which hit the market relatively recently. But if you can't find this apple (and they sell out fast), try a Fuji or Pink Lady.

Fresh cranberries are hard to find outside of holiday seasons in fall and winter. When you find them, buy extra and wash, dry and freeze the cranberries in freezer bags for use all year round. Make sure to transfer some to the refrigerator to thaw the night before you want to use them in this recipe.

1 tsp	onion flakes	5 mL
1 tbsp	warm water	15 mL
1 lb	trimmed boneless skinless turkey breast, chilled (see page 49)	500 g
1 lb	untrimmed boneless skinless turkey thighs, chilled	500 g
1 cup	finely chopped peeled sweet-tart apple (such as Honeycrisp)	250 mL
¼ cup	finely chopped fresh cranberries	60 mL
2½ tsp	kosher salt	12 mL
½ tsp	freshly ground white pepper	2 mL
2 tbsp	pure maple syrup	30 mL
¼ cup	water	60 mL
4 to 5 feet	32/35 mm hog casing, soaked (see page 49)	120 to 150 cm

1. In a small bowl, combine onion flakes and warm water. Let stand for about 20 minutes or until softened.

2. Meanwhile, cut turkey breast and thighs into pieces small enough to fit in the throat of your grinder, keeping them separate. Using the coarse grinder plate, grind turkey breast into a large bowl or stand mixer bowl. Using the fine grinder plate, grind turkey thighs into the same bowl.

3. Add apple, cranberries, salt, pepper, maple syrup and onion flakes mixture to the ground turkey. Using your hands or the stand mixer paddle attachment, mix until seasonings are evenly distributed. Add ¼ cup (60 mL) water and mix until a handful of the mixture holds together.

4. In a small skillet, over medium-high heat, sauté a small amount of the sausage mixture until no longer pink. Taste the sample, then adjust seasonings as desired.

5. Stuff sausage mixture into prepared casing as directed on page 51. Twist into 8 links, each about 6 inches (15 cm) in length.

Health Facts

Cranberries are high in essential nutrients, especially vitamin C and manganese, and in phytonutrients. A 2011 study reported that cranberry extract induced cancer cell suicide, known as apoptosis, in prostate cancer cells.

Thanksgiving Turkey Sausages

Many North Americans celebrate Thanksgiving by roasting a turkey with all the traditional trimmings. In these sausages, along with the turkey itself, you'll find all the traditional herbs and flavorings used to make the stuffing.

MAKES 9 SAUSAGES

Tip

For an even stronger herb flavor, substitute packaged stuffing mix for the bread crumbs, but reduce the salt in the recipe to 1½ tsp (7 mL).

Health Facts

Diosmetin, one of the phenolic acids found in sage, has several biologic effects, including antiviral, anticarcinogenic and antidementia. A 2003 study reported that sage improved memory in young adults, a possible link to its antidementia effects.

1 tsp	vegetable oil	5 mL
¼ cup	finely chopped onion	60 mL
¼ cup	finely chopped celery	60 mL
1 tsp	onion flakes	5 mL
1 tbsp	warm water	15 mL
1 lb	trimmed boneless skinless turkey breast, chilled (see page 49)	500 g
1 lb	untrimmed boneless skinless turkey thighs, chilled	500 g
1 cup	dry bread crumbs	250 mL
2½ tsp	kosher salt	12 mL
1 tsp	freshly cracked black pepper	5 mL
1 tsp	ground rubbed sage	5 mL
1 tsp	dried marjoram	5 mL
½ tsp	garlic powder	2 mL
½ cup	water	125 mL
4 to 5 feet	32/35 mm hog casing, soaked (see page 49)	120 to 150 cm

1. In a small skillet, heat oil over medium-high heat. Add onion and celery; cook, stirring, for about 6 minutes or until tender. Let cool completely.

2. Meanwhile, in a small bowl, combine onion flakes and warm water. Let stand for about 20 minutes or until softened.

3. Cut turkey breast and thighs into pieces small enough to fit in the throat of your grinder, keeping them separate. Using the coarse grinder plate, grind turkey breast into a large bowl or stand mixer bowl. Using the fine grinder plate, grind turkey thighs into the same bowl.

4. Add onion mixture, bread crumbs, salt, pepper, sage, marjoram, garlic powder and onion flakes mixture to the ground turkey. Using your hands or the stand mixer paddle attachment, mix until seasonings are evenly distributed. Add ½ cup (125 mL) water and mix until a handful of the mixture holds together.

5. In a small skillet, over medium-high heat, sauté a small amount of the sausage mixture until no longer pink. Taste the sample, then adjust seasonings as desired.

6. Stuff sausage mixture into prepared casing as directed on page 51. Twist into 9 links, each about 6 inches (15 cm) in length.

Holiday Turkey Sausages

These sausages were inspired by a cranberry sauce recipe created by Detroit restaurateur and chef Jimmy Schmidt, of the famous Rattlesnake Club. Many ingredient additions and deletions later, it's still a family favorite during the holidays when turkey is featured on the menu.

**MAKES
9 SAUSAGES**

Tip

You can buy frozen mangos, but they're not as flavorful as fresh. Timing can be tricky with fresh mangos — to improve the odds that one will be perfect when you're ready to make sausage, buy several mangos at different stages of ripeness. Color is not an indication of ripeness; mangos are ready when they are slightly soft to the touch and give off a fragrant scent.

1 tsp	onion flakes	5 mL
1 tbsp	warm water	15 mL
1 lb	trimmed boneless skinless turkey breast, chilled (see page 49)	500 g
1 lb	untrimmed boneless skinless turkey thighs, chilled	500 g
1 cup	finely diced mango	250 mL
¼ cup	finely minced golden raisins	60 mL
¼ cup	finely minced dried cranberries	60 mL
2½ tsp	kosher salt	12 mL
1 tsp	freshly cracked black pepper	5 mL
¼ cup	Grand Marnier liqueur	60 mL
4 to 5 feet	32/35 mm hog casing, soaked (see page 49)	120 to 150 cm

1. In a small bowl, combine onion flakes and warm water. Let stand for about 20 minutes or until softened.

2. Meanwhile, cut turkey breast and thighs into pieces small enough to fit in the throat of your grinder, keeping them separate. Using the coarse grinder plate, grind turkey breast into a large bowl or stand mixer bowl. Using the fine grinder plate, grind turkey thighs into the same bowl.

3. Add mango, raisins, cranberries, salt, pepper and onion flakes mixture to the ground turkey. Using your hands or the stand mixer paddle attachment, mix until seasonings are evenly distributed. Add liqueur and mix until a handful of the mixture holds together.

4. In a small skillet, over medium-high heat, sauté a small amount of the sausage mixture until no longer pink. Taste the sample, then adjust seasonings as desired.

5. Stuff sausage mixture into prepared casing as directed on page 51. Twist into 9 links, each about 6 inches (15 cm) in length.

Health Facts

Mangos are high in vitamin C and vitamin A in the form of beta-carotene, a superstar among antioxidants. In addition, a 2014 study reported that one of mango's many phytonutrients, mangiferin, enhanced the growth of insulin-producing cells, suggesting that it may help prevent and/or treat diabetes.

Game and Fish Sausages

It should be apparent by now that you can stuff just about anything into a casing and make delicious sausages. Our two sausage experts have experimented with all types of game meat, from antelope to yak, and have come up with creative recipes to turn it into a variety of tasty products. This chapter provides the basics on using many of these meats to make sausages.

With the exception of the fish sausages (which are poached), all of the sausages in this chapter taste best if they are refrigerated for at least 1 day before they are cooked.

Duck Sausages

The Chinese were likely the first to domesticate ducks, and duck meat has long been favored throughout Asia. These days, duck hunting is a popular sport. As with other types of game fowl, duck has no white meat and is similar to dark meat from chicken or turkey.

**MAKES
6 SAUSAGES**

Tips

If you are a duck hunter and will be making these sausages often, try using different types of preserves and dried fruit. For example, dried cranberries would combine well with orange marmalade.

If you decide to use table salt in place of kosher salt, use 1½ tsp (7 mL), as table salt has a higher density.

1½ lbs	untrimmed boneless skinless wild or farm-raised duck breast, chilled (see page 50)	750 g
8 oz	untrimmed boneless skinless chicken thighs, chilled	250 g
¼ cup	strawberry preserves	60 mL
2 tbsp	finely minced dried cherries	30 mL
1 tbsp	finely minced fresh thyme	15 mL
1 tbsp	finely minced fresh chives	15 mL
2 tsp	grated orange zest	10 mL
2 tsp	kosher salt	10 mL
1 tsp	freshly cracked black pepper	5 mL
1 tsp	garlic powder	5 mL
¼ cup	water	60 mL
4 to 5 feet	32/35 mm hog casing, soaked (see page 49)	120 to 150 cm

1. Cut duck breast and chicken thighs into pieces small enough to fit in the throat of your grinder, keeping them separate. Using the coarse grinder plate, grind duck breast into a large bowl or stand mixer bowl. Using the fine grinder plate, grind chicken thighs into the same bowl.

2. Add preserves, cherries, thyme, chives, orange zest, salt, pepper and garlic powder to the ground meat. Using your hands or the stand mixer paddle attachment, mix until seasonings are evenly distributed. Add water and mix until a handful of the mixture holds together.

3. In a small skillet, over medium-high heat, sauté a small amount of the sausage mixture until no longer pink. Taste the sample, then adjust seasonings as desired.

4. Stuff sausage mixture into prepared casing as directed on page 51. Twist into 6 links, each about 6 inches (15 cm) in length.

Health Facts

Duck meat's nutritional profile is similar to that of chicken thighs, with 1 oz (30 g) of lean meat providing 35 calories, 6 grams of protein and 1 gram of fat.

Goose Sausages

Geese are among the most popular waterfowl for hunters. The meat is all dark and relatively lean. Farm-raised domesticated goose does not have a gamey flavor; some people describe it as roast beef–like. As for wild goose, some say it's delicious, while others consider it "best stuffed into sausage."

Tips

Goat cheese is highly perishable because of its high moisture content. Whether opened or unopened, it should be used within 2 to 3 weeks.

Blackberries make a good substitute for blueberries, depending on what is in season.

If you would rather not use beer, you can substitute water.

1 lb	trimmed boneless skinless goose breast, chilled (see page 49)	500 g
1 lb	untrimmed boneless skinless chicken thighs, chilled	500 g
4 oz	goat cheese, crumbled	125 g
¼ cup	blueberries	60 mL
2 tsp	kosher salt	10 mL
2 tsp	freshly cracked black pepper	10 mL
1 tsp	dried marjoram	5 mL
1 tsp	ground coriander	5 mL
½ tsp	ground cinnamon	2 mL
¼ tsp	ground nutmeg	1 mL
½ cup	dark beer (porter or stout)	125 mL
4 to 5 feet	32/35 mm hog casing, soaked (see page 49)	120 to 150 cm

1. Cut goose breast and chicken thighs into pieces small enough to fit in the throat of your grinder, keeping them separate. Using the coarse grinder plate, grind goose breast into a large bowl or stand mixer bowl. Using the fine grinder plate, grind chicken thighs into the same bowl.

2. Add cheese, blueberries, salt, pepper, marjoram, coriander, cinnamon and nutmeg to the ground meat. Using your hands or the stand mixer paddle attachment, mix until seasonings are evenly distributed. Add beer and mix until a handful of the mixture holds together.

3. In a small skillet, over medium-high heat, sauté a small amount of the sausage mixture until no longer pink. Taste the sample, then adjust seasonings as desired.

4. Stuff sausage mixture into prepared casing as directed on page 51. Twist into 7 links, each about 6 inches (15 cm) in length.

Health Facts

Domesticated goose meat provides 46 calories, 6.5 grams of protein and 2 grams of fat per 1 oz (30 g), which qualifies it as a lean meat. Although wild goose is not listed in nutrient databases, its nutrient content would be similar or even lower in fat and calories.

Wild Turkey Sausages

Turkey hunting remains a popular sport, especially in the fall as North Americans prepare for Thanksgiving feasts. You can also purchase farm-raised "wild" turkey at specialty stores, though usually only during the autumn months. Even this turkey meat is significantly different from that of the more common domesticated birds found in all grocery stores.

Tips

For a leaner version of these sausages, substitute ¼ cup (60 mL) dry white wine for the cream.

If you use your hands to mix the ground meat, have a bowl of water nearby in which to dip your fingers. This will help keep them from getting too sticky.

Health Facts

Wild turkey breast contains 32 calories, 6 grams of protein and 1 gram of fat per 1 oz (30 g), making it a very lean meat.

2¼ cups	water, divided	550 mL
¼ cup	diced carrots	60 mL
1 lb	trimmed boneless skinless wild turkey breast, chilled (see page 49)	500 g
1 lb	untrimmed boneless skinless turkey or chicken thighs, chilled	500 g
2 tbsp	finely chopped fresh parsley	30 mL
2 tsp	kosher salt	10 mL
1 tsp	freshly cracked black pepper	5 mL
1 tsp	onion powder	5 mL
1 tsp	garlic powder	5 mL
½ tsp	celery seeds	2 mL
¼ cup	heavy or whipping (35%) cream	60 mL
4 to 5 feet	32/35 mm hog casing, soaked (see page 49)	120 to 150 cm

1. In a small saucepan, bring 2 cups (500 mL) water to a boil. Add carrots and cook for 6 minutes or until slightly tender. Drain, plunge into a bowl of ice water and let cool completely.

2. Meanwhile, cut turkey breast and thighs into pieces small enough to fit in the throat of your grinder, keeping them separate. Using the coarse grinder plate, grind turkey breast into a large bowl or stand mixer bowl. Using the fine grinder plate, grind thighs into the same bowl.

3. Add carrots, parsley, salt, pepper, onion powder, garlic powder and celery seeds to the ground meat. Using your hands or the stand mixer paddle attachment, mix until seasonings are evenly distributed. Add cream and the remaining water; mix until a handful of the mixture holds together.

4. In a small skillet, over medium-high heat, sauté a small amount of the sausage mixture until no longer pink. Taste the sample, then adjust seasonings as desired.

5. Stuff sausage mixture into prepared casing as directed on page 51. Twist into 7 links, each about 6 inches (15 cm) in length.

Pheasant Sausages

Pheasant was domesticated centuries ago in several parts of the world, but it's also a favorite of those who enjoy bird hunting. The meat has long been considered a delicacy, with many celebrated chefs creating famous recipes. Domesticated pheasant is similar to chicken, although its breast meat is even leaner. Wild pheasant has the expected gamey flavor, which increases with the age of the bird.

Tips

If you are using wild pheasant and want to use the entire bird, you can use 1 lb (500 g) each of trimmed breast and untrimmed thigh meat.

If you decide to use table salt in place of kosher salt, use 1½ tsp (7 mL), as table salt has a higher density.

Health Facts

Pheasant (both thigh and breast meat) provides 38 calories, 7 grams of protein and 1 gram of fat per 1 oz (30 g), making it a very lean meat.

2¼ cups	water, divided	550 mL
¼ cup	diced carrots	60 mL
2 lbs	untrimmed pheasant thighs, chilled (see page 50)	1 kg
1 tbsp	finely chopped fresh thyme	15 mL
1 tbsp	finely chopped fresh parsley	15 mL
2 tsp	kosher salt	10 mL
1 tsp	freshly ground white pepper	5 mL
1 tsp	onion powder	5 mL
1 tsp	garlic powder	5 mL
1 tsp	sweet paprika	5 mL
½ tsp	celery seeds	2 mL
¼ cup	heavy or whipping (35%) cream	60 mL
4 to 5 feet	32/35 mm hog casing, soaked (see page 49)	120 to 150 cm

1. In a small saucepan, bring 2 cups (500 mL) water to a boil. Add carrots and cook for 6 minutes or until slightly tender. Drain, plunge into a bowl of ice water and let cool completely.

2. Meanwhile, cut pheasant into pieces small enough to fit in the throat of your grinder. Using the coarse grinder plate, grind pheasant into a large bowl or stand mixer bowl.

3. Add carrots, thyme, parsley, salt, pepper, onion powder, garlic powder, paprika and celery seeds to the ground pheasant. Using your hands or the stand mixer paddle attachment, mix until seasonings are evenly distributed. Add cream and the remaining water; mix until a handful of the mixture holds together.

4. In a small skillet, over medium-high heat, sauté a small amount of the sausage mixture until no longer pink. Taste the sample, then adjust seasonings as desired.

5. Stuff sausage mixture into prepared casing as directed on page 51. Twist into 7 links, each about 6 inches (15 cm) in length.

Venison Sausages

Hunters fortunate enough to bag a deer will save the steaks and roasts and use all other meat (generally called venison trim) to make sausage. Non-hunters may find a local source of venison, but in areas where no such source exists, the only recourse is the Internet. Be warned, though: you'll pay top dollar online, especially with shipping charges.

MAKES 7 SAUSAGES

Tips

If you cannot find 24/26 mm sheep casing, 32/25 mm hog casing will work just fine, though you'll end up with 8 links instead of 7. The sheep casing gives the sausage a more tender bite, but some people prefer the wider diameter of the hog casing.

How long to make your sausage links is really up to you, although we suggest 6 inches (15 cm) for this recipe. Keep in mind that this is a rough guideline, and that you may have to adjust the length up or down so that you don't end up with one link smaller than the rest.

1 tbsp	dried juniper berries	15 mL
2¼ cups	water, divided	550 mL
1 lb	venison trim, chilled (see page 50)	500 g
1 lb	trimmed boneless pork shoulder blade roast, chilled	500 g
½ cup	chopped morel mushrooms or shiitake mushroom caps	125 mL
1 tbsp	finely minced garlic	15 mL
1 tbsp	mustard seeds	15 mL
2 tsp	finely minced fresh sage	10 mL
2 tsp	finely minced fresh rosemary	10 mL
2 tsp	kosher salt	10 mL
1 tsp	freshly cracked black pepper	5 mL
4 to 5 feet	24/26 mm sheep casing, soaked (see page 49)	120 to 150 cm

1. In a small saucepan, bring juniper berries and 2 cups (500 mL) water to a boil. Reduce heat to low, cover and simmer for 10 minutes or until berries are rehydrated. Drain berries and let cool completely, then mince.

2. Meanwhile, cut venison and pork into pieces small enough to fit in the throat of your grinder. Using the coarse grinder plate, grind meat into a large bowl or stand mixer bowl.

3. Add juniper berries, mushrooms, garlic, mustard seeds, sage, rosemary, salt and pepper to the ground meat. Using your hands or the stand mixer paddle attachment, mix until seasonings are evenly distributed. Add the remaining water and mix until white strands appear in the mixture and a handful of the mixture holds together.

4. In a small skillet, over medium-high heat, sauté a small amount of the sausage mixture until no longer pink. Taste the sample, then adjust seasonings as desired.

5. Stuff sausage mixture into prepared casing as directed on page 51. Twist into 7 links, each about 6 inches (15 cm) in length.

Health Facts

Venison is a very lean meat, with 1 oz (30 g) containing just 47 calories, 9 grams of protein and 0 grams of fat, regardless of the cut (shoulder or tenderloin).

Elk Sausages

Elk meat is not considered venison even though the elk is a member of the deer family. As with venison, you may find a local source, depending on your area. If not, elk meat is available for purchase online, though it is quite expensive. Elk trim is generally used for sausage making, but any cut will work.

**MAKES
7 SAUSAGES**

Tips

Mushrooms add an umami flavor that contributes nicely to the elk meat. Any type of mushroom will work in this recipe, so feel free to use your favorite in place of the portobellos.

You can vary the flavor of these sausages by using different dried fruits in place of the blueberries.

1 lb	elk meat trim, chilled (see page 50)	500 g
1 lb	trimmed boneless pork shoulder blade roast, chilled	500 g
½ cup	chopped portobello mushroom caps	125 mL
2 tbsp	finely minced dried blueberries	30 mL
1 tbsp	finely minced garlic	15 mL
1 tbsp	mustard seeds	15 mL
2 tsp	finely minced fresh sage	10 mL
2 tsp	finely minced fresh rosemary	10 mL
2 tsp	kosher salt	10 mL
1 tsp	freshly cracked black pepper	5 mL
¼ cup	water	60 mL
4 to 5 feet	32/35 mm hog casing, soaked (see page 49)	120 to 150 cm

1. Cut elk and pork into pieces small enough to fit in the throat of your grinder. Using the coarse grinder plate, grind meat into a large bowl or stand mixer bowl.

2. Add mushrooms, blueberries, garlic, mustard seeds, sage, rosemary, salt and pepper to the ground meat. Using your hands or the stand mixer paddle attachment, mix until seasonings are evenly distributed. Add water and mix until white strands appear in the mixture and a handful of the mixture holds together.

3. In a small skillet, over medium-high heat, sauté a small amount of the sausage mixture until no longer pink. Taste the sample, then adjust seasonings as desired.

4. Stuff sausage mixture into prepared casing as directed on page 51. Twist into 7 links, each about 6 inches (15 cm) in length.

Health Facts

Elk is a very lean meat, with all cuts providing about 32 calories, 7 grams of protein and 0 grams of fat per 1 oz (30 g).

Moose Sausages

The moose is the largest member of the deer family, with an adult male weighing in at 1,800 pounds (820 kg). The flavor of the meat varies with the season. When leafy green plants are in season, the meat tastes similar to grass-fed beef. In fall or winter, when moose munch on twigs and conifers, the meat takes on a gamey flavor. If you want moose meat and are not a hunter, you'll most likely need to purchase it online, unless you live in an area where it is locally available.

MAKES
MAKES 6 SAUSAGES

Tips

Make sure the moose meat is trimmed of all visible fat, as the fat would impart an unpleasant gamey flavor.

If you can't find beef fat, you can substitute 4 oz (125 g) high-fat ground beef.

1¾ lbs	moose meat trim, chilled (see page 50)	875 g
4 oz	beef fat (see tip, at left), chilled	125 g
2 tbsp	finely minced garlic	30 mL
2 tbsp	finely chopped fresh tarragon	30 mL
1 tbsp	mustard seeds	15 mL
1 tbsp	onion powder	15 mL
2 tsp	sweet paprika	10 mL
2 tsp	kosher salt	10 mL
1 tsp	freshly cracked black pepper	5 mL
1 tsp	ground coriander	5 mL
¼ tsp	ground allspice	1 mL
¼ cup	water	60 mL
4 to 5 feet	32/35 mm hog casing, soaked (see page 49)	120 to 150 cm

1. Cut moose meat and beef fat into pieces small enough to fit in the throat of your grinder. Using the coarse grinder plate, grind moose meat and beef fat into a large bowl or stand mixer bowl.

2. Add garlic, tarragon, mustard seeds, onion powder, paprika, salt, pepper, coriander and allspice to the ground meat mixture. Using your hands or the stand mixer paddle attachment, mix until seasonings are evenly distributed. Add water and mix until white strands appear in the mixture and a handful of the mixture holds together.

3. In a small skillet, over medium-high heat, sauté a small amount of the sausage mixture until no longer pink. Taste the sample, then adjust seasonings as desired.

4. Stuff sausage mixture into prepared casing as directed on page 51. Twist into 6 links, each about 6 inches (15 cm) in length.

Health Facts

Like venison and elk, moose is a very lean meat, with 1 oz (30 g) providing 30 calories, 6 grams of protein and 0 grams of fat.

Bison Sausages

People often confuse buffalo with bison. While both belong to the same family, the American bison lives only in North America. Most of the meat available in North America, even when called "buffalo," is actually bison. If you enjoy this meat and don't have a local supplier, it's available for purchase online.

Tips

You can substitute cooked fresh or frozen corn kernels for the canned corn.

If you like your sausages spicy, you can add twice as much (or more!) of the cayenne pepper and chipotle pepper.

Health Facts

There are slight differences in the nutritional profile of bison meat, depending on the cut, but on average, it provides 49 calories, 9 grams of protein and 0 grams of fat per 1 oz (30 g), making it a very lean meat.

1 lb	trimmed bison roast, chilled (see page 49)	500 g
1 lb	trimmed boneless pork shoulder blade roast, chilled	500 g
¼ cup	drained canned corn kernels	60 mL
¼ cup	finely chopped fresh cilantro	60 mL
2 tsp	sweet paprika	10 mL
2 tsp	kosher salt	10 mL
2 tsp	freshly cracked black pepper	10 mL
1 tsp	cayenne pepper	5 mL
1 tsp	finely ground coffee	5 mL
1 tsp	ground cumin	5 mL
1 tsp	chili powder	5 mL
1 tsp	onion powder	5 mL
1 tsp	garlic powder	5 mL
½ tsp	dried thyme	2 mL
½ tsp	ground chipotle pepper	2 mL
2 tbsp	apple cider vinegar	30 mL
2 tbsp	water	30 mL
4 to 5 feet	32/35 mm hog casing, soaked (see page 49)	120 to 150 cm

1. Cut bison and pork into pieces small enough to fit in the throat of your grinder. Using the coarse grinder plate, grind meat into a large bowl or stand mixer bowl.

2. Add corn, cilantro, paprika, salt, black pepper, cayenne, coffee, cumin, chili powder, onion powder, garlic powder, thyme and chipotle pepper to the ground meat. Using your hands or the stand mixer paddle attachment, mix until seasonings are evenly distributed. Add vinegar and water; mix until white strands appear in the mixture.

3. In a small skillet, over medium-high heat, sauté a small amount of the sausage mixture until no longer pink. Taste the sample, then adjust seasonings as desired.

4. Stuff sausage mixture into prepared casing as directed on page 51. Twist into 6 links, each about 6 inches (15 cm) in length.

Bear Sausages

Bears conjure up an image of a lumbering beast that packs on fat to get ready for hibernation. So you might be surprised to learn that bear meat is lean. If you don't want to face down a bear yourself on a hunt, you'll likely have to purchase the meat online. This meat definitely qualifies as "gamey," and it's flavor varies depending on what the bear was feasting on prior to its demise.

**MAKES
6 SAUSAGES**

Tips

Be meticulous about trimming off the bear fat, as it is likely to impart an undesirable flavor.

If you use your hands to mix the ground meat, have a bowl of water nearby in which to dip your fingers. This will help keep them from getting too sticky.

How long to make your sausage links is really up to you, although we suggest 6 inches (15 cm) for this recipe. Keep in mind that this is a rough guideline, and that you may have to adjust the length up or down so that you don't end up with one link smaller than the rest.

1 lb	trimmed bear meat, chilled (see page 49)	500 g
8 oz	trimmed boneless pork shoulder blade roast, chilled	250 g
8 oz	85/15 boneless beef shoulder, chilled	250 g
2 tbsp	finely minced garlic	30 mL
2 tsp	finely minced fresh rosemary	10 mL
1 tsp	finely minced fresh oregano	5 mL
2 tsp	kosher salt	10 mL
2 tsp	freshly cracked black pepper	10 mL
2 tsp	curry powder	10 mL
1 tsp	onion powder	5 mL
1 tsp	finely grated orange zest	5 mL
¼ cup	liquid honey	60 mL
2 tbsp	Dijon mustard	30 mL
2 tbsp	water	30 mL
4 to 5 feet	32/35 mm hog casing, soaked (see page 49)	120 to 150 cm

1. Cut bear, pork and beef into pieces small enough to fit in the throat of your grinder. Using the coarse grinder plate, grind meat into a large bowl or stand mixer bowl.

2. Add garlic, rosemary, oregano, salt, pepper, curry powder, onion powder and orange zest to the ground meat. Using your hands or the stand mixer paddle attachment, mix until seasonings are evenly distributed. Add honey, mustard and water; mix until white strands appear in the mixture and a handful of the mixture holds together.

3. In a small skillet, over medium-high heat, sauté a small amount of the sausage mixture until no longer pink. Taste the sample, then adjust seasonings as desired.

4. Stuff sausage mixture into prepared casing as directed on page 51. Twist into 6 links, each about 6 inches (15 cm) in length.

Health Facts
Bear is a lean meat, with 1 oz (30 g) providing 46 calories, 5.5 grams of protein and 2 grams of fat.

Bass Sausages

The term "bass" encompasses a number of different fish species, some freshwater and some saltwater. Popular bass species include largemouth, smallmouth and striped bass. Of all game fish, the largemouth bass is the best known and most popular in North America.

MAKES 6 SAUSAGES

Tips

For a bit of smoke flavor, try adding ½ tsp (2 mL) liquid smoke with the coriander.

Fish sausages are highly perishable, so make sure to freeze whatever you don't plan to eat within 2 days.

Health Facts

One ounce (30 g) of freshwater bass contains 28 calories, 5 grams of protein and 1 gram of fat, with some of the fat being omega-3 fatty acids. The American Heart Association recommends eating a 3½-oz (100 g) serving of fish twice weekly to reduce the risk of cardiovascular disease.

• Meat thermometer

2 lbs	boned skinless bass, chilled (see page 50)	1 kg
2 tsp	kosher salt	10 mL
2	large eggs	2
2 tbsp	crushed ice	30 mL
2 tbsp	water	30 mL
1 tbsp	hot pepper flakes	15 mL
1 tsp	freshly cracked black pepper	5 mL
1 tsp	ground ginger	5 mL
1 tsp	garlic powder	5 mL
⅛ tsp	ground coriander	0.5 mL
4 to 5 feet	32/35 mm hog casing, soaked (see page 49)	120 to 150 cm

1. Cut fish into pieces small enough to fit in the throat of your grinder. Using the coarse grinder plate, grind fish into a large bowl or stand mixer bowl.

2. Add salt to the ground fish. Using your hands or the stand mixer paddle attachment, mix until salt is evenly distributed. Let stand for 10 minutes.

3. Add eggs, ice and water; mix until evenly distributed. Add hot pepper flakes, black pepper, ginger, garlic powder and coriander; mix until evenly distributed.

4. In a small skillet, over medium-high heat, sauté a small amount of the sausage mixture until firm and opaque. Taste the sample, then adjust seasonings as desired.

5. Stuff sausage mixture into prepared casing as directed on page 51. Twist into 6 links, each about 6 inches (15 cm) in length. Cut links apart.

6. In a large shallow pan of simmering water (200°F to 205°F/93°C to 96°C), poach sausages for 15 to 20 minutes, topping up water if level dips, until sausages reach an internal temperature of 180°F (82°C).

7. Transfer sausages to a bowl of cold water and let stand until the internal temperature of the sausages drops to 70°F (21°C), refreshing cold water as necessary to cool the sausages quickly. Meanwhile, bring the pan of water to a boil.

8. Add sausages to the boiling water for 1 minute to tighten the casings. Drain and let cool completely, then wipe dry with paper towels and refrigerate for up to 2 days or freeze.

Lake Whitefish Sausages

This slender fish is one of the most important to the fishing industry in North America and swims in numerous lakes throughout the continent. One of its nicknames is "humpback," because its head is small in comparison to the length of its body.

Tips

If you decide to use table salt in place of kosher salt, use 1½ tsp (7 mL), as table salt has a higher density.

Fish sausages are highly perishable, so make sure to freeze whatever you don't plan to eat within 2 days.

Health Facts

Lake whitefish contains 38 calories, 5 grams of protein and 2 grams of fat per 1 oz (30 g). Of the fat, 28% is in the form of omega-3 fatty acids.

• **Meat thermometer**

2 lbs	boned skinless lake whitefish, chilled (see page 50)	1 kg
2 tsp	kosher salt	10 mL
2	large eggs	2
2 tbsp	crushed ice	30 mL
2 tbsp	water	30 mL
2 tbsp	finely chopped fresh dill	30 mL
1 tbsp	finely grated lemon zest	15 mL
1 tsp	freshly ground white pepper	5 mL
1 tsp	garlic powder	5 mL
½ tsp	sweet paprika	2 mL
4 to 5 feet	32/35 mm hog casing, soaked (see page 49)	120 to 150 cm

1. Cut fish into pieces small enough to fit in the throat of your grinder. Using the coarse grinder plate, grind fish into a large bowl or stand mixer bowl.

2. Add salt to the ground fish. Using your hands or the stand mixer paddle attachment, mix until salt is evenly distributed. Let stand for 10 minutes.

3. Add eggs, ice and water; mix until evenly distributed. Add dill, lemon zest, pepper, garlic and paprika; mix until evenly distributed.

4. In a small skillet, over medium-high heat, sauté a small amount of the sausage mixture until firm and opaque. Taste the sample, then adjust seasonings as desired.

5. Stuff sausage mixture into prepared casing as directed on page 51. Twist into 6 links, each about 6 inches (15 cm) in length. Cut links apart.

6. In a large shallow pan of simmering water (200°F to 205°F/93°C to 96°C), poach sausages for 15 to 20 minutes, topping up water if level dips, until sausages reach an internal temperature of 180°F (82°C).

7. Transfer sausages to a bowl of cold water and let stand until the internal temperature of the sausages drops to 70°F (21°C), refreshing cold water as necessary to cool the sausages quickly. Meanwhile, bring the pan of water to a boil.

8. Add sausages to the boiling water for 1 minute to tighten the casings. Drain and let cool completely, then wipe dry with paper towels and refrigerate for up to 2 days or freeze.

Vegetarian and Vegan Sausages

Even if you're a dedicated meat eater, you're going to want to try some of these vegetarian sausages. In addition to being delicious, they provide an array of nutrients and phytonutrients that are important for optimal health. The majority of these recipes include nuts, cheese or a legume or legume product, such as chickpeas, lentils or seitan, to make them a good source of protein, allowing you to use them as a meat replacement in a balanced meal.

Perhaps the most important component of vegetarian sausages is the binder, which will hold all the other ingredients in your sausages together. We have included two binder recipes in this chapter — one vegetarian and one vegan — which can be used interchangeably in the sausage recipes, although the vegetarian binder will yield at least two more links, depending on the diameter of the cellulose casing.

We used Butcher & Packer 30 mm casing for these sausages. It comes in compacted 70-foot (21 m) sticks. For each recipe, you'll need about 4 to 5 feet (120 by 150 cm), so you should get about 14 to 17 batches of sausages from each stick. If you have difficulty finding a specific diameter, it will not affect sausage quality, just the number of links.

Vegetarian Sausage Binder

A binder is a crucial component of vegetarian sausages, as it holds all the other ingredients together. This vegetarian version is a good choice for sausage recipes that include cheese or other non-vegan ingredients.

**MAKES ABOUT
4¾ CUPS
(1.175 L)**

Tips

All of the less common ingredients in this recipe are readily available online and in natural foods stores and some supermarkets with well-stocked natural foods sections.

The only similarity between potato flour and potato starch is that they are both potato products. Potato flour is made from the whole potato, including skin, a process in which the potatoes are usually cooked, then dried, and ground. Potato starch is only the dried starch component of peeled raw potatoes, a fine white powder most similar to cornstarch. The flour confers potato flavor, absorbs moisture in recipes, and has some thickening power. The starch has no potato flavor and is a potent thickener for sauces, again similar to cornstarch.

3	large eggs	3
2½ tbsp	water	37 mL
2 tbsp	vegetable oil	30 mL
6 tbsp	powdered soy protein	90 mL
4 tsp	potato flour	20 mL
1½ tbsp	xanthan gum	22 mL
3 cups	cooked short-grain white rice, cooled	750 mL

1. In a large bowl, whisk together eggs, water and oil. Using a wooden spoon, stir in soy protein, potato flour and xanthan gum until well blended. Stir in rice until well combined.

Vegan Sausage Binder

This vegan binder can be used in any of the recipes in this chapter, but is an especially good choice for sausages that otherwise contain only vegan ingredients.

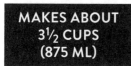
Tip

All of the less common ingredients in this recipe are readily available online and in natural foods stores and some supermarkets with well-stocked natural foods sections.

1 cup	dry texturized vegetable protein (TVP)	250 mL
1 cup	boiling water	250 mL
6 tbsp	powdered soy protein	90 mL
3 tbsp	guar gum	45 mL
¼ cup	vegan powdered egg replacer	60 mL
9 tbsp	water	135 mL
3 tbsp	vegetable oil	45 mL

1. Place texturized vegetable protein in a saucepan and gradually stir in boiling water. Heat over medium heat, stirring constantly, until liquid is absorbed. Remove from heat and let cool completely.
2. In a large bowl, combine soy protein and guar gum.
3. In a small bowl, combine egg replacer and 9 tbsp (135 mL) water until well blended. Stir in oil.
4. Add the oil mixture to the soy protein mixture, stirring until well blended. Stir in the rehydrated texturized vegetable protein until well blended.

Black Bean Breakfast Sausages

Black beans make a great sausage ingredient. Add in some barley, maple syrup and herbs, and you have the start to a great breakfast.

Tips

For vegan sausages, replace the Vegetarian Sausage Binder with 3½ cups (875 mL) Vegan Sausage Binder (page 225). Omit step 2 and just taste and adjust seasonings as needed. The yield will decrease to 10 sausages. Use within 1 week.

There are three main types of barley: hulled, pot and pearl. Hulled barley has only the tough outer covering removed and is considered the whole grain, whereas pot and pearl barley have both been processed. Pot barley is processed for a shorter time than pearl barley and retains some of the bran. Although hulled barley takes the longest to cook, it is the best choice as it has more fiber and other essential nutrients and phytonutrients. Any type of barley will work in this recipe.

1 cup	rinsed drained canned black beans	250 mL
4¾ cups	Vegetarian Sausage Binder (page 224)	1.125 L
1 cup	cooked barley (see tip, at left), cooled	250 mL
2 tbsp	finely minced fresh sage	30 mL
2 tsp	kosher salt	10 mL
2 tsp	freshly cracked black pepper	10 mL
1 tsp	hot pepper flakes	5 mL
1 tsp	dried thyme	5 mL
1 tsp	sweet paprika	5 mL
1 tsp	onion powder	5 mL
3 tbsp	pure maple syrup	45 mL
	30 mm shirred stick cellulose casing	

1. In a large bowl, mash beans with a pastry blender or potato masher until only slightly chunky. Stir in sausage binder, barley, sage, salt, black pepper, hot pepper flakes, thyme, paprika, onion powder and maple syrup until well combined.

2. In a small skillet, over medium-high heat, sauté a small amount of the sausage mixture until thoroughly heated and egg is set. Taste the sample, then adjust seasonings as desired.

3. Stuff sausage mixture into casing as directed on page 51. Twist into 12 links, each about 6 inches (15 cm) in length.

4. In a large shallow pan of gently simmering water, poach sausages for 10 minutes or until sausages reach an internal temperature of 160°F (71°C). Do not allow water temperature to rise above 170°F (77°C).

5. Remove sausages from water and let cool completely. Refrigerate overnight or for up to 3 days before using. Gently peel off casing before cooking or eating.

Health Facts

Barley is high in fiber, niacin, manganese, selenium and iron. It also contains phytonutrients that act as antioxidants, as well as beta-glucan, which helps lower blood glucose.

Vegan Harvest Sausages

Nothing brings a crisp autumn day to mind like a mix of apples and cranberries. Sauerkraut, another fall favorite, supplies beneficial bacteria to support gut and immune health. This interesting blend of fall flavors, in sausage form, makes a delightfully healthy addition to any meal.

MAKES 9 SAUSAGES

Tips

For vegetarian sausages, replace the Vegan Sausage Binder with 4¾ cups (1.125 L) Vegetarian Sausage Binder (page 224). Before tasting and adjusting seasonings in step 2, you will need to sauté a small amount of the sausage mixture until thoroughly heated and egg is set. In step 4, cook the sausages until they reach an internal temperature of 160°F (71°C). The yield will increase to 11 sausages. Use within 3 days.

Cranberries and walnuts make perfect partners with a powerful punch of antioxidants. Keep a mix of coarsely chopped dried cranberries and walnuts in the freezer for a quick addition to almost any recipe.

4 oz	prepared sauerkraut	120 g
1	small Granny Smith apple, peeled and diced	1
3½ cups	Vegan Sausage Binder (page 225)	875 mL
2 tbsp	finely minced dried cranberries	30 mL
2 tbsp	finely chopped walnuts	30 mL
1 tbsp	finely minced garlic	15 mL
1 tbsp	packed brown sugar	15 mL
2 tsp	mustard seeds	10 mL
2 tsp	freshly cracked black pepper	10 mL
1½ tsp	kosher salt	7 mL
1 tsp	caraway seeds	5 mL
	30 mm shirred stick cellulose casing	

1. Drain sauerkraut and press out excess liquid, then roughly chop. Measure out 1 cup (250 mL).

2. In a large bowl, stir together sauerkraut, apple, sausage binder, cranberries, walnuts, garlic, brown sugar, mustard seeds, pepper, salt and caraway seeds until well combined. Taste and adjust seasonings as desired.

3. Stuff sausage mixture into casing as directed on page 51. Twist into 9 links, each about 6 inches (15 cm) in length.

4. In a large shallow pan of gently simmering water, poach sausages for 10 minutes or until hot in the center. Do not allow water temperature to rise above 170°F (77°C).

5. Remove sausages from water and let cool completely. Refrigerate overnight or for up to 1 week before using. Gently peel off casing before cooking or eating.

Health Facts

Walnuts contain omega-3 fatty acids, which may be why they help protect against heart disease. In a 2004 study, researchers fed human subjects walnuts for 4 weeks and found improvements in blood cholesterol levels and blood vessel functioning.

Nutty Vegan Sausages

These nutritious and tasty sausages will satisfy vegans and sausage lovers alike. Pair them with brown rice or whole-grain pasta for a complete meal rich in protein.

**MAKES
10 SAUSAGES**

Tips

For vegetarian sausages, replace the Vegan Sausage Binder with 4¾ cups (1.125 L) Vegetarian Sausage Binder (page 224). Before tasting and adjusting seasonings in step 1, you will need to sauté a small amount of the sausage mixture until thoroughly heated and egg is set. In step 4, cook the sausages until they reach an internal temperature of 160°F (71°C). The yield will increase to 12 sausages. Use within 3 days.

Almond flour is made with blanched almonds (where the skin has been removed), whereas almond meal can be made with either whole or blanched almonds. The consistency is slightly different, but either product can be used in most recipes. Both will remain fresh in the refrigerator for up to 6 months.

3½ cups	Vegan Sausage Binder (page 225)	875 mL
1 cup	almond meal (see tip, at left)	250 mL
¼ cup	finely chopped walnuts	60 mL
¼ cup	finely chopped roasted unsalted cashews	60 mL
2 tsp	finely minced fresh thyme	10 mL
2 tsp	sweet smoked paprika	10 mL
2 tsp	kosher salt	10 mL
1 tsp	freshly ground white pepper	5 mL
1 tsp	curry powder	5 mL
1 tsp	ground cinnamon	5 mL
½ tsp	ground allspice	2 mL
⅓ cup	olive oil	75 mL
	30 mm shirred stick cellulose casing	

1. In a large bowl, stir together sausage binder, almond meal, walnuts, cashews, thyme, paprika, salt, pepper, curry powder, cinnamon, allspice and oil until well combined. Taste and adjust seasonings as desired.

2. Stuff sausage mixture into casing as directed on page 51. Twist into 10 links, each about 6 inches (15 cm) in length.

3. In a large shallow pan of gently simmering water, poach sausages for 10 minutes or until hot in the center. Do not allow water temperature to rise above 170°F (77°C).

4. Remove sausages from water and let cool completely. Refrigerate overnight or for up to 1 week before using. Gently peel off casing before cooking or eating.

Health Facts

You may have heard that incomplete protein foods, such as legumes and most grains, need to be combined at the same meal in order for the body to use the protein effectively. However, recent research has revealed that we actually have up to 24 hours to consume the complete array of all nine essential amino acids that make up a complete protein.

Grilled Cheese Sausages

Combining bread and cheese and applying heat has been a tradition for millennia. The ancient Romans included several variations on the theme in their cookbooks. In North America, grilled cheese sandwiches became a staple in the 1920s, when sliced bread and processed cheese became widely available. These novel vegetarian sausages incorporate a traditional "go with" snack, pretzels, to make a great centerpiece to a casual meal.

MAKES 13 SAUSAGES

Tips

You can use either oil-packed or dry-packed sun-dried tomatoes. If you use oil-packed, drain well before mincing and measuring. An opened container of oil-packed tomatoes will remain fresh in the refrigerator for up to 6 months. The oil will turn into a white solid, but it will liquefy in 30 minutes at room temperature. To store dry-packed tomatoes, squeeze any air out of the bag before sealing it; this will keep them fresh for about a year in the refrigerator.

A tasty and traditional accompaniment to grilled cheese sandwiches, tomato soup, also works well with these sausages.

4¾ cups	Vegetarian Sausage Binder (page 224)	1.125 L
1 cup	crushed pretzels	250 mL
½ cup	finely chopped sun-dried tomatoes (see tip, at left)	125 mL
½ cup	shredded Cheddar cheese	125 mL
½ cup	shredded provolone cheese	125 mL
½ cup	shredded Swiss cheese	125 mL
1 tsp	kosher salt	5 mL
1 tsp	freshly ground white pepper	5 mL
1 tsp	garlic powder	5 mL
	30 mm shirred stick cellulose casing	

1. In a large bowl, stir together sausage binder, pretzels, sun-dried tomatoes, Cheddar, provolone, Swiss cheese, salt, pepper and garlic powder until well combined.

2. In a small skillet, over medium-high heat, sauté a small amount of the sausage mixture until thoroughly heated and egg is set. Taste the sample, then adjust seasonings as desired.

3. Stuff sausage mixture into casing as directed on page 51. Twist into 13 links, each about 6 inches (15 cm) in length.

4. In a large shallow pan of gently simmering water, poach sausages for 10 minutes or until sausages reach an internal temperature of 160°F (71°C). Do not allow water temperature to rise above 170°F (77°C).

5. Remove sausages from water and let cool completely. Refrigerate overnight or for up to 3 days before using. Gently peel off casing before cooking or eating.

Health Facts

Tomatoes have become famous for their content of the potent antioxidant lycopene, which is even more concentrated in sun-dried tomatoes. This important carotenoid compound is linked to many health benefits, especially prevention of prostate cancer.

Woodland Mushroom Sausages

Because of their high content of umami components, which stimulate the savory taste sense, mushrooms are the perfect ingredient in vegetarian recipes. These sausages evoke an autumnal forage on a crisp morning in search of wild mushrooms.

**MAKES
12 SAUSAGES**

Tips

You can use just about any mushrooms in this recipe, either alone or as a blend. Portobellos have a particularly meaty texture.

Certain mushrooms, such as shiitakes and portobellos, require special trimming, as not all parts of these mushrooms have an appetizing texture. To trim shiitake mushrooms, cut or twist off the stems (you can save the stems to make stock, if desired). For portobellos, twist off the stems, then remove the black gills inside the caps by scraping them off with the edge of a spoon.

- Preheat oven to 375°F (190°C)
- Rimmed baking sheet

1 lb	mixed gourmet mushrooms (such as shiitake, portobello, oyster and chanterelle)	500 g
2 tbsp	olive oil	30 mL
1 tbsp	balsamic vinegar	15 mL
2 tsp	kosher salt	10 mL
1 tsp	freshly cracked black pepper	5 mL
4¾ cups	Vegetarian Sausage Binder (page 224)	1.125 L
¼ cup	finely chopped fresh basil	60 mL
1 tsp	finely chopped fresh rosemary	5 mL
1 tsp	sweet paprika	5 mL
1 tsp	onion powder	5 mL
Pinch	crushed saffron threads	Pinch
2 tbsp	roasted garlic paste (see page 47)	30 mL
	30 mm shirred stick cellulose casing	

1. Remove or trim mushroom stems as necessary (see tip, at left) and chop mushrooms into uniform pieces. In a bowl, toss mushrooms with oil, vinegar, salt and pepper. Spread in a single layer on baking sheet. Roast in preheated oven for 15 minutes or until starting to brown. Let cool, then finely mince.

2. In a large bowl, stir together roasted mushrooms, sausage binder, basil, rosemary, paprika, onion powder, saffron and garlic paste until well combined.

3. In a small skillet, over medium-high heat, sauté a small amount of the sausage mixture until thoroughly heated and egg is set. Taste the sample, then adjust seasonings as desired.

For vegan sausages, replace the Vegetarian Sausage Binder with 3½ cups (875 mL) Vegan Sausage Binder (page 225). Omit step 3 and just taste and adjust seasonings as needed. The yield will decrease to 10 sausages. Use within 1 week.

4. Stuff sausage mixture into casing as directed on page 51. Twist into 12 links, each about 6 inches (15 cm) in length.

5. In a large shallow pan of gently simmering water, poach sausages for 10 minutes or until sausages reach an internal temperature of 160°F (71°C). Do not allow water temperature to rise above 170°F (77°C).

6. Remove sausages from water and let cool completely. Refrigerate overnight or for up to 3 days before using. Gently peel off casing before cooking or eating.

Health Facts

Shiitake mushrooms have a long history of use as a medicinal plant. Although much of the attention had been on the mushrooms' immune system benefits, more recent studies also point to heart and blood vessel benefits. For example, shiitakes may prevent immune cells from binding to the lining of blood vessels, protecting against atherosclerosis.

Abruzzi Cannellini Sausages

Bringing together many ingredients common to the Abruzzo region of central Italy, these sausages make a great addition to a meatless Italian meal. The generous amounts of basil stimulate the umami taste, so no one will miss the meat.

MAKES
13 SAUSAGES

Tips

For vegan sausages, replace the Vegetarian Sausage Binder with 3½ cups (875 mL) Vegan Sausage Binder (page 225) and use a grated vegan cheese alternative in place of the pecorino Romano. Omit step 3 and just taste and adjust seasonings as needed. The yield will decrease to 11 sausages. Use within 1 week.

If you can only find smaller or larger cans of cannellini beans, you will need 1¾ cups (425 mL) drained beans for this recipe.

The taste of fennel seeds has become associated with Italian sausages, so regular meat eaters may find that adding fennel seeds to vegetarian sausages increases their enjoyment.

- Food processor (optional)

1	can (15 oz/425 mL) cannellini (white kidney) beans, drained and rinsed	1
4¾ cups	Vegetarian Sausage Binder (page 224)	1.125 L
½ cup	diced seeded peeled tomatoes	125 mL
½ cup	roughly chopped fresh basil	125 mL
½ cup	freshly grated Pecorino Romano cheese	125 mL
2 tbsp	finely minced garlic	30 mL
2 tsp	freshly cracked fennel seeds	10 mL
2 tsp	kosher salt	10 mL
1 tsp	freshly cracked black pepper	5 mL
1 tsp	dried oregano	5 mL
2 tbsp	tomato paste	30 mL
	30 mm shirred stick cellulose casing	

1. In food processor, purée beans to a paste-like consistency. (Or mash to a paste-like consistency with a pastry blender or potato masher.)

2. In a large bowl, stir together bean purée, sausage binder, tomatoes, basil, cheese, garlic, fennel seeds, salt, pepper, oregano and tomato paste until well combined.

3. In a small skillet, over medium-high heat, sauté a small amount of the sausage mixture until thoroughly heated and egg is set. Taste the sample, then adjust seasonings as desired.

4. Stuff sausage mixture into casing as directed on page 51. Twist into 13 links, each about 6 inches (15 cm) in length.

5. In a large shallow pan of gently simmering water, poach sausages for 10 minutes or until sausages reach an internal temperature of 160°F (71°C). Do not allow water temperature to rise above 170°F (77°C).

6. Remove sausages from water and let cool completely. Refrigerate overnight or for up to 3 days before using. Gently peel off casing before cooking or eating.

Health Facts

Studies show that the flavonol kaempferol, contained in fennel seeds, has powerful anti-inflammatory properties. A 2015 review discussed potential uses of kaempferol to combat chronic diseases that involve inflammation, such as cardiovascular disease and diabetes.

Florentine Sausages

These sausages bring together all of Florence's traditional ingredients to make a delicious centerpiece to your meal.

Tip

For vegan sausages, replace the Vegetarian Sausage Binder with 3½ cups (875 mL) Vegan Sausage Binder (page 225). Omit step 3 and just taste and adjust seasonings as needed. The yield will decrease to 10 sausages. Use within 1 week.

Health Facts

In addition to a high vitamin and mineral content, artichokes contain the compound cynarin, which studies show has a cholesterol-lowering effect and may ease the symptoms of irritable bowel syndrome.

- Preheat oven to 400°F (200°C)
- Rimmed baking sheet, oiled

5	medium plum (Roma) tomatoes, cut into ¼-inch (0.5 cm) thick slices	5
1 tbsp	balsamic vinegar	15 mL
1½ tsp	olive oil	7 mL
	Kosher salt and freshly cracked black pepper	
4¾ cups	Vegetarian Sausage Binder (page 224)	1.125 L
2 oz	thawed frozen chopped spinach, excess liquid squeezed out	60 g
½ cup	finely chopped drained canned artichoke hearts	125 mL
¼ cup	finely chopped fresh basil	60 mL
1 tbsp	granulated sugar	15 mL
2 tsp	dried oregano	10 mL
1 tsp	hot pepper flakes	5 mL
1 tsp	onion powder	5 mL
	30 mm shirred stick cellulose casing	

1. Arrange tomatoes in a single layer on prepared baking sheet. In a small bowl, combine vinegar and oil; brush evenly over tomatoes. Season lightly with salt and black pepper. Roast in preheated oven for 8 to 10 minutes or until tomatoes start to shrivel and color. Let cool completely, then finely chop.

2. In a large bowl, stir together roasted tomatoes, sausage binder, spinach, artichokes, basil, sugar, oregano, 2 tsp (10 mL) salt, 1 tsp (5 mL) black pepper, hot pepper flakes and onion powder until well combined.

3. In a small skillet, over medium-high heat, sauté a small amount of the sausage mixture until thoroughly heated and egg is set. Taste the sample, then adjust seasonings as desired.

4. Stuff sausage mixture into casing as directed on page 51. Twist into 12 links, each about 6 inches (15 cm) in length.

5. In a large shallow pan of gently simmering water, poach sausages for 10 minutes or until sausages reach an internal temperature of 160°F (71°C). Do not allow water temperature to rise above 170°F (77°C).

6. Remove sausages from water and let cool completely. Refrigerate overnight or for up to 3 days before using. Gently peel off casing before cooking or eating.

Polenta Portobello Sausages

Food journalist Waverly Root writes of how the ancient Etruscans prepared a grain mush with the consistency of porridge, and while it didn't sound particularly appetizing, "on it the Roman Legions conquered the world." With polenta and the other traditional Italian ingredients, these sausages will make you, too, feel like you can conquer the world.

MAKES 13 SAUSAGES

Tips

For vegan sausages, replace the Vegetarian Sausage Binder with 3½ cups (875 mL) Vegan Sausage Binder (page 225). Omit step 3 and just taste and adjust seasonings as needed. The yield will decrease to 11 sausages. Use within 1 week.

You may see two different spellings for the mushrooms in this recipe: "portobello" and "portabella." The latter may refer to the smaller immature mushrooms, which are also called cremini mushrooms. However, most people use the terms interchangeably in reference to the fully matured large mushrooms.

¼ cup	olive oil, divided	60 mL
1 cup	finely chopped portobello mushrooms	250 mL
4¾ cups	Vegetarian Sausage Binder (page 224)	1.125 L
½ cup	cornmeal	125 mL
¼ cup	finely chopped fresh basil	60 mL
¼ cup	finely chopped sun-dried tomatoes (see tip, page 229)	60 mL
2 tsp	kosher salt	10 mL
2 tsp	freshly cracked black pepper	10 mL
2 tsp	onion powder	10 mL
1 tsp	garlic powder	5 mL
½ cup	ready-to-use vegetable broth	125 mL
2 tbsp	tomato paste	30 mL
	30 mm shirred stick cellulose casing	

1. In a small skillet, heat 2 tbsp (30 mL) oil over medium heat. Add mushrooms and cook, stirring, for 8 minutes or until lightly browned. Let cool completely.

2. In a large bowl, stir together mushrooms, sausage binder, cornmeal, basil, sun-dried tomatoes, salt, pepper, onion powder, garlic powder, broth and tomato paste until well combined. Let stand for 10 minutes.

3. In the same skillet, over medium-high heat, sauté a small amount of the sausage mixture until thoroughly heated and egg is set. Taste the sample, then adjust seasonings as desired.

4. Stuff sausage mixture into casing as directed on page 51. Twist into 13 links, each about 6 inches (15 cm) in length.

5. In a large shallow pan of gently simmering water, poach sausages for 10 minutes or until sausages reach an internal temperature of 160°F (71°C). Do not allow water temperature to rise above 170°F (77°C).

6. Remove sausages from water and let cool completely. Refrigerate overnight or for up to 3 days before using. Gently peel off casing before cooking or eating.

Health Facts

Like other mushrooms, portobellos are a good source of fiber, B vitamins and essential minerals. They are low in calories, and meaty-textured portobellos make a great meat replacer.

Spicy Sicilian Chickpea Sausages

Chickpeas are a staple legume throughout the Mediterranean, and in these sausages, they get top billing as the main ingredient.

MAKES 10 SAUSAGES

Tips

For vegan sausages, replace the Vegetarian Sausage Binder with 3½ cups (875 mL) Vegan Sausage Binder (page 225). Omit step 3 and just taste and adjust seasonings as needed. The yield will decrease to 8 sausages. Use within 1 week.

How long to make your sausage links is really up to you, although we suggest 6 inches (15 cm) for this recipe. Keep in mind that this is a rough guideline, and that you may have to adjust the length up or down so that you don't end up with one link smaller than the rest.

* Food processor (optional)

1 cup	rinsed drained canned chickpeas	250 mL
4¾ cups	Vegetarian Sausage Binder (page 224)	1.125 L
¼ cup	finely chopped green bell pepper	60 mL
2 tbsp	hot pepper flakes	30 mL
1 tbsp	finely chopped fresh oregano	15 mL
2 tsp	kosher salt	10 mL
2 tsp	freshly cracked black pepper	10 mL
2 tsp	freshly cracked fennel seeds	10 mL
2 tbsp	roasted garlic paste (see page 47)	30 mL
	30 mm shirred stick cellulose casing	

1. In food processor, purée chickpeas to a paste-like consistency. (Or mash to a paste-like consistency with a pastry blender or potato masher.)

2. In a large bowl, stir together chickpea purée, sausage binder, green pepper, hot pepper flakes, oregano, salt, black pepper, fennel seeds and garlic paste until well combined.

3. In a small skillet, over medium-high heat, sauté a small amount of the sausage mixture until thoroughly heated and egg is set. Taste the sample, then adjust seasonings as desired.

4. Stuff sausage mixture into casing as directed on page 51. Twist into 10 links, each about 6 inches (15 cm) in length.

5. In a large shallow pan of gently simmering water, poach sausages for 10 minutes or until sausages reach an internal temperature of 160°F (71°C). Do not allow water temperature to rise above 170°F (77°C).

6. Remove sausages from water and let cool completely. Refrigerate overnight or for up to 3 days before using. Gently peel off casing before cooking or eating.

Health Facts

A 2015 review discussed the potential for garlic, and its phytonutrients, as a treatment in metabolic syndrome. Metabolic syndrome is characterized by high blood pressure, insulin resistance and abnormal blood cholesterol levels, which together can lead to type 2 diabetes. The authors concluded that, given data showing garlic may reduce blood pressure and cholesterol, this area of study holds promise.

Greek Kalamata Sausages

The southern Greek city of Kalamata is the birthplace of the kalamata olive, which has become associated with Greek cuisine. Like other olives, it is bitter when picked and must be cured (a process of fermentation in a brine solution), which accounts for the high salt content. Along with other notable Greek ingredients, kalamata olives form the base of these delicious vegetarian sausages.

**MAKES
9 SAUSAGES**

Tips

For vegan sausages, replace the Vegetarian Sausage Binder with 3½ cups (875 mL) Vegan Sausage Binder (page 225). In place of the feta cheese, use ¼ cup (60 mL) crumbled soft tofu and increase the salt by ¼ tsp (1 mL). Omit step 3 and just taste and adjust seasonings as needed. The yield will decrease to 7 sausages. Use within 1 week.

You can purchase kalamata olives in bulk at specialty stores. Before purchasing them prepacked into a bulk container, ask for a sample and avoid them if the olives are soft or mushy. If the bulk olives are packed in oil, store them in the refrigerator and use within 2 weeks. Jarred brine-packed olives can be safely stored in the refrigerator for up to 2 months.

4¾ cups	Vegetarian Sausage Binder (page 224)	1.125 L
½ cup	finely chopped pitted drained kalamata olives	125 mL
¼ cup	grated carrots	60 mL
¼ cup	finely chopped red bell pepper	60 mL
¼ cup	crumbled feta cheese	60 mL
2 tbsp	finely minced garlic	30 mL
1 tbsp	grated lemon zest	15 mL
1 tbsp	finely chopped fresh thyme	15 mL
2 tsp	freshly cracked black pepper	10 mL
1 tsp	kosher salt	5 mL
1 tsp	ground cumin	5 mL
1 tsp	curry powder	5 mL
	30 mm shirred stick cellulose casing	

1. In a large bowl, stir together sausage binder, olives, carrots, red pepper, cheese, garlic, lemon zest, thyme, pepper, salt, cumin and curry powder until well combined.

2. In a small skillet, over medium-high heat, sauté a small amount of the sausage mixture until thoroughly heated and egg is set. Taste the sample, then adjust seasonings as desired.

3. Stuff sausage mixture into casing as directed on page 51. Twist into 9 links, each about 6 inches (15 cm) in length.

4. In a large shallow pan of gently simmering water, poach sausages for 10 minutes or until sausages reach an internal temperature of 160°F (71°C). Do not allow water temperature to rise above 170°F (77°C).

5. Remove sausages from water and let cool completely. Refrigerate overnight or for up to 3 days before using. Gently peel off casing before cooking or eating.

Health Facts

Traditional medicines in the Mediterranean region often made use of olives, especially for problems involving inflammation, such as allergic reactions. Recent research has shown that compounds in olives combat inflammation by blocking histamine, which the body releases in high amounts during allergic reactions and in inflammation.

Persian Chickpea Sausages

Persian cuisine uses a delicate balance of sweet and sour flavors. These vegetarian sausages rely on traditional spices, as well as the rich taste of pomegranate syrup.

Tips

For vegan sausages, replace the Vegetarian Sausage Binder with 3½ cups (875 mL) Vegan Sausage Binder (page 225). Omit step 3 and just taste and adjust seasonings as needed. The yield will decrease to 8 sausages. Use within 1 week.

Some people leave opened pomegranate syrup in the cupboard, but it's best to err on the side of safety and refrigerate it. This is even more important if you make your own syrup (see tip, page 193).

- Food processor (optional)

¾ cup	rinsed drained canned chickpeas	175 mL
4¾ cups	Vegetarian Sausage Binder (page 224)	1.125 L
2 oz	thawed frozen chopped spinach, excess liquid squeezed out	60 g
¼ cup	dried red currants	60 mL
2 tbsp	finely minced garlic	30 mL
2 tsp	kosher salt	10 mL
1 tsp	freshly cracked black pepper	5 mL
1 tsp	ground cumin	5 mL
1 tsp	curry powder	5 mL
¼ cup	tahini	60 mL
1 tbsp	pomegranate syrup (pomegranate molasses)	15 mL
	30 mm shirred stick cellulose casing	

1. In food processor, purée chickpeas to a paste-like consistency. (Or mash to a paste-like consistency with a pastry blender or potato masher.)

2. In a large bowl, stir together chickpea purée, sausage binder, spinach, currants, garlic, salt, pepper, cumin, curry powder, tahini and pomegranate syrup until well combined.

3. In a small skillet, over medium-high heat, sauté a small amount of the sausage mixture until thoroughly heated and egg is set. Taste the sample, then adjust seasonings as desired.

4. Stuff sausage mixture into casing as directed on page 51. Twist into 10 links, each about 6 inches (15 cm) in length.

5. In a large shallow pan of gently simmering water, poach sausages for 10 minutes or until sausages reach an internal temperature of 160°F (71°C). Do not allow water temperature to rise above 170°F (77°C).

6. Remove sausages from water and let cool completely. Refrigerate overnight or for up to 3 days before using. Gently peel off casing before cooking or eating.

Health Facts

A 2015 review on the health effects of various fruit juices reported on the benefits of pomegranate juice. Based on its nutrient and phytonutrient content, pomegranate juice appears to confer protection against cancer, cardiovascular disease and hypertension.

Lebanese Majadra Sausages

Lentils are the base for these savory vegetarian sausages inspired by a traditional Lebanese dish. Majadra is made by caramelizing onions in olive oil, then adding lentils and spices and cooking until tender.

Tips

For vegan sausages, replace the Vegetarian Sausage Binder with 3½ cups (875 mL) Vegan Sausage Binder (page 225). Omit step 4 and just taste and adjust seasonings as needed. The yield will decrease to 11 sausages. Use within 1 week.

When buying olive oil, look for specific details on the label. "Extra virgin" refers to oil from the first pressing, with no heat applied. It is darkest in color and lowest in acidity. "Virgin" refers to oil made from riper olives with slightly higher acidity. Extra virgin olive oil contains more of the phytonutrients that may help fight chronic disease.

⅔ cup	dried brown lentils, rinsed	150 mL
3 cups	water	750 mL
1 tbsp	olive oil	15 mL
1	small onion, finely chopped	1
4¾ cups	Vegetarian Sausage Binder (page 224)	1.125 L
2 tbsp	finely minced fresh mint	30 mL
2 tbsp	finely chopped drained roasted red bell pepper	30 mL
2 tbsp	finely minced sun-dried tomatoes (see tip, page 229)	30 mL
1 tbsp	curry powder	15 mL
2 tsp	kosher salt	10 mL
2 tsp	freshly cracked black pepper	10 mL
1 tsp	ground cumin	5 mL
½ tsp	ground cinnamon	2 mL
½ tsp	ground allspice	2 mL
¼ tsp	ground coriander	1 mL
	30 mm shirred stick cellulose casing	

1. In a medium saucepan, combine lentils and water. Bring to a boil over high heat. Reduce heat to medium, cover tightly and simmer for 15 to 20 minutes or until lentils are tender. Drain off any excess water.

2. In a large skillet, heat oil over medium heat. Add onion and cook, stirring often, for about 10 minutes or until browned and caramelized. Add lentils and cook, stirring, for 5 minutes to blend the flavors. Let cool completely, then transfer to a large bowl and mash with a pastry blender or potato masher.

3. In a large bowl, stir together lentil mixture, sausage binder, mint, roasted pepper, sun-dried tomatoes, curry powder, salt, pepper, cumin, cinnamon, allspice and coriander until well combined.

4. In a small skillet, over medium-high heat, sauté a small amount of the sausage mixture until thoroughly heated and egg is set. Taste the sample, then adjust seasonings as desired.

5. Stuff sausage mixture into casing as directed on page 51. Twist into 13 links, each about 6 inches (15 cm) in length.

Tip

How long to make your sausage links is really up to you, although we suggest 6 inches (15 cm) for this recipe. Keep in mind that this is a rough guideline, and that you may have to adjust the length up or down so that you don't end up with one link smaller than the rest.

6. In a large shallow pan of gently simmering water, poach sausages for 10 minutes or until sausages reach an internal temperature of 160°F (71°C). Do not allow water temperature to rise above 170°F (77°C).

7. Remove sausages from water and let cool completely. Refrigerate overnight or for up to 3 days before using. Gently peel off casing before cooking or eating.

Health Facts

A 2015 study of extra virgin olive oil reported that a 10-gram dose lowered blood levels of glucose and LDL ("bad") cholesterol after meals. Both of these effects could work together to lower the risk for cardiovascular disease.

Saag Aloo Sausages

In India, *saag* is a dish consisting of leafy greens, such as spinach and mustard greens, and numerous spices. These sausages are based on the potato version, *saag aloo*. They make a hearty vegetarian meal when served with side dishes of rice and legumes.

Tips

For vegan sausages, replace the Vegetarian Sausage Binder with 3½ cups (875 mL) Vegan Sausage Binder (page 225). Omit step 3 and just taste and adjust seasonings as needed. The yield will decrease to 11 sausages. Use within 1 week.

If you prefer to use fresh greens, use 2 cups (500 mL) each spinach and mustard greens. Add to 8 cups (2 L) boiling water, reduce heat and simmer for 15 minutes. Drain, let cool and press out excess liquid.

Try different greens to change up the recipe. One traditional *saag* recipe uses chopped cooked broccoli; other choices might include cooked collard greens or kale.

4 oz	russet potato, peeled and diced	125 g
8 oz	seitan, finely chopped	250 g
4¾ cups	Vegetarian Sausage Binder (page 224)	1.125 L
1 cup	thawed frozen chopped spinach, excess liquid squeezed out	250 mL
1 cup	thawed frozen chopped mustard greens, excess liquid squeezed out	250 mL
1 tbsp	curry powder	15 mL
2 tsp	finely minced garlic	10 mL
2 tsp	kosher salt	10 mL
1 tsp	freshly ground white pepper	5 mL
1 tsp	ground turmeric	5 mL
1 tsp	ground coriander	5 mL
1 tsp	ground cumin	5 mL
	30 mm shirred stick cellulose casing	

1. Place potato in a small saucepan and add enough cold water to cover by 1 inch (2.5 cm). Bring to a boil over high heat. Reduce heat and simmer for 15 to 20 minutes or until fork-tender. Drain and let cool completely.

2. In a large bowl, stir together potato, seitan, sausage binder, spinach, mustard greens, curry powder, garlic, salt, pepper, turmeric, coriander and cumin until well combined.

3. In a small skillet, over medium-high heat, sauté a small amount of the sausage mixture until thoroughly heated and egg is set. Taste the sample, then adjust seasonings as desired.

4. Stuff sausage mixture into casing as directed on page 51. Twist into 14 links, each about 6 inches (15 cm) in length.

5. In a large shallow pan of gently simmering water, poach sausages for 10 minutes or until sausages reach an internal temperature of 160°F (71°C). Do not allow water temperature to rise above 170°F (77°C).

6. Remove sausages from water and let cool completely. Refrigerate overnight or for up to 3 days before using. Gently peel off casing before cooking or eating.

Health Facts

Mustard greens fall in the cruciferous vegetable family, which means that they contain powerful phytonutrients with antioxidant and anti-inflammatory effects.

Kimchi Brats

Korean historians believe that kimchi was created in the seventh century, and this ancient food has not only endured but has recently become popular worldwide. These sausages bring kimchi's distinctive flavor to your table as a flavorful contribution to a healthy meal.

**MAKES
11 SAUSAGES**

Tip

For vegan sausages, replace the Vegetarian Sausage Binder with 3½ cups (875 mL) Vegan Sausage Binder (page 225). Omit step 2 and just taste and adjust seasonings as needed. The yield will decrease to 9 sausages. Use within 1 week.

4¾ cups	Vegetarian Sausage Binder (page 224)	1.125 L
1⅔ cups	roughly chopped drained kimchi	400 mL
½ cup	roughly chopped mung bean sprouts	125 mL
1 tbsp	finely minced gingerroot	15 mL
1 tbsp	hot pepper flakes	15 mL
2 tsp	garlic powder	10 mL
2 tsp	freshly cracked black pepper	10 mL
1 tsp	kosher salt	5 mL
2 tsp	soy sauce	10 mL
	30 mm shirred stick cellulose casing	

1. In a large bowl, stir together sausage binder, kimchi, bean sprouts, ginger, hot pepper flakes, garlic powder, pepper, salt and soy sauce until well combined.

2. In a small skillet, over medium-high heat, sauté a small amount of the sausage mixture until thoroughly heated and egg is set. Taste the sample, then adjust seasonings as desired.

3. Stuff sausage mixture into casing as directed on page 51. Twist into 11 links, each about 6 inches (15 cm) in length.

4. In a large shallow pan of gently simmering water, poach sausages for 10 minutes or until sausages reach an internal temperature of 160°F (71°C). Do not allow water temperature to rise above 170°F (77°C).

5. Remove sausages from water and let cool completely. Refrigerate overnight or for up to 3 days before using. Gently peel off casing before cooking or eating.

Health Facts

Kimchi is one of many fermented foods gaining popularity because of its probiotic content. In addition, since it is made with cabbage, garlic, ginger and hot pepper, it conveys the anticancer and cardioprotective benefits of the various phytonutrients in those ingredients.

Curried Lentil Sausages

The combination of spices in curry powders varies by region, but the main spices are coriander, cumin and turmeric. In these sausages, the curry powder adds a rich fragrance and intense flavor to the lentils and sweet potatoes, for a delightful taste experience.

**MAKES
14 SAUSAGES**

Tips

For vegan sausages, replace the Vegetarian Sausage Binder with 3½ cups (875 mL) Vegan Sausage Binder (page 225). Omit step 4 and just taste and adjust seasonings as needed. The yield will decrease to 12 sausages. Use within 1 week.

If you're in a hurry, you can use canned lentils in place of dried. After cooking, the lentils in this recipe yield about 2½ cups (625 mL). A 15-oz (425 mL) can of lentils, after draining, yields about 1¼ to 1½ cups (300 to 375 mL), so you'll need to use part of a second can.

1¼ cups	dried brown lentils, rinsed	300 mL
3 cups	water	750 mL
1	5-inch (12.5 cm) sweet potato (unpeeled), cut into dice	1
1 tbsp	olive oil	15 mL
1	small onion, finely chopped	1
¼ cup	red wine	60 mL
4¾ cups	Vegetarian Sausage Binder (page 224)	1.125 L
¼ cup	finely chopped fresh cilantro	60 mL
2 tbsp	grated lemon zest	30 mL
2 tbsp	curry powder	30 mL
2 tsp	ground cumin	10 mL
2 tsp	kosher salt	10 mL
1 tsp	freshly cracked black pepper	5 mL
1 tsp	cayenne pepper	5 mL
2 tbsp	roasted garlic paste (see page 47)	30 mL
	30 mm shirred stick cellulose casing	

1. In a medium saucepan, combine lentils and water. Bring to a boil over high heat. Reduce heat to medium, cover tightly and simmer for 15 to 20 minutes or until lentils are tender. Drain off any excess water and let cool completely.

2. Place sweet potato in a medium saucepan and add enough cold water to cover. Bring to a boil over high heat. Reduce heat to medium-low, cover and simmer for 20 minutes or until tender. Drain and let cool completely.

3. In a large skillet, heat oil over medium heat. Add onion and cook, stirring often, for about 8 minutes or until browned and caramelized. Stir in wine, scraping up any browned bits from the bottom of the pan. Let cool completely

4. In a large bowl, stir together lentils, onion mixture, sweet potato, sausage binder, cilantro, lemon zest, curry powder, cumin, salt, black pepper, cayenne and garlic paste until well combined.

5. In the same skillet, over medium-high heat, sauté a small amount of the sausage mixture until thoroughly heated and egg is set. Taste the sample, then adjust seasonings as desired.

Tip

How long to make your sausage links is really up to you, although we suggest 6 inches (15 cm) for this recipe. Keep in mind that this is a rough guideline, and that you may have to adjust the length up or down so that you don't end up with one link smaller than the rest.

6. Stuff sausage mixture into casing as directed on page 51. Twist into 14 links, each about 6 inches (15 cm) in length.

7. In a large shallow pan of gently simmering water, poach sausages for 10 minutes or until sausages reach an internal temperature of 160°F (71°C). Do not allow water temperature to rise above 170°F (77°C).

8. Remove sausages from water and let cool completely. Refrigerate overnight or for up to 3 days before using. Gently peel off casing before cooking or eating.

Health Facts

Lentils are an excellent source of fiber and several minerals, and a good source of protein. A 2014 study on the effects of several legumes reported that a lentil-based diet reduced blood pressure in rats with high blood pressure.

Malaysian Satay Sausages

Satay is enjoyed throughout Asia, with both Indonesia and Malaysia claiming it as their invention. Food historians tend to side with Indonesia, but Malaysians take special pride in their version of this skewered spiced meat. These sausages have all the traditional ingredients except the meat. Enhance their authenticity by serving them on skewers with a side of Spicy Peanut Sauce (see recipe, opposite).

**MAKES
11 SAUSAGES**

Tips

For vegan sausages, replace the Vegetarian Sausage Binder with 3½ cups (875 mL) Vegan Sausage Binder (page 225). Omit step 2 and just taste and adjust seasonings as needed. The yield will decrease to 9 sausages. Use within 1 week.

If you decide to use table salt in place of kosher salt, use 1½ tsp (7 mL), as table salt has a higher density.

1 cup	rinsed drained canned kidney beans	250 mL
4¾ cups	Vegetarian Sausage Binder (page 224)	1.125 L
½ cup	crushed roasted unsalted peanuts	125 mL
¼ cup	finely chopped fresh cilantro	60 mL
2 tbsp	Malaysian vegetable curry powder	30 mL
2 tsp	ground cumin	10 mL
2 tsp	kosher salt	10 mL
1 tsp	freshly cracked black pepper	5 mL
1 tsp	onion powder	5 mL
2 tbsp	roasted garlic paste (see page 47)	30 mL
	30 mm shirred stick cellulose casing	

1. In a large bowl, mash beans with a pastry blender or potato masher until only slightly chunky. Stir in sausage binder, peanuts, cilantro, curry powder, cumin, salt, pepper, onion powder and garlic paste until well combined.

2. In a small skillet, over medium-high heat, sauté a small amount of the sausage mixture until thoroughly heated and egg is set. Taste the sample, then adjust seasonings as desired.

3. Stuff sausage mixture into casing as directed on page 51. Twist into 11 links, each about 6 inches (15 cm) in length.

4. In a large shallow pan of gently simmering water, poach sausages for 10 minutes or until sausages reach an internal temperature of 160°F (71°C). Do not allow water temperature to rise above 170°F (77°C).

5. Remove sausages from water and let cool completely. Refrigerate overnight or for up to 3 days before using. Gently peel off casing before cooking or eating.

Health Facts

A large 2015 study had high praise for the peanut. Among men and women aged 40 to 79 years, those who ate more peanuts had a lower risk of dying from cardiovascular disease.

Spicy Peanut Sauce

**MAKES ABOUT
5 CUPS (1.25 L)**

Tip

This sauce can be stored in airtight containers in the refrigerator for up to 2 weeks or in the freezer for up to 4 months.

Everyone will enjoy this spicy dipping sauce with the Malaysian Satay Sausages. Leftovers are wonderful for topping a fresh spinach or mixed green salad.

¼ cup	peanut or sesame oil	60 mL
5	green onions, finely chopped	5
2	cloves garlic, finely chopped	2
2 tbsp	finely grated gingerroot	30 mL
⅓ cup	packed brown sugar	75 mL
1 tsp	hot pepper flakes	5 mL
2 cups	water	500 mL
1 cup	creamy natural peanut butter	250 mL
½ cup	soy sauce	125 mL
½ cup	apple cider vinegar	125 mL

1. In a large saucepan, heat oil over medium heat. Add green onions, garlic and ginger; cook, stirring, for 2 minutes.
2. Stir in brown sugar, hot pepper flakes, water, peanut butter, soy sauce and vinegar; bring to a boil. Reduce heat and simmer, stirring often, for 20 minutes or until slightly thickened and flavors are blended.

Dirty Rice and Bean Sausages

The inspiration for these sausages is the Creole dish dirty rice, which gets its rather unfortunate name from the color given to the rice by the other ingredients in the dish.

Tips

For vegan sausages, replace the Vegetarian Sausage Binder with 3½ cups (875 mL) Vegan Sausage Binder (page 225). Add 1 cup (250 mL) cooked long-grain white rice, cooled, with the sausage binder. Omit step 4 and just taste and adjust seasonings as needed. Use within 3 days.

When choosing bell peppers, select those that have unwrinkled skin and no blemishes.

Health Facts

Red beans (and their larger cousin, kidney beans) are an excellent source of molybdenum. This essential mineral helps the body detoxify and may help prevent tooth decay.

• Food processor (optional)

1 tbsp	vegetable oil	15 mL
½ cup	finely chopped onion	125 mL
½ cup	finely chopped red bell pepper	125 mL
¾ cup	rinsed drained canned red beans	175 mL
4¾ cups	Vegetarian Sausage Binder (page 224)	1.125 L
2 tsp	kosher salt	10 mL
2 tsp	freshly cracked black pepper	10 mL
2 tsp	garlic powder	10 mL
½ tsp	celery seeds	2 mL
½ tsp	mustard seeds	2 mL
½ tsp	cayenne pepper	2 mL
¼ tsp	chili powder	1 mL
	30 mm shirred stick cellulose casing	

1. In a small skillet, heat oil over medium heat. Add onion and red pepper; cook, stirring, for 10 minutes or until pepper is tender. Let cool completely.

2. In food processor, purée beans to a paste-like consistency. (Or mash to a paste-like consistency with a pastry blender or potato masher.)

3. In a large bowl, stir together onion mixture, bean purée, sausage binder, salt, black pepper, garlic powder, celery seeds, mustard seeds, cayenne and chili powder until well combined.

4. In the same skillet, over medium-high heat, sauté a small amount of the sausage mixture until thoroughly heated and egg is set. Taste the sample, then adjust seasonings as desired.

5. Stuff sausage mixture into casing as directed on page 51. Twist into 10 links, each about 6 inches (15 cm) in length.

6. In a large shallow pan of gently simmering water, poach sausages for 10 minutes or until sausages reach an internal temperature of 160°F (71°C). Do not allow water temperature to rise above 170°F (77°C).

7. Remove sausages from water and let cool completely. Refrigerate overnight or for up to 3 days before using. Gently peel off casing before cooking or eating.

PART 4

MEAL PLANNING
MADE EASY

Creating Meal Plans

Most of us have busy lives these days, juggling more activities than we can really handle without dropping some. This means we sometimes relegate meals to the bottom of the task list, and that means we probably eat less healthfully than we want to. It probably also means that we spend more money on food than we want to, since eating on the run usually involves relying on pricey convenience items that come up short on nutrition.

With a bit of advance preparation, your homemade sausages can be a convenient focal point for quick, healthy meals. If you prepare a variety of sausages and store them in your freezer, you will always have nutritious protein options on hand to build a meal around or to augment a recipe.

Putting It All Together

Since the sausage recipes include various types of protein from different meat, poultry and vegetable sources, you could easily have sausages every day of the week for a series of healthy meals. However, that might get a bit dull. Our sample weekly dinner plan shows how you could incorporate sausages into your evening meal each night, but feel free to substitute other items on some of the days to avoid sausage burnout.

A great way to use sausages is as an ingredient in another dish, as with Monday's stew and Sunday's lasagna in the sample plan. Sausages are a convenient and quick way to start or augment a recipe. And you'll get the benefit of the meat protein, vitamins and minerals, without eating a large portion of meat. Remember, the healthiest approach is to eat a variety of foods each day and through the week, and this applies to your homemade sausages, too.

Before You Head to the Grocery Store

The first step toward healthier and quicker meals is a menu plan. It doesn't have to be elaborate and detailed; even a basic menu plan will make grocery

SAMPLE WEEKLY DINNER PLAN

	MONDAY	TUESDAY	WEDNESDAY	
Entrée	Stew made with sliced North African Sausage	Barbecue Sausage	Rice pilaf with sliced Kafta Sausage	
Side Dish	Couscous	Macaroni and cheese	Sautéed peas and mushrooms	
Vegtable	Sliced carrots	Cabbage slaw	Spinach salad	

shopping and meal preparation easier. If you spend a small amount of time up front doing this basic task, your day-to-day meal preparation will be a breeze.

You can use the sample menu plan below as a template for designing your own. Breakfast and lunch are fairly routine for many people, but you can add these to your menu plan if you like. For most of us, it's dinner that presents the most challenges. If you typically include dessert in your evening meal, you can add another row to your menu plan for that.

Before you start filling in your menu plan, first make a list of "Possible Choices," listing all of the entrées, side dishes and vegetable dishes you like. Your list should include at least 10 different entrées, enabling you to have a 2-week menu cycle. Most people can put up with repetition of vegetables and side dishes but not of the main course.

The next step is to do an inventory of the food you already have on hand. You'll save a significant amount of money by using up your existing inventory, especially perishable items that need to be eaten soon. Compare your "Possible Choices" list with your inventory and see what dishes you can make with items you have available. Fill in some of the spaces in your menu plan with these choices.

As you fill in the remaining spaces with other selections from your "Possible Choices" list, start a grocery shopping list that includes everything you need to prepare all of your selections for the week. If you like technology and have a smartphone, many free apps will generate a shopping list for you. Or you can create one the old-fashioned way: on paper.

At the Grocery Store and Back Home

When purchasing packaged foods, compare food labels, checking for specific information to help you choose nutrient-dense options. Select products that are higher in key nutrients, such as protein, fiber, vitamins C and A, iron, calcium and potassium, and lower in added sugars and sodium.

When you prepare meals and, on a smaller scale, fill up your plate, the best evidence suggests that a healthy mix of foods is 50% vegetables, 25% protein foods and 25% high-fiber whole grains. If you're trying to manage your weight, keep fat intake to moderate levels, usually 30% of your total calories for the day.

THURSDAY	FRIDAY	SATURDAY	SUNDAY
Aloha Chicken Sausage	Saag Aloo Sausage	Philly Chicken Sausage	Whole-grain lasagna made with sliced Spicy Sicilian Sausage
Jasmine rice	Oven-baked diced potatoes	Whole-grain hoagie bun	
Steamed asparagus	Steamed broccoli	Buttered corn	Marinated green beans

Perfect Pairings

When it comes to pairing a sausage with a side dish and a vegetable, think about ingredients in the sausage, particularly the protein choice, spices and herbs. For perfect pairings, it is best to avoid repeating ingredients, to avoid strong flavors in more than one food item and to stay within the flavor palette or ethnic profile of the sausage.

As an example, let's say you want to plan a meal around a Kimchi Brat. This vegetarian sausage contains a spicy ingredient, kimchi. As much as you might be a fan of pasta aglio e olio, which is pasta with lots of garlic and olive oil, it wouldn't work as a side dish for the Kimchi Brat because garlic and kimchi are both heady ingredients and the combination would overpower even the most devoted fans of both foods. In contrast, teaming the Kimchi Brat with a bowl of steamed basmati rice, which has a delicate, fragrant flavor, creates a pairing that works on every level.

PERFECT SAUSAGE PAIRINGS

PROTEIN	SAUSAGE	SIDE DISH	VEGETABLE
Pork	Bandiera	Whole wheat linguine	Roasted beet greens
	Barbecue	Oven fries	Corn on the cob
	Curry	Jasmine rice	Peas and carrots
	Green Chorizo	Red beans and rice	Brussels sprout salad
	Jamaican Jerk	Fried brown rice	Cauliflower
	Pennsylvania Dutch	Baked beans	Buttered parsnips
	Pork Roast	Whole-grain biscuits and gravy	French-style green beans
	Ramen	Japanese noodles	Sautéed snow peas
Beef	Cheeseburger	Sweet potato oven fries	Cabbage slaw
	Golabki Brat	Long-grain rice	Brussels sprouts
	Meatloaf	Mashed herbed red potatoes	Parsley carrots
	North African	Couscous	Sautéed greens
	Steak Siciliano	Tricolor rotini	Roasted peppers
	Weisswurst	Roasted acorn squash	Green beans

PROTEIN	SAUSAGE	SIDE DISH	VEGETABLE
Lamb	Australian Kransky	Baked beans	Cauliflower
	Contadina	Penne rigate	Artichokes
	Easter Lamb	Roasted red potatoes	Asparagus
	Gyro	Whole-grain pita	Spinach salad
	Loukaniko	Rice in tomato sauce	Sliced beets
	Milanese	Whole-grain vermicelli	Marinated green beans
	Moussaka	Couscous	Early peas
	Persian Lamb	Basmati rice	Sautéed mixed greens
Chicken or Turkey	Aloha Chicken	Brown rice	Sliced carrots
	Athenian Chicken	Couscous	Roasted eggplant
	Autumn Harvest Turkey	Quinoa and brown rice	Butternut squash
	Gorgonzola Chicken	Baked sweet potatoes	Green beans
	Holiday Turkey	Whole-grain stuffing and wild rice	Buttered corn
	Parmesan Chicken	Whole wheat angel hair pasta	Sautéed kale and onion
	Persian Chicken	Basmati rice	Sautéed spinach
	Piedmont Pollo	Sautéed polenta	Zucchini
	Thai Chicken	Jasmine rice	Broccoli
Vegetarian	Abruzzi Cannellini	Whole-grain rotini	Roasted eggplant
	Dirty Rice and Beans	Roasted red potatoes	Broccoli
	Florentine	Risotto	Sautéed mushrooms
	Greek Kalamata	Rice pilaf	Roasted tomatoes
	Vegan Harvest	Quinoa	Butternut squash
	Lebanese Majadra	Pan-sautéed pita bread	Roasted red peppers
	Malaysian Satay	Long-grain rice	Gingered green beans
	Saag Aloo	Curried rice	Peas
	Spicy Sicilian Chickpea	Angel hair pasta with garlic and olive oil	Marinated green beans

Sausage-Making Glossary

Binding: The process by which sausage ingredients maintain a stable emulsion between the fat and water.

Blood sausage: A type of sausage made with blood and varying amounts of meat, along with a wide assortment of additional ingredients, depending on the country of origin.

Brine: A solution of salted water often used to soak meat but also used as an ingredient.

Brisket: A cut of beef or veal from the lower front portion of the chest. It is used to make corned beef and sausages, and is often smoked over wood or charcoal. Brisket is a tough cut of meat due to its high collagen content, which softens when heated. If the fat cap is left intact, this further tenderizes the meat. Without the fat cap, brisket is a lean cut of meat.

Cartilage: A type of connective tissue found in many areas of animal carcasses. It is often ground in commercial sausages, resulting in somewhat elastic, tough particles. It is not used in home sausage making.

Casing: Natural casings are prepared pig, cow or sheep intestines that meat is stuffed into to make sausages. Sheep casings are the smallest and most fragile; cow intestines are the largest and thickest. Pork casings are the best suited for most sausage making. Natural casings are permeable and fragile when wet, but strengthen and become impermeable upon drying. Other types of casing include collagen, cellulose and synthetic, some of which are edible and some of which need to be peeled off the sausage before eating.

Cross-contamination: The unintentional transfer of microbes from one food to another by various means, such as product-to-product contact, human handling or contact with equipment or utensils. It can cause foodborne illness because the contaminated food may not undergo further processing to destroy the microbes. An example of cross-contamination is using a cutting board to cut raw chicken and then, without adequate cleaning, using the same cutting board to chop lettuce, which will not be cooked to destroy the microbes.

Curing: The process of making dried sausages, which requires the use of specific compounds, known as curing salts, sometimes with the added step of smoking. The main purpose of curing salts is to prevent the growth of a pathogenic bacterium, *Clostridium botulinum*, which causes potentially fatal botulism in humans.

Dried sausages: A type of sausage produced from cured, fermented and sometimes smoked meats, which are not otherwise cooked or heat-processed.

Drying chamber: A room or unit in which temperature and humidity are controlled to facilitate drying of sausages.

Emulsion: A mixture of a water-based solvent, fat and an agent (emulsifier) that binds the other two substances into a permanent solution. An example is mayonnaise, a mixture of vinegar (water-based), oil (fat) and egg yolks, which contain the emulsifier lecithin. In sausage making, a meat emulsion is a mixture of finely chopped meat, water, spices and curing agents, held together by a very specific process.

Extraction: A process in sausage making in which the myosin protein in the muscle fibers of the meat is released as a result of mechanical action and partial dissolution of the protein by salt. As the protein molecules are liberated from the tissue, they form cross-links with each other, leading to visible white strands in the meat mixture.

Fat cap: The layer of fat on the surface of a cut of meat. It can vary in thickness from $1/4$ to $1/2$ inch (0.5 to 1 cm).

Fermentation: The breakdown of chemicals, performed by microbes such as yeast and bacteria. In the production of dried sausages, fermentation refers to the process by which friendly bacteria consume nutrients in the meat and prevent the growth of pathogens and microbes that would cause spoilage.

Grinder: The mechanism used to grind the meat in sausage making. It may be a hand-operated, electric or a specialized attachment to a stand mixer.

Grinder plate: A circular metal component of a grinder with holes that the meat is pushed through. The size of the holes determines whether the meat is finely or coarsely ground.

HACCP (hazard analysis critical control points): A systematic approach to reducing the risk of foodborne illness by identifying, evaluating and controlling potential safety hazards. It has become the industry gold standard, used by virtually all institutions involved in food production and food service.

Herbs and spices: Herbs are the leafy parts of a plant, dried or fresh. Examples include basil, cilantro, bay leaves, parsley, rosemary and thyme. Spices can be any other portion of the plant, such as berries, roots, seeds, flower buds or flower stamens, and are usually dried. Examples include peppercorns, ginger, cloves, nutmeg and saffron.

Lactobacillus: A genus of bacteria that produce lactic acid. Many *Lactobacillus* species are important to human health and to the production of fermented foods. In sausage making, specific cultures are added to fermented sausages to produce a characteristic flavor and aroma.

Meat: Skeletal muscle from various animals (such as cattle, sheep and pigs) or muscle from the tongue, diaphragm, heart or esophagus.

Meat by-products: Any part of an animal intended for human consumption that does not fit the definition of "meat," including lips, snouts, ears, skin, spleen, heart, liver and fat.

Myosin: A protein in muscle tissue that is a primary component of the muscle fibers.

Pathogenic: The ability to cause disease in humans.

Potentially hazardous foods (PHFs): In the HACCP model, these are foods that can support rapid bacterial growth and increase the potential for foodborne illness.

Ready to eat: A type of sausage that has been cooked during production and does not require further cooking before consumption.

Ripening: The period of time in the production of dried sausages during which the meat undergoes biochemical and physical changes that lead to a shelf-stable product. The longer the ripening time, the lower the moisture content of the sausages. As sausages ripen, their flavor becomes more concentrated and their texture gets firmer.

Sausage: A product typically made of ground or chopped meat, meat by-products and various seasonings.

Shelf-stable: A term for products, such as dried sausages, that have undergone adequate processing to destroy all microbes so that they can be stored in a sealed container at room temperature.

Smear: The adhesion of fat (or gristle) in the grinder and inside the casing in the sausages, caused by heat from the friction of grinding. Smear is more likely if fat content is too high. This causes straining of the grinder and may even damage it. The grinder must be disassembled and the parts run under warm water. Before reassembling the grinder, run the parts under very cold water. To avoid smear, start with partially frozen meat and cold equipment, don't exceed the fat content indicated in the recipe, use sharp blades and consider keeping an extra set of blades on hand to swap out if needed.

Stuffer: A tool that holds casing in place during the stuffing of ground meat to produce sausages. A stuffer may be a separate tool or an attachment for a meat grinder.

Nutrition and Health Glossary

Anthocyanins: Pigment compounds that comprise a class of flavonoids contained in most plants. Anthocyanins vary in color from red to blue depending on the amount of acid in the plant. They are powerful antioxidants and may help fight chronic diseases in which oxidative damage plays a key role. Foods that are high in anthocyanins include açaí, blueberries, blue corn, eggplant, raspberries and some types of grapes.

Anti-inflammatory: A compound that counteracts inflammation, which is characterized by swelling, redness, pain and a sense of heat in an area of the body. Inflammation is a protective reaction to injury, infection, disease or irritation of a body tissue. However, when inflammation affects more than a localized tissue and becomes chronic, it is an underlying cause of many diseases, in particular cardiovascular disease.

Antimicrobials: Substances in food that prevent the growth of a variety of microorganisms. Antimicrobials may be naturally occurring compounds in the food or additives put in by manufacturers. Microbes that cause spoilage and foodborne illness include bacteria, yeasts, molds and fungi. Historically, sugar, salt and various spices were added to preserve food.

Antioxidant: A compound that prevents oxidative damage (see page 257) by becoming oxidized itself. Essential nutrients that act as antioxidants include vitamin C, vitamin E and selenium. Numerous phytonutrients, including carotenoids and polyphenols, also have antioxidant activity.

Arginine: An amino acid that is not considered essential, as the body can make it, although under some circumstances, an individual may not produce it in adequate amounts. It is a starting compound in the synthesis of nitric oxide.

Beta-carotene: A yellow-orange pigment in the carotenoid family, found in a variety of vegetables and fruits. It has powerful antioxidant activity, and the body can convert it to active vitamin A. In North America, beta-carotene provides the average person with roughly 50% of their vitamin A intake. Good sources of beta-carotene include dark leafy greens, such as kale and spinach, carrots, broccoli and apricots. *See also* Carotenoids.

Beta-caryophyllene: A phytonutrient contained in the essential oils of numerous plants. Researchers have suggested potential health benefits related to its functions as an anti-inflammatory, antibiotic, antioxidant, anticarcinogenic and local anesthetic.

Calorie (or kilocalorie): A unit of measure of energy from food, which is also expressed as kilojoules (kJ). The conversion between calorie and kilojoule is 1 calorie = 4.184 kilojoules.

Capsaicin: A phytonutrient in hot peppers that produces a burning sensation. It is the active ingredient in pepper spray, used in self-defense. Studies indicate that it has many important functions, including antioxidant, analgesic, anti-inflammatory and anticancer activities.

Carbohydrate: A nutrient that serves as the most important energy source for the body. One gram of carbohydrate provides 4 calories (16.7 kJ). The different types of carbohydrate are starches, sugars and dietary fiber. Sugars are known as simple carbohydrates because of their small size compared to the more complex starch molecules. Sugars include fructose (from fruit) and lactose (from milk). The term "added sugars" encompasses a variety of sugars that are added to commercial food products, especially sucrose, which consists of glucose and fructose. Complex carbohydrates incorporate numerous sugar and other molecules bound together, sometimes in the presence of dietary fiber (see page 256).

Cardiovascular disease (CVD): A disease that affects the heart and/or blood vessels. Two major forms of CVD that claim the most lives in industrialized countries are myocardial infarction (heart attack) and cerebrovascular accident (stroke). High blood pressure, or hypertension, is a form of CVD and is a major risk factor for both heart attack and stroke. Two important underlying processes of CVD, inflammation and oxidative damage, are important from a food and nutrition standpoint in that the compounds and nutrients in foods can either promote or impede these processes.

Carnitine: An important compound that humans can synthesize under normal conditions, so it's not an essential nutrient. Carnitine carries long-chain fatty acids into the mitochondria of the cells in the production of energy. Meat is an excellent source of carnitine.

Carnosic acid and carnosol: Compounds contained in sage and rosemary that have antimicrobial, antioxidant and anticancer activity.

Carotenoids: A group of over 600 phytonutrients found in plants, consisting of two main subgroups: carotenes and xanthophylls. Of these, humans can convert 50 to vitamin A. Carotenoids have varying degrees of biologic activity as antioxidants, immune stimulants and inhibitors of cellular proliferation, a key step in the development of cancer.

Cholesterol: An important component of cell membranes and the starting compound from which the body synthesizes some hormones. It is found in animal foods and is also made by the liver. It is carried in the bloodstream by lipoprotein compounds. The major lipoproteins are high-density lipoprotein (HDL), which carries cholesterol away from the arteries, and low-density lipoprotein (LDL), which carries cholesterol into circulation. In their roles as carriers, HDL is protective against heart disease, while high levels of LDL are thought to increase risk.

Daily value (DV): A North American reference standard for food labeling that indicates a food's content of specific nutrients and compounds in comparison to the recommended standards for dietary intake.

Diabetes mellitus: A disease caused by either a lack of the hormone insulin or an inadequate response to insulin resulting in high levels of glucose in the blood. Diabetes is a major risk factor for cardiovascular disease and is the leading cause of amputations, blindness and kidney disease. Two major types of diabetes include type 1 (which tends to arise in childhood) and type 2 (which typically occurs in adulthood). People with type 1 must have an external source of insulin or have a pancreas transplant; those with type 2 can sometimes control the disease with diet and exercise or oral medications.

Dietary fiber: Plant compounds that humans can't digest, including cellulose, hemicellulose, lignans, pectins, gums and mucilages. Fiber can be classified as two main types, soluble and insoluble. Both types are digested by the bacteria that inhabit the human intestinal tract, so they are considered prebiotics, promoting the growth of bacteria that may have beneficial health effects. Insoluble fiber absorbs water in the colon, making stools easier to eliminate and helping to prevent constipation. Insoluble fiber is found in vegetables, wheat bran and whole-grain breads and cereals. Soluble fiber appears to reduce blood glucose and blood cholesterol. It is found in fruits, legumes, oats and barley.

Dietary reference intakes (DRIs): A North American set of recommendations for nutrient intake established by the Institute of Medicine. The DRIs include four levels: estimated average requirement (EAR), recommended dietary allowance (RDA), adequate intake (AI), and tolerable upper intake level (UL). The RDA and AI are recommended levels of intake based on age and sex that meet the needs of up to 98% of the healthy population. They are differentiated by the degree of scientific consensus on the level established, with RDA having more evidence than AI. The EAR represents a level that meets the needs of about half the population; the UL is a level above which safety from toxicity cannot be guaranteed.

Fat: Chemical compounds, also known as triglycerides, that are consumed in foods (dietary fat) and are the main form of energy storage in the human body (adipose tissue). A triglyceride molecule consists of three fatty acids and glycerol. One gram of dietary fat provides 9 calories. In foods, fat adds to flavor, texture and mouth feel, a term that describes a creamy sensation in the mouth when one is eating a food containing fat. Fat also contributes to satiety, a feeling of fullness after a meal.

Fatty acids (FAs): Compounds that make up a fat molecule. Some fatty acids are saturated with hydrogen atoms; others are unsaturated, containing varying numbers of double bonds in place of some of the hydrogen atoms. The consumption of saturated fats is thought by some to be linked to cardiovascular disease because of their ability to raise blood cholesterol levels. The body can produce certain fatty acids, but not others; the latter are considered essential nutrients — they must be provided by diet. The essential fatty acids (EFAs) are linoleic acid and alpha-linolenic acid. Their functions include reproduction, growth, skin integrity and fat metabolism.

Fiber: *See* Dietary fiber.

Flavonols: Plant compounds with antioxidant activity and beneficial effects on blood circulation and blood pressure. Some of these compounds include kaempferol, myricetin and quercetin.

Free radical: *See* Reactive oxygen species.

Glycemic index (GI): A measure of the increase in blood glucose and insulin as a result of eating a food that contains some form of carbohydrate in comparison to a food designated as the standard, often white bread. In general, foods with a lower GI are those that are high in protein, fat and fiber. Research indicates that a high-GI diet promotes cardiovascular disease, liver disease, diabetes, some types of cancers and obesity. For people with diabetes, a lower-GI diet may help control blood glucose. Low-GI foods include legumes, vegetables, some fruits and whole-grain breads and cereals.

Glycemic load (GL): A system for ranking foods that considers the glycemic index. The method for determining GL is as follows: GL = GI × carbohydrate content (grams per serving) ÷ 100.

Lycopene: A carotenoid that is one of the most potent antioxidants but cannot be converted to active vitamin A. Lycopene may help prevent some types of cancer and has even been used in the treatment of early-stage prostate cancer. The best food sources are tomatoes, watermelon and red peppers. Interestingly, lycopene is best absorbed when the food has been exposed to intense heat, as when tomatoes are made into pasta sauce or ketchup.

Minerals: Inorganic elements present in both foods and the human body. Essential minerals are those that must be obtained through the diet. Recommended levels of intake have been established for 15 essential minerals.

Nitric oxide: A compound made by all the cells of the body using L-arginine, an amino acid, as the starting compound. Dietary intake of nitrate and nitrite provide another source of starting compounds for the synthesis of nitric oxide. One of nitric oxide's key functions is as a potent relaxing factor in blood vessels, controlling blood pressure and reducing the potential for a heart attack. Nitric oxide also plays an important role in blood clotting cell function, nerve conduction and immune function.

Nutrient density: A description of the quality of a food that compares its level of nutrients to the energy it provides. Although no standard for the term exists, nutrient-dense foods are generally considered to be those low in energy relative to a high level of essential nutrients and health-promoting phytonutrients.

Nutrients: Compounds needed for specific body functions and necessary for life. The body can make some nutrients; others, called essential nutrients, must be consumed in the diet. Essential nutrients are grouped into six categories: carbohydrates, protein, fats, vitamins, minerals and water.

Oxidative damage/oxidative stress: The damage that arises in body tissues as the result of reactive oxygen species (ROS) coming into contact with body compounds (such as DNA and lipoproteins) and tissues (such as the cell membrane) through the process of oxidation. The oxidizing compounds can arise from pollution, exposure to sunlight, cigarette smoke or oxidized compounds in foods. In addition, the immune system generates ROS as a means of defense, and they are also produced in normal metabolism and during intense exercise. Oxidative stress refers to an imbalance between ROS and the body's antioxidant defenses. Oxidative damage and stress are involved in cardiovascular disease, diabetes, cancer and many other diseases.

Phenols (phenolic compounds): A large group of plant compounds consisting of several subgroups. Studies have shown that phenols have important biologic effects, including antioxidant, anti-inflammatory and anticancer activities, to help prevent chronic diseases.

Phytonutrient (phytochemical): Any plant compound that is not an essential nutrient. Many phytonutrients may provide beneficial health effects via a wide range of biologic activities.

Phytosterols: Plant compounds that are chemically similar to cholesterol and appear to lower blood cholesterol by blocking intestinal absorption of dietary cholesterol from foods. Phytosterols are divided into two groups: sterol esters and stanol esters. They are used as food additives in margarine products and are also sold separately as supplements.

Polyphenol: Plant compounds that are divided into several groups under two main divisions of flavonoids and nonflavonoids. Many polyphenols demonstrate antioxidant, anti-inflammatory and anticancer effects that may help protect against chronic diseases.

Prebiotic: A food or supplement that contains compounds that serve as a food source for the bacteria that colonize the intestinal tract, promoting their growth. Prebiotics are usually divided into the two groups: inulins and fructo-oligosaccharides (FOS).

Probiotic: Live bacterial cultures consumed in foods, such as yogurt and fermented products, that colonize the intestinal tract and may be beneficial for health.

Protein: A nutrient made up of individual amino acids, nine of which are considered essential nutrients. One gram of protein provides 4 calories. Protein is the major structural component of muscle and most other tissues in the body, and its functions include catalyzing metabolic reactions, antibodies and hormones. "Protein quality" refers to the extent to which a food provides the nine essential amino acids at an adequate level. In general, protein from animal sources is of higher quality than protein from most plant sources. The highest-quality protein, which serves as a standard for comparison, is albumen, the protein in egg white.

Reactive oxygen species (ROS): Highly unstable compounds that can induce oxidative damage to cell membranes, DNA and lipids in the body. They may play a role in the development of many chronic diseases, including cardiovascular disease, diabetes and cancer.

Resveratrol: An important phytonutrient that may be involved in slowing the aging process. It is also a potent antioxidant. High levels of resveratrol are found in red and black grapes, and therefore in some types of wines.

Rosmarinic acid, rosmaridiphenol, rosmanol: Phytonutrients with antimicrobial, antioxidant and anti-inflammatory activity, found primarily in rosemary but also in other plants.

Umami: The fifth basic human taste, along with sweet, sour, salty and bitter. Many different types of foods, from both plants and animals, stimulate this taste, which is described as imparting a meat-like flavor. The word *umami* is a Japanese word meaning "delicious."

Ursolic acid: A plant compound that exhibits anticancer properties and may protect the heart and blood vessels. Food sources include apples, basil, cranberries, rosemary, oregano and prunes.

Vitamins: A class of essential nutrients that do not provide energy but are necessary for life. If a particular vitamin is not consumed in the diet, a deficiency results, which can be reversed by subsequent consumption of the vitamin. Each vitamin has specific functions, many of which regulate the body's chemical reactions.

Resources

Nutrition, Food Science and Health

Health Canada, "Food and Nutrition": www.hc-sc.gc.ca/fn-an/index-eng.php

Linus Pauling Institute: http://lpi.oregonstate.edu

Livestrong, "Diet and Nutrition": www.livestrong.com/scat/diet-and-nutrition

Nutri-Facts: www.nutri-facts.org/eng

Science of Cooking: www.scienceofcooking.com

Sugar-and-Sweetener-Guide: www.sugar-and-sweetener-guide.com

USDA, "Food and Nutrition": www.usda.gov/wps/portal/usda/usdahome?navid=food-nutrition

The World's Healthiest Foods: www.whfoods.com/index.php

Food Safety

Health Canada, "Food Safety": www.hc-sc.gc.ca/fn-an/securit/index-eng.php

Todar's Online Textbook of Bacteriology: http://textbookofbacteriology.net/index.html

University of Florida IFAS Extension, "HACCP: An Overview": http://edis.ifas.ufl.edu/fs122

USDA, "Food Safety": www.usda.gov/wps/portal/usda/usdahome?navid=food-safety

U.S. FDA, "Refrigerator Temperatures: Cold Facts about Food Safety": www.fda.gov/Food/ResourcesForYou/Consumers/ucm253954.htm

Sausage Making Information and Supplies

Best Meat Grinder Reviews: http://bestmeatgrinderreviewsguide.com

Franco's Famous Sausage Making: www.sausagemaking.org

Let's-Make-Sausage: www.lets-make-sausage.com

McCormick: www.mccormick.com/Spices-and-Flavors

Randolph Packing Co., "Authentic Sausage Flavor Profiles": http://randolphpacking.com/rpc_recipes/authentic-sausage-flavor-profiles

Sonoma Mountain Sausages, "Homemade Sausages": http://lpoli.50webs.com/index.htm

Sopressata.org: www.sopressata.org

University of Connecticut, "Home Sausage Making": http://animalscience.uconn.edu/extension/publications/sausage.htm

University of Minnesota Extension, "Venison: Making Summer and Smoked Sausage": www.extension.umn.edu/food/food-safety/preserving/meat-fish/venison-making-summer-and-smoked-sausage

Walton's Everything But the Meat: www.waltonsinc.com

References

Books

Adams, Martin R., and Maurice O. Moss. *Food Microbiology*, 3rd ed. Cambridge, UK: Royal Society of Chemistry Publishing, 2008.

Albala, Ken. *Beans: A History*. New York: Berg, 2007.

Batt, Carl A., and Mary-Lou Tortorello. *Food Encyclopedia of Microbiology*, 2nd ed. Burlington, MA: Elsevier Ltd., 2014.

Charley, Helen, and Connie Weaver. *Foods: A Scientific Approach*, 3rd ed. Upper Saddle River, NJ: Prentice Hall, 1997.

Coe, Sophie D. *America's First Cuisines*. Austin: University of Texas Press, 1994.

Counihan, Carole. *Around the Tuscan Table: Food, Family, and Gender in Twentieth-Century Florence*. New York: Routledge, 2004.

Evans, Simon, and Paul Burkhardt. *BrainFit for Life: A User's Guide to Life Long Brain Health and Fitness*. Milan, MI: River Pointe Publications, 2008.

Knechtges, Paul L. *Food Safety: Theory and Practice*. Burlington, MA: Jones & Bartlett Learning, 2012.

Mahan, L. Kathleen, Sylvia Escott-Stump and Janice L. Raymond. *Krause's Food and the Nutrition Care Process*, 13th ed. St. Louis, MO: Elsevier Health Sciences, 2011.

Marchello, Martin, and Julie Garden-Robinson. *The Art and Practice of Sausage Making*. Fargo: North Dakota State University Extension Service FN-176, 2012.

Reinhard, Tonia. *Superfoods: The Healthiest Foods on the Planet*, 2nd ed. Toronto: Firefly Books, 2014.

Rombauer, Irma S., Marion Rombauer Becker and Ethan Becker. *The Joy of Cooking*. New York: Scribner, 1997.

Root, Waverley. *The Food of Italy*. New York: Vintage Books, 1992.

Salloum, Habeeb. *From the Lands of Figs and Olives*. New York: Interlink Books, 1995.

Savic, I.V. *Small-Scale Sausage Production*. Rome: Food and Agriculture Organization of the United Nations, 1985.

Journal Articles

Bryan NS. Letter by Bryan regarding article, "Red and processed meat consumption and risk of incident coronary heart disease, stroke, and diabetes mellitus: A systematic review and meta-analysis." *Circulation*, 2011 Jan 25; 123 (3): e16.

Carlson MH, Halvorsen BL, Holte K, et al. The total antioxidant content of more than 3100 foods, beverages, spices, herbs and supplements used worldwide. *Nutr J*, 2010 Jan 22; 9: 3.

Cheynier V. Polyphenols in foods are more complex than often thought. *Am J Clin Nutr*, 2005 Jan; 81 (1 Suppl): 223S–29S.

DiNicolantonio JJ, Lucan SC. The wrong white crystals: Not salt but sugar as aetiological in hypertension and cardiometabolic disease. *Open Heart*, 2014; 1: e000167.

Fadda S, López C, Vignolo G. Role of lactic acid bacteria during meat conditioning and fermentation: Peptides generated as sensorial and hygienic biomarkers. *Meat Sci*, 2010 Sep; 86 (1): 66–79.

Harcombe Z, Baker JS, Cooper SM, et al. Evidence from randomised controlled trials did not support the introduction of dietary fat guidelines in 1977 and 1983: A systematic review and meta-analysis. *Open Heart*, 2015 Jan 29; 2 (1): e000196.

Hyson DA. A comprehensive review of apples and apple components and their relationship to human health. *Adv Nutr*, 2011 Sep; 2 (5): 408–20.

Kennedy DO, Wightman EL. Herbal extracts and phytochemicals: Plant secondary metabolites and the enhancement of human brain function. *Adv Nutr*, 2011 Jan; 2 (1): 32–50.

Manach C, Scalbert A, Morand C, et al. Polyphenols: Food sources and bioavailability. *Am J Clin Nutr*, 2004 May; 79 (5): 727–47.

Mentreddy SR. Medicinal plant species with potential antidiabetic properties. *J Sci Food and Agricul*, 2007 Apr; 87 (5): 743–50.

Milkowski A, Garg HK, Coughlin JR, Bryan NS. Nutritional epidemiology in the context of nitric oxide biology: A risk-benefit evaluation for dietary nitrite and nitrate. *Nitric Oxide*, 2010 Feb 15; 22 (2): 110–19.

Nychas GJ, Dillon VM, Board RG. Glucose, the key substrate in the microbial changes occurring in meat and certain meat products. *Biotechnol Appl Biochem*. 1988 Jun; 10 (3): 203–31.

Pesch B, Kendzia B, Gustavsson P, et al. Cigarette smoking and lung cancer — relative risk estimates for the major histological types from a pooled analysis of case-control studies. *Int J Cancer*, 2012 Sep 1; 131 (5): 1210–19.

Websites

Centers for Disease Control and Prevention. "Guideline for Disinfection and Sterilization in Healthcare Facilities, 2008." Retrieved July 2, 2015, from www.cdc.gov/hicpac/Disinfection_Sterilization/6_0disinfection.html.

Clemson Cooperative Extension. "Safe Handling of Beef." Retrieved July 30, 2015, from www.clemson.edu/extension/hgic/food/food_safety/handling/hgic3504.html.

Clemson Cooperative Extension. "Safe Handling of Lamb." Retrieved July 31, 2015, from www.clemson.edu/extension/hgic/food/food_safety/handling/hgic3509.html.

Clemson Cooperative Extension. "Safe Handling of Pork." Retrieved July 3, 2015, from www.clemson.edu/extension/hgic/food/food_safety/handling/hgic3511.html.

Clemson Cooperative Extension. "Safe Handling of Poultry." Retrieved July 30, 2015, from www.clemson.edu/extension/hgic/food/food_safety/handling/hgic3512.html.

The Cook's Thesaurus. "Sausages." Retrieved June 10, 2015, from www.foodsubs.com/MeatcureSausage.html.

Food Safety.gov. "Storage Times for the Refrigerator and Freezer." Retrieved June 29, 2015, from www.foodsafety.gov/keep/charts/storagetimes.html.

LEO Network. "British Culture, British Customs and British Traditions." Retrieved July 6, 2015, from www.learnenglish.de/culture/foodculture.html.

Liguria Foods. "The History of Pepperoni." Retrieved August 4, 2015, from http://liguriafoods.com/the-history-of-pepperoni.

Medscape. "Saturated Fat and CAD: It's Complicated," by Tricia Ward. February 9, 2015. Available at www.medscape.com/viewarticle/839360.

National Academies Press. "Dietary Reference Intakes for Water, Potassium, Sodium, Chloride, and Sulfate." Retrieved June 16, 2015, from www.nap.edu/catalog/10925/dietary-reference-intakes-for-water-potassium-sodium-chloride-and-sulfate.

National Pork Board. "The History of Pork." Retrieved July 11, 2015, from www.porkbeinspired.com/about-the-national-pork-board/the-history-of-pork.

Taste of Lisboa. "Sausages from Portugal." Retrieved July 6, 2015, from www.tasteoflisboa.com/eng/blog/like/article/85#.Vphcsf32a71.

Todar's Online Textbook of Bacteriology. "Nutrition and Growth of Bacteria." Retrieved July 2, 2015, from http://textbookofbacteriology.net/nutgro.html

UCLA, Louise M. Darling Biomedical Library. "Spices: Exotic Flavors & Medicines." Retrieved June 29, 2015, from http://unitproj.library.ucla.edu/biomed/spice/index.cfm.

University of Florida IFAS Extension. "HACCP: An Overview." Retrieved July 2, 2015, from http://edis.ifas.ufl.edu/fs122.

University of Michigan School of Public Health. "Relative Risk." Retrieved June 1, 2015, from http://practice.sph.umich.edu/micphp/epicentral/relative_risk.php.

Wedliny Domowe. "History of Polish Sausages." Retrieved June 1, 2015, from www.meatsandsausages.com/sausages-by-country/polish-sausages/history.

Other References

Meat Processing, North American Division. *Best Practices for Cooked Sausage: Controlling the Process for Safety and Quality #588*. November 2003.

Personal interview with Dr. Tilakavati Karupaiah, Associate Professor and Clinical Coordinator of Health Sciences at the National University of Malaysia, on June 6, 2015.

Pork Checkoff. *Quick Facts: The Pork Industry at a Glance*. Des Moines, IA: National Pork Board, 2009–2011. Retrieved July 11, 2015, from www.extension.umn.edu/youth/mn4-H/events/project-bowl/docs/pb-gl-Quick-Facts-The-Pork-Industry-at-a-Glance.pdf.

Suddath, Claire. "A Brief History of Buffalo Wings." *Time*, September 3, 2009. Retrieved August 5, 2015, from http://time.com/3957370/buffalo-wings.

U.S. Department of Agriculture, Food Safety and Inspection Service, and Association of Food and Drug Officials, U.S. Food and Drug Administration (FDA). *Safe Practices for Sausage Production*. September 1999.

Whoriskey P. "The U.S. Government Is Poised to Withdraw Longstanding Warnings about Cholesterol." *Washington Post*, February 10, 2015. Retrieved June 1, 2015, from www.washingtonpost.com/blogs/wonkblog/wp/2015/02/10/feds-poised-to-withdraw-longstanding-warnings-about-dietary-cholesterol.

World Cancer Research Fund /American Institute for Cancer Research. Continuous Update Project Report. *Food, Nutrition, Physical Activity, and the Prevention of Colorectal Cancer*. 2011.

Library and Archives Canada Cataloguing in Publication

Reinhard, Tonia, author
   The complete art & science of sausage making : 150 healthy homemade recipes from chorizo to hot dogs / Tonia Reinhard, MS, RD, FAND with Brendan Reinhard & Brent Mitchell.

Includes index.
ISBN 978-0-7788-0535-9 (paperback)

1. Cooking (Sausages). 2. Sausages. 3. Cookbooks.
I. Reinhard, Brendan, 1983–, author II. Mitchell, Brent, 1985–, author III. Title.
IV. Title: Complete art and science of sausage making.

TX749.5.S28R45 2016   641.6'6   C2016-900244-6

Recipe Index

Health Index

in meat, 14
saturated, 25, 26, 27–28
in sausages, 15, 28, 41, 49
fatback, 41–42
fat cap, 43, 253
fatty acids, 25, 27, 120, 170, 256
fennel seeds, 70, 124, 232
fenugreek, 77, 177
fermentation, 15–17, 253
feta cheese, 128
fiber (dietary), 32, 256
flavonols, 256
food poisoning, 17, 22, 56–60
freezing, 53–54, 57
fructooligosaccharides (FOS), 138
frying, 55

G

GABA (gamma-aminobutyric acid), 133
galangal, 156
game meats, 44–45
garlic, 47–48, 72, 152, 184, 187, 235
genetics, 26–27
ginger, 129, 206
glucosinolates, 98
glycemic index/load (GI/GL), 256
glycogen, 14
glycolysis (anaerobic), 14
goose, 213
green tea, 151

H

HACCP (hazard analysis critical control points), 56–60, 253
health
diet and, 19–21
glossary of terms, 254–58
risks to, 20–21, 23
sausages and, 19–32
heart disease, 24, 25, 255
herbs, 17, 253. *See also specific herbs*
Hippocrates, 64, 115
honey, 166, 205
hop extract, 137

I

inositol hexaphosphate, 150
iron (dietary), 32
isothiocyanates, 98, 115

K

kaempferol, 232
Karupaiah, Tilakavati, 28
ketchup, 163
Keys, Ancel, 26

L

lactic acid, 14, 16, 253
Lactobacillus, 253
lake whitefish, 222
lamb, 43–44
lectins, 162
legumes, 32, 150, 243, 246
lentils, 243
lignans, 178
limes, 195
linoleic acid, 25
Listeria monocytogenes, 57
lycopene, 127, 149, 161, 163, 187, 229, 257

M

macadamia nuts, 197
mace, 66, 147
mangos, 210
marjoram, 74, 96, 110, 204
meal planning, 248–50
meat, 13–14, 15, 253. *See also specific meats*
buying, 40, 57
by-products, 253
health benefits, 32
processed, 21, 22
trimming, 40–41, 42–43, 49–50
Milkowski, Andrew, 24
minerals, 257
mint, 154, 180
molasses, 135, 139
molybdenum, 246
moose, 218
MSG (monosodium glutamate), 131
mushrooms, 151, 162, 231, 234
mustard greens, 240

mustard seeds, 115, 160
myofibrils, 14
myoglobin, 13–14, 17, 43
myosin, 14, 15, 253
myristicin, 147

N

naringenin, 111
Nestle, Marion, 26
nitrates/nitrites, 16–17, 21–24
in curing salts, 47
food sources, 23–24
health benefits, 23, 24
negative press, 21–22
nitrogen, 22
nitrogen oxide compounds, 22–23, 257
nitroglycerin (glyceryl trinitrate), 24
nitrosamines, 21, 22
nitrosomyoglobin, 17
nutmeg, 159
nutrient density, 257
nutrients, 257
in sausages, 31–32
nutrigenetics, 27
nutrigenomics, 26–27
nutrition glossary, 254–58

O

oats, 73, 106, 112
olive oil, 48, 172, 239
olives, 236
omega fatty acids, 25, 27, 120, 170
onions, 152, 157, 165, 200
orange zest, 142
oregano, 121, 191
oxidative stress/damage, 257
oxymyoglobin, 43

P

pan-frying, 55
paprika, 48, 125
parsley, 76, 79, 113, 176
pathogens, 253
peanuts, 244
pepper (black), 71, 104
peppers (bell), 127, 161
pheasant, 215

phenols, 18, 257
PHFs (potentially hazardous foods), 253. *See also* HACCP
phytonutrients, 32, 257
phytosterols, 257
pimentón, 48
pineapple, 132, 133
pine nuts, 118
piperine, 71
pistachios, 181
polyphenols, 200, 257
pomegranates, 193, 237
pork, 40–42
portobello mushrooms, 234
potassium chloride, 30
potassium nitrate (saltpeter), 17, 24
potatoes, 109
prebiotics, 258
probiotics, 57, 258
propolis, 205
protein, 15, 30–31, 258
  in animal foods, 13–14, 30
  combining, 228
  extraction of, 15
  vegetarian, 30, 46

Q

quercetin, 123, 157

R

RDA (recommended dietary allowance), 28–29, 31
research, 19–21, 22–23
  epidemiologic studies, 20, 23
  media reporting of, 20
  in nutrition, 26–27
resveratrol, 258
ricotta cheese, 122
ripening, 253

risk (relative), 20–21, 23
ROS (reactive oxygen species), 258
rosemary, 136, 183
rosmarinic acid, 258
rutin, 70, 123

S

saffron, 116
sage, 114, 209
saliva, 23
salt, 16, 28–30
  in sausage making, 15, 29–30, 47
saltpeter (potassium nitrate), 17, 24
Sardinia, 27
sausages, 253
  fat in, 15, 28, 41, 49
  freezing and thawing, 53–54
  and health/diet, 19–32
  as nutrient source, 31–32
  pairing with other foods, 250–51
  ready-to-eat, 253
  salt in, 15, 29–30, 47
  shelf-stable, 253
  storing, 53–54, 57–58
  vegetarian, 32, 226–46
shiitake mushrooms, 231
sodium, 28. *See also* nitrates/nitrites; salt
spices, 17, 253. *See also* specific spices
spinach, 81, 173
strawberries, 108
sulforaphane, 145
sumac, 192

T

tarragon, 111
tea (green), 151

temperature. *See also* thermometers
  of drying chamber, 39
  of meat, 15, 50
  of refrigerator, 58
  during sausage making, 57
terpinolene, 204
thermometers
  for meat, 37
  for refrigerator, 58
thyme, 64, 97
thymol, 64, 121
tomatoes, 149, 187, 203, 229
turkey, 44, 50
turmeric, 91, 194. *See also* curcumin

U

umami, 258
ursolic acid, 191, 258

V

vegans, 30
vegetables. *See also specific vegetables*
  cruciferous, 98, 240
venison, 216
vinegar, 80
vitamins, 32, 258

W

walnuts, 227
whitefish, 222
wine, 148
World Cancer Research Fund International, 23

Z

zinc (dietary), 32